Ten Lectures on the Essence of Being "Individuality, Value, and the Absolute"

Ten Lectures on the Essence of Being "Individuality, Value, and the Absolute"

Metaphysics of Individuality and Value with Philosophical Self-Reflection and Existence Guide

(*Illustrated, Refined & Edited*)

B. Bosanquet

Copyright Notice for Readers

Publication Year: 2026
Publisher: DD Books
ISBN: 9789372441840

Edition: First Edition, 2026
Contact: ddsalesglobal@gmail.com

Book: Ten Lectures on The Essence of Being
Author: B. Bosanquet
Price: Rs 500/-

Table of Content

Reader Note

In an age where individuality often dissolves under the pressure of conformity, and value is measured in material success rather than inner truth, B. Bosanquet's "Ten Lectures on the Essence of Being" invites us to pause and rediscover the deeper architecture of existence. This profound work is not simply a treatise on philosophy—it is a meditation on what it means to be a conscious, self-aware individual living in a meaningful world. Through ten intellectually charged and beautifully reasoned lectures, Bosanquet explores the intricate relationships between individuality, universality, value, freedom, and the Absolute—concepts that form the living pulse of human understanding.

The book opens by grounding the reader in the central human experiences—attention, perception, and awareness—that guide our exploration of being.

As Bosanquet progresses, he leads us beyond abstract generalizations into what he calls the "Concrete Universal"—a unity where individuality and the whole of existence interpenetrate rather than oppose one another. He dismantles the false divide between necessary and contingent truths, showing that reality is not a dry network of laws, but a living totality whose every part resonates with purpose and value.

In later lectures, Bosanquet draws readers into a remarkable intellectual ascent—from the teleology of finite consciousness, to the bodily foundation of mind, and then into the heart of self-consciousness itself.

Through lucid reasoning and poetic insight, he portrays the self not as a detached spectator of the world, but as an active participant in the unfolding logic of the cosmos.

When he reaches the theme of the Self and the Absolute, the reader feels a genuine awakening—an understanding that individuality, far from being isolated, is the very medium through which the Absolute expresses itself.

For readers who seek more than intellectual stimulation, this book offers an inner dialogue—a conversation with the eternal. Bosanquet's discussion of freedom, initiative, and value restores the dignity of personal agency, showing that our truest freedom arises not from chaos or rebellion, but from harmony with the larger order of Being.

His argument that individuality is the logical criterion of value provides a timeless moral compass, suggesting that worth is never arbitrary—it is born from coherence, integrity, and the unity of self with the whole.

Each lecture builds upon the last like a symphony of thought, leading to the culminating synthesis in "Nature, the Self, and the Absolute."

Here, the reader perceives how matter, mind, and spirit converge into one radiant vision of totality—how all experience, from the smallest perception to the highest ideal, forms the pulse of the Absolute itself.

This is not light reading—it is a work for thinkers, seekers, and reflective souls. But those who open their minds and hearts to Bosanquet's vision will find immense reward.

The prose is dense yet musical, the reasoning rigorous yet intimate. Each page calls the reader to contemplate their own being—Who am I in relation to the whole? What is the true measure of value?

To read Ten Lectures on the Essence of Being is to walk through the corridors of one's own consciousness, guided by a philosopher who sees life not as a problem to solve, but as a unity to understand and embrace. This is philosophy in its purest sense: alive, illuminating, and transformative.

Publisher's Note

When B. Bosanquet first delivered his Ten Lectures on the Essence of Being, he sought not merely to instruct but to awaken a deeper understanding of the human condition. His purpose was to reveal the subtle harmony between individuality and universality, between finite experience and the Absolute.

In this new edition, our goal as publishers has been to present this remarkable philosophical journey in a form that remains faithful to Bosanquet's profound vision while opening its insights to the modern reader.

At a time when philosophy risks becoming fragmented and overly technical, Bosanquet's work reminds us of its living purpose: to clarify, unify, and illuminate the meaning of existence.

Each lecture unfolds with remarkable logical precision yet retains a lyrical depth, exploring ideas that continue to resonate today—identity and difference, freedom and necessity, the mind-body relation, and the nature of value.

His method is not to dictate truths but to lead the reader into reflection, allowing each insight to emerge naturally through dialectical discovery.

The publisher's task in reviving such a work is both an honor and a responsibility. Our editorial team has carefully preserved

Bosanquet's rich philosophical tone, while ensuring clarity for contemporary audiences.

The original text's complexity is respected—not simplified, but illuminated with clean typography, accessible annotations, and thoughtful structure.

The aim is not to modernize Bosanquet's philosophy, but to make it vividly present, enabling readers to experience its elegance without linguistic barriers.

Why, in our era of speed and distraction, should one turn to such a text?

Because Ten Lectures on the Essence of Being speaks to the enduring questions of human existence: What makes each individual unique? How do we find value in a world of flux?

How can freedom coexist with necessity? In his exploration of these timeless issues, Bosanquet bridges philosophy, psychology, and art—showing that thought itself is a living creative act.

Modern readers will find that Bosanquet's concept of the Concrete Universal resonates strongly with current discussions in cognitive science, aesthetics, and systems theory.

His notion of value as coherence within individuality anticipates modern ethical and existential thought, while his treatment of freedom prefigures contemporary debates about determinism and agency.

Thus, although the lectures belong to the late idealist tradition, their relevance extends far beyond their time.

This edition stands as part of our ongoing commitment to reviving philosophical classics that challenge, inspire, and endure. It is our belief that Bosanquet's work, though intricate, rewards the attentive reader with both intellectual illumination and personal insight.

His vision of the self as a "world in miniature"—an active center of meaning—remains a profound antidote to the fragmentation of modern life.

We invite readers, scholars, and seekers alike to approach this book not as an academic relic, but as a living text. Its voice may come from another century, but its spirit speaks urgently to ours. May this edition serve as both a tribute to Bosanquet's genius and a bridge between eternal philosophy and contemporary understanding—a reminder that the quest for truth, individuality, and value remains as vital today as ever.

Introduction

There are books that inform, books that question, and then there are books that transform the very way we see ourselves. Ten Lectures on the Essence of Being belongs to this rare category. It is not merely a treatise on metaphysics—it is a journey through the inner landscape of consciousness, where philosophy and life intertwine. B. Bosanquet, one of the leading figures of British Idealism, undertakes here a daring exploration of the nature of individuality, the structure of value, and the unity of the Absolute. His goal is not to construct an abstract system, but to help us perceive the logic of being as something alive, organic, and self-revealing.

From the first lecture, Bosanquet draws readers into a world where experience itself becomes the clue to ultimate reality. The "central experiences" he speaks of are not distant metaphysical puzzles—they are the familiar sensations, desires, and reflections that constitute our daily existence. Yet through them, he shows how the finite self, when properly understood, mirrors the infinite order of the cosmos. Every thought, emotion, and act becomes part of a grand pattern—a universal rhythm through which the Absolute expresses itself.

The idea of the Concrete Universal, which runs like a golden thread through the book, overturns our ordinary understanding of opposites. Instead of seeing individuality as separate from the whole, Bosanquet reveals it as the living embodiment of universality. A person is not a fragment cut off from reality but a focal point where the entire logic of being converges. This concept, profound in its simplicity, transforms how we view freedom, morality, and the purpose of life itself.

The later lectures intensify this vision. When Bosanquet examines teleology, he challenges us to reconsider purpose—not as a mechanical chain of cause and effect, but as the unfolding of perfection through finite forms. The discussion of the bodily basis of mind restores dignity to human embodiment, portraying the body not as a prison of the soul but as the very medium of its revelation. Through self-consciousness, he shows how awareness itself becomes the architect of reality, turning introspection into metaphysical insight.

In the climactic lectures—"The Self and the Absolute," "Freedom and Initiative," and "Nature, the Self, and the Absolute"—Bosanquet fuses logic, psychology, and spirituality into one luminous whole. Freedom emerges not as rebellion against necessity, but as the self's joyful recognition of its place in the cosmic order. Individuality becomes both the expression and the proof of value, and nature is reimagined as the visible language of spirit.

By the end, readers are left with a profound realization: to understand being is to understand oneself. The search for truth and the search for self are one and the same. Bosanquet's prose, while deeply intellectual, possesses a moral and emotional power that transcends academic boundaries. His philosophy calls not just for comprehension, but for transformation—for the reader to become, through reflection, more truly what they are.

To open this book is to step into an interior conversation that spans centuries—a dialogue between self and world, between the human and the divine. For the modern reader weary of fragmentation and relativism, it offers a refreshing vision of unity: a world where reason and feeling, science and art, individuality and the Absolute coexist in harmony. Ten Lectures on the Essence of Being is, ultimately, a mirror for the thinking soul. It asks not only "What is the nature of reality?" but also "How can I live in harmony with it?" The reader who accepts this challenge will find here both intellectual rigor and spiritual illumination—a rare synthesis of logic and life that continues to inspire, question, and enlighten.

Lecture–1
Introduction: The Central Experiences

This opening lecture invites the reader into philosophy not as an escape from life, but as a deeper confrontation with it. It establishes why central human experiences—love, struggle, value, and growth—are the true gateways to understanding individuality and the Absolute, and why only a philosophy rooted in lived reality can guide the whole mind.

Sets the foundation by outlining the core human experiences that guide the inquiry into individuality, value, and the Absolute

The philosophical journey we are embarking upon together, as described by Lord Gifford, addresses some of the most profound and enduring needs of the human mind. It calls upon us to investigate the fundamental nature of the one Reality within which we exist, the duty and destiny of finite beings as revealed through their connection to this Reality, and perhaps most crucially, our knowledge of this Reality itself. This knowledge, however, must be more than a mere abstract concept; it must be real, carry deep conviction, and be genuinely felt - a profound experience, not just the empty framework of a theory.

This emphasis on avoiding a "mere framework of a theory" highlights what I see as the double task of philosophy.

On one hand, we cannot abandon serious and systematic thinking, for it provides the essential justification for extending our beliefs beyond the superficial aspects of life. Indeed, we *must* construct the framework of a theory. Yet, there is something more, something that is not separate from this structure, but rather its "living spirit and inner energy". This "something" is our attitude to experience, or more precisely, the particular kind of experience through which each of us most directly feels our continuity with reality. While theories are valuable only as they embody this subjective selection and point of view, it's also true that our chosen attitude or selective experience would collapse into a mere mood unless it is concentrated and shaped into a serious philosophical theory. This is the classic interplay of matter and form – their absolute interdependence and the impossibility of conceiving one apart from the other. Therefore, our discussions will demand the highest efforts in rigorous thought to convey a knowledge that carries deep conviction and appeals to our entire being, truly embodying Lord Gifford's original intent.

To clearly delineate the philosophical attitude we aim to establish, it's helpful to begin by describing it through negatives, by identifying tendencies we must resist. We start with the need for proportion, centrality, and sanity in selecting experiences that shape our outlook, contrasting them with those that are overly specialized, scattered, or capricious. It is often considered wise to avoid the "obvious," and in a certain sense, we too will argue against a superficial understanding of it. However, there is a distinct kind of "obviousness" that is not about mere immediacy, but about centrality and dominance – a truth that is neither easy to grasp nor safe to ignore. Consider, for example, a wood or a crowd; both seem obvious, yet it's famously difficult "to see the wood for the trees," or to understand the mind of a society. These examples, though simple, illustrate what I mean by a familiar yet often neglected obvious fact.

Thus, our fundamental principle, almost a truism, is that in our approach to experience and the world, we must "put central things at the centre". We must respect the significance of these "neglected obvious" truths and take as our standard those values recognized by human beings when life is at its fullest and the soul at its highest point of development. Of course, a critic might object that terms like "rank" and "value" presuppose our conclusion. What *are* these central things? What is the soul's "highest stretch"? These are questions that will be fully addressed later when we develop our attitude as a logical theory. For now, however, we simply insist that life contains certain central and dominant experiences whose importance is undeniable, even though they are rarely given full recognition in formal philosophy, except by the greatest thinkers. Too often, philosophy fails to focus the complete conviction that a courageous and open person gathers from the world. Instead, it tends to be impatient, enslaved by superficial oppositions, and prone to fragmenting its subject, rather than strivi for an approach to life that is sane, central, profound, and complete.

For instance, it is difficult to find philosophical doctrines that represent as wide and free an impression of the world as that recently expressed by a gifted student of Shakespeare. To put it simply: we undeniably receive a tremendous impression of evil from the world, but equally, an overwhelming impression of good. The challenge arises in trying to separate the two, for good and evil belong to each other; they cannot be torn apart.

Instead of patiently exploring experience and striving to account for the most expansive and courageous outlook of the soul, theory often rushes in, based on superficial appearances. It might then argue that "black is white," or "white is black," or that the whole is merely a "patchwork of both, producing nothing more than grey". But such arguments fail to capture our central impression; they fail to confront the complete, sane, and courageous experience. The facts, as we truly experience them, are more akin to beauty and ugliness - you cannot neatly divide them. Rather, you must open your eyes to the "higher obvious" and recognize these greater experiences as they are, seeing sublimity and splendour shining through the very lines of horror and squalor.

Perhaps you cannot "solve the problem" of good and evil, but you can perceive that the whole belongs together in a way that superficial judgments completely miss.

This applies to "good" and "evil" in the universe. Experiences such as mere moral good, pleasure, or justice only take you part of the way.

Even the finest logic cannot construct a universe from these alone; in fact, the finest logic refuses to work with such limited material. The material must be richer in quality if it is ever to rise to a higher form. Thus, the higher—yet still obvious and central—experiences carry us further, towards such realities as strength and endurance, love and sacrifice, the creation and fulfilment of souls.

As Ruskin noted, there's a significant loss when thinking is seen as the "work of cowards" rather than the "work of soldiers". We observe this same principle in intellectual understanding. While we certainly perceive error everywhere, we simultaneously hold onto truth.

The central experience, which can be called the "arduousness of reality," is something we often admit verbally but rarely truly confront in our philosophical reasoning. We tend to retreat into some form of rest and refuge, relying on a "solid core" we call fact, or surrendering to the "flow of indeterminacy" we call life. In doing so, we remain blind to the "open secret" that all life worth living should make clear, just as a forest or a crowd is apparent to the eye. What is familiar and fundamental often eludes precise perception.

The greatest philosophers are those who succeed in recognizing these simple and fundamental truths. I am convinced that a lack of sympathetic insight often prevents many from understanding that being correct in one's overarching view of values requires a higher intellectual character and greater effort than simply writing volumes of clever arguments. While logical development is essential, no amount of skill can compensate for a flawed approach to life. It is not merely a matter of weak "matter" and strong "form," or vice versa. Philosophy, like poetry, is an inseparable combination of matter and form, reflecting either a sound or defective outlook on life in both its spirit and structure. As I put it, "Bad taste is bad logic, and bad logic is bad taste". To be truly right, as the greatest minds are, means having navigated countless intellectual attempts, discarded the inadequate ones, and returned to the center enriched by these failures.

Now, turning briefly to the negative aspects of central human experience, we observe a clear fact: nowhere, in asserting our connection with reality, do we stand on truly solid ground. By this, I mean ground on which we could simply remain if we chose. Experience alone tells us nothing certain; there are countless "immediates," and nothing is exempt from being immediate. If "immediate" means the primary fact or naive apprehension, then the lesson is clear: immediacy cannot provide stability. There is no rest or salvation in life or logic by withdrawing from engagement with the world, whether in personal matters, international politics, or moral and spiritual service. To possess reality is a difficult task; stability and solidity come not at the beginning, but only as we engage with broader perspectives.

This truth is obvious, yet, as we shall see in the lives of many extraordinary people, obvious truths are often neglected. The greatest truths are frequently acknowledged but not truly believed. If this obvious nature of our dominant experience—taken as the deepest clue to all else—were fully understood, we would not encounter arguments such as "the stream cannot rise above its source" or "in seeking the Absolute, we abandon our given self". Critics who claim we are replacing substance with shadow misunderstand. We must continually return to the fundamental facts of existence to remind ourselves that reality lies in the opposite sense: shadow and substance are interconnected, not opposed, contrary to how Plato's dualism is sometimes interpreted. Plato's universe, in essence, is unified, and the human soul, when self-centered, remains largely alienated from it.

From this understanding, our human journey—our "Pilgrim's Progress"—is inevitably adventurous. Attempting to cling to an initial, solid ground is impossible and would lead only to stagnation, a "City of Destruction". The belief in an inherent, pre-existing self or fact that can be retained while seeking higher truths is an illusion unsupported by real experience. Every person, in their work, learning, religion, or even in sin, embarks on a journey to reshape the self, acquire understanding, and transform the world. It is in this adventure—not apart from it—that we truly develop the personality we assume to possess at birth. These may seem like familiar platitudes, like "We have no abiding city here," but it is remarkable how much philosophy ignores or denies these common human experiences.

We will now briefly examine some common illusions, which I call the "centrifugal type"—negative attitudes that help shape our discussion.

First, I want to firmly reject what I see as the ultimate denial in philosophy—il gran rifiuto("the great refusal"). I refer here to a passage written by Professor William James, a thinker of immense influence. To be fair, James's ultimate moral conclusion is very similar to my own. Yet, I identify this "great refusal" in his critique of traditional philosophical studies and his call for a new, different philosophy. The passage recounts a student's perception: that entering a philosophy classroom meant stepping into a universe entirely different from the "tangled, messy, painful, and confusing" world of concrete personal experiences found outside in the street. The philosophical world, in contrast, was described as "simple, clean, and noble," devoid of contradictions, a "marble temple shining on a hill". The student viewed this philosophical world not as an explanation of our actual universe, but as a "carefully constructed addition built upon it—a kind of classical sanctuary where the rational mind takes refuge from the intolerably confused, gothic character of mere facts. It is something else altogether—a substitute for it, a remedy, an escape".

Philosophical Refuge Pyramid

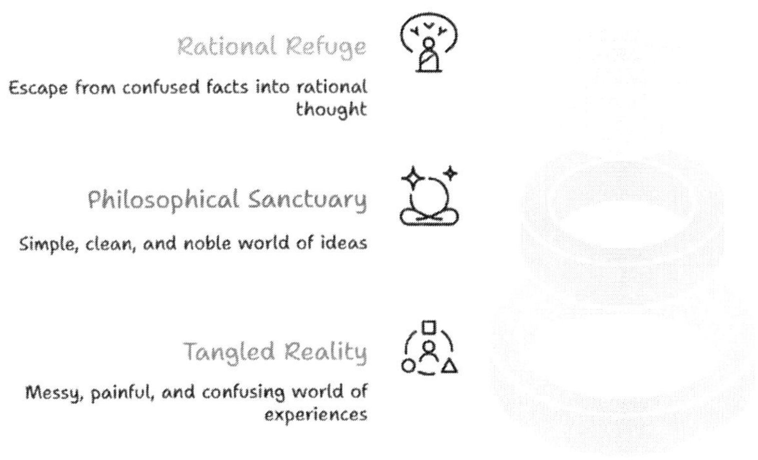

I recall my shock and disappointment when James used this passage to support Pragmatism, rather than as a powerful opening to explain the true nature of philosophy in the hands of great thinkers. I presume your experience is similar to mine: when you express to your professors that philosophical systems seem far removed from real life, they likely try to show you that this gap is not real. They strive to demonstrate that the perceived disconnect is instead a result of insufficient serious attention given to life's facts, compared with the breadth, patience, insight, and sympathy now being asked of you. This new effort transforms experience itself.

As your perspective shifts, your language about life changes, and you begin to glimpse insights into the thought of great philosophers whose understanding of life stands in relation to our own as "the ocean to a small stream".

You discover how even the smallest point in lived experience opens out into vast problems and unexpected depths, learning, as Plato said, the "alphabet of the ethical, social, and ultimately metaphysical world".

Philosophy is the formal embodiment of the "penetrative imagination". It deals with the true meaning of things, transforming them through deeper illumination.

Throughout this course, we must reject this "ultimate denial," this gran rifiuto, which treats great philosophies as if they are abstractions alien to life. It is the "great refusal" when life turns its back on its own richest and deepest experiences, a phenomenon that sadly becomes more common the greater the experiences are.

Secondly, we must also resist—firmly and without compromise—any attempt to treat immediacy, understood as something excluding reflection or mediation, as an absolute and reliable foundation. This applies whether immediacy is presented as a simple object of perception (a "solid fact"), as a vague, creative impulse called "life," or as an isolated, impenetrable subject of experience called "self".

All three forms of immediacy can be criticized in the same way: they appear to be arbitrary refuges or fearful retreats from the real movement of the world. What is often feared in that movement is the unsettling breakdown of the supposed solidity of "fact" or "self," or else the demand to recognize continuity and determinacy. In every case, these retreats connect closely with a deeper philosophical pessimism. By pessimism, I don't mean just a mood, but the deeper claim that there is a radical break between real existence and the principle of perfection.

Does this imply that a true philosopher must be an optimist? I hope the answer will unfold later, but let me anticipate briefly. The decisive fact is that both our best and our worst belong to one universe.

We have no basis for imagining another universe where either could exist separately. We cannot fairly compare cases of good and evil until we have understood what these words truly mean in their full reality and connection.

To say we would prefer a universe with only good and no evil may be nothing more than a meaningless hypothesis. Our real task is to discover what the true best of *our* universe is, once the worst has been taken into account.

Until we have delved into the depths of this question, we are not equipped to pass judgment on the universe, for we do not yet know what its true claim to "the best" actually is. While our current ideas of good and bad have some value, our present notions vary so widely and contain within themselves a principle of growth that could carry our judgment far beyond our first and simplest ideas. Thus, the claim to judge the universe based on immediacy is one of the very attitudes we must reject.

Thirdly, if, in clinging to immediacy, we accept the apparent self as a solid starting point and demand fulfillment for it in the same material terms, then we find ourselves dealing with questions of justice, ethics, and purpose (teleology). Without detailing these doctrines now, let me point out that certain clear and central experiences in our lives already reveal the limitations of this approach.

Take the idea of Justice, for example. Many gloomy philosophies or novels rest on a "tired demand for justice"—that is, the claim that there should be a proportionate balance between a person's wants and their fortune, with the repeated question, "Why? Why should A suffer when B does not?". We feel this attitude to be out of tune with the spirit of the stronger souls we admire—those who welcome life's differences and see in every demand for endurance an opportunity. Justice, as thus demanded, is simply compensation for being what you are. But in a universe full of differentiation, such a principle cannot stand. It would trap the individual in their finite limits, whereas their true power lies in transcending those limits—by embracing the whole reality in which they are placed.

So it is with Ethics and Teleology. We clearly see their value and necessity, but we must also recognize that they cannot describe the character of the whole universe; they apply only to its finite members.

Their essence is captured in the paradox: "The end is progress," an inconsistency that reveals itself in many ways. A teleology can never be ultimate; it expresses nothing more than the necessity of change based on a given situation that demands alteration.

Daily life convinces us that ethical struggle, justice, and teleology are useful only so long as they serve a purpose—as tools for the necessary self-assertion of the finite mind. But once that limit is passed, or once those aspects are subordinated, only love and pity remain—or again, faith and triumph.

We feel, and often admit, that moral judgment and failure do not represent the full value of a person. A man's true worth and reality go much deeper. Good, we feel, requires and includes ethical struggle, but it is far more than that—for without this "more," the struggle itself would be impossible.

Fourthly, it has always been a mistake of simple prima facie (surface-level) judgment to divide the tension of real life into pure delight and pure misery—heaven and hell—treating the first as the perfection of experience, and the second as complete failure. Such a conception, as we shall see, always ends by restoring unity, usually by making the misery of the lost somehow contribute to the happiness of the saved.

All views that imagine pain and struggle as merely leading up to a happiness from which they are later excluded share this absurdity. When Plato said that neither pleasure nor pain were suitable experiences for divine beings—indicating, of course, not a neutral condition, but something beyond both—he expressed the obvious demand of the mind at any higher stage of development.

It seems clear that we oppose the basic necessities of the better life if we interpret the Absolute as heaven, as though it were simply a future of enjoyment rewarding the struggles of time. Tension and satisfaction, we know, can be greatly transformed in their character, and imagining them as perfectly united is beyond our present experience. Yet, reason does not suggest, nor experience indicate, that satisfaction could ever exist without tension. Humanity at its best, in freely seeking its fullest satisfaction, has pointed toward something deeper. The value of poetic tragedy shows us something of what a truly satisfying experience must involve.

I do not claim that the most perfect tragedy is such an experience, but the near-supreme rank of tragedy among the greatest achievements of the human mind is a fact of profound significance, though rarely recognized in general philosophy.

If we truly believe that humanity is progressing toward a stage of happiness where it will draw painless enjoyment from tragedy—without ever having shared in tragic experience—then we are not far from the doctrine that the torments of hell somehow contribute to the pleasures of heaven.

The moral of this is that when we begin from everyday experience, we are always tempted to separate effort (endeavor) from fulfillment (fruition).

But in all higher attainments of mind—such as socially realized morality or aesthetic enjoyment—we find this separation to be impossible. And if we imagine it possible, it ruins the experience. You cannot, so to speak, hold to Optimism or Pessimism alone. If you want a pure heaven, you must also have a pure hell to balance it. If pain and struggle are not allowed to shape and be shaped by fulfillment, then they must be left aside, isolated, like the endless torment of Tantalus.

Lastly, an opinion, supported by thinkers I deeply respect, seems to me completely untenable: the doctrine that philosophy gives hope, but not guidance.

So far as this principle serves as a warning against rigid dogmatism—against expecting philosophy to provide practical prescriptions in detail—it seems perfectly sound. But as formulated by its distinguished proponents, it goes further. In the same mistaken way as before, perfection is identified with happiness, free from anything resembling pain, and it places great emphasis on the likelihood of happiness emerging as the crowning achievement of time. Thus, we are subtly lured away from thinking of the Absolute as the guiding spirit and principle of our world, and away from the conviction that the general trend of our higher experiences points us toward true perfection.

We are promised a vague "harmony"—that is the "hope" philosophy offers. But this promise is so general, and its terms so abstract, that the concrete system of values—values that should remain present within our actual lives to guide us toward the best—is left out entirely.

This, I believe, comes from accepting too quickly some immediate fact as the basis of our ideal—from taking pleasure as the model of harmony. If we do this, we divide life into separate pieces and fail to use one half of experience as a part of our ideal, and so we lose the "heartbeat of the Absolute within our actual world". We fail to see that the best things in our own lives truly connect with what is best in the universe, that their deepest tendencies can be traced in our surroundings, and that in ultimate reality they are not reversed, but transformed in the very direction we already glimpse.

Now, to draw towards a conclusion, I will sum up in a few positive statements—still as description and anticipation—the critical points of the attitude I intend to maintain as faithful to our most sane and central experiences. Later, I will work them out in technical detail, but for now, I will strive for plainness.

First, the most important thing is the level and fullness of mind attained. The destiny and separate survival of particular minds is of lesser importance, serving only as instruments toward that greater end. I am convinced that this conviction is deeply rooted in the best parts of everyday thought, though often overshadowed by less real conventions.

What a person truly cares about—at least at their best—can be described as making the most of the trust they have received.

They do not value themselves as isolated, self-identical beings, but rather as inheritors of gifts, circumstances, and surroundings concentrated in them—gifts they are called to raise to their highest potential. This attitude is like the true noble, in whom noblesse oblige—a sense of duty in nobility—is a guiding force. Similarly, all people, in their own way, are trustees of the world's powers and circumstances. Even suffering and deprivation are opportunities, and the question is always: "What can I make of them?".

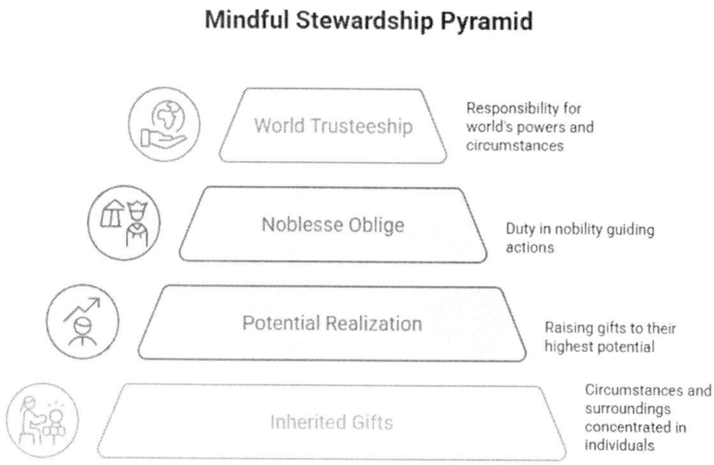

This is the primary, simple, and also the truest perspective. A healthy mind does not dwell on bare personality or on separate destiny. Its concern is with the work to be done, the truth to be known, the feeling to be experienced—in short, the completeness of experience, the individual's contribution to it, and their participation in it.

At every point, the fabric of experience is continuous; no individual can truly separate their part from the whole. To equate the preservation of values with the survival of separate personalities strikes me as a most extraordinary assumption. Indeed, the more one realizes this continuity, the less one cares about the separateness of individual contributions. Often, both the individual and others realize that the credit for ideas or discoveries belongs neither to the one who receives it, nor to the one best suited for it, highlighting the cooperative element in experience which cannot be overestimated.

This insight also affects how we think about unfulfilled promise: through unnoticed contributions to the collective mind, much is preserved that might otherwise seem lost. In some cases, what appears to be only "half" has turned out to be "more than the whole".

Take the passion of love as an example. Here, even if one argues that the lover loses themselves in the other, the particular being of the beloved remains the very heart of the emotion.

The destiny, permanence, and even immortality of the beloved seem more important than anything else in the universe. And yet, as in all higher experiences, the beloved matters not just as an individual, but as the embodiment of something greater.

Love transforms the beloved into a whole world. This, in truth, is what the desire for eternity really means, bringing with it a deep transformation.

A great writer once said that hate, like fire, makes even rubbish deadly, and it is equally true that love, like fire, makes the poorest things radiant. It is, one might almost say, "the Absolute itself appearing in person". At any rate, one central lesson—both in life and in theory—is this: the level and quality of mind matters far more than the mere survival of its separate centers.

Secondly, in more technical terms, this principle means that Logic—or the spirit of totality—is the key to reality, value, and freedom.

The root of this principle lies in the connection between the satisfactions of experience, their stability and self-maintenance, and the nature of creative initiative. Creative initiative is change, while stability and self-maintenance are its counterpart in duration.

The desire to free the mind's initiative from all conditions sometimes goes so far that it forgets this: every inference—a typical act of mind—must rest on data or premises. Likewise, the creation of a work of art is empty if it does not already involve some vision or premonition of the unity which makes it, when complete, a true logical whole.

The logical spirit—the drive of parts to transcend themselves and merge into wholes—is the birth-impulse of initiative, just as it is the lifeblood of stable existence. The degree to which this spirit is embodied in any world or system determines its value, its satisfaction, its reality, and the creative effort by which it is sustained.

The "good" of the universe must be something that belongs to the whole world, not just to a single member within it. This point is very important and becomes clear even in a comparatively simple matter like the difference between morality in an individual person and morality in the state. A member of a world—whether relatively or absolutely—depends on that world for his existence, and his task is given by it.

But the world itself, which stands as the ultimate condition of things, has a very different task. Its role is to support within itself all the organs and conditions needed to make a world possible. The individual, as a member of this world, is bound by his surroundings, which set his task, and his good is determined by his relation to his task—by how he responds to his surroundings. But the world's "good" cannot possibly be the same as his.

The "good" of the world must include making the individual's good possible. And if the world were "good" in exactly the same way we expect a person to be, then our human goodness would not even be possible. We should think of the universe rather as the birthplace and theatre of goodness—or more than that, as the totality in which goodness exists—rather than being good itself in the same way we are. Its excellence lies in being great in possibilities, beyond what the finite soul can ever fully grasp.

This way, the soul always finds more than it can master—always finds scope for its greatest effort and highest worship. We could never be satisfied with a universe designed only to make us "good"—a world where sin, endurance, and aspiration were carefully measured to suit us, so that we could clearly see it was all planned for our benefit.

In such a case, we would feel ourselves, in our finiteness, to be the true lords and masters, as if the world existed only for us. But this would leave us miserable, because the goal would not be reached: we would have nothing greater than ourselves to contemplate.

We need something above us—something to challenge us, to inspire us to dare, to act, and to hope. We are finite beings, which means we are incomplete and not made to be absolute ends in ourselves.

This applies even to the State; it is not a mere contrivance, but deals with a complex network of lives, bringing about both greatness and conflict. Its task is to maintain a system of life that allows many-sided excellence to grow within it.

As Browning wrote: "Oh, dread succession to a dizzy post, Sad sway of sceptre whose mere touch appals, Ghastly dethronement, cursed by those the most On whose repugnant brow the crown next falls".

In other words, goodness by itself cannot be the ultimate moral end. If we try to make it so, it becomes empty and collapses into nothing.

The world that provides the conditions for our goodness cannot exist simply for the sake of goodness; it must direct that goodness toward some larger, concrete purpose or nature. A world's excellence must certainly include the excellence of its members, and must have a connection or kinship with them. But its greatness is of another order—it must go beyond them while sustaining them. It is, in fact, the greatness of souls.

Thirdly, the universe is not a place meant simply for pleasure, nor is it a place only made up of probation and justice. From the highest point of view—at least concerning finite beings—it is a place for soul-making.

Our best experiences clearly show us this truth. We see for ourselves that mere pleasure, or even the strict sense of moral reward and punishment, are only small parts of what truly matters to the fully capable mind. Both are included, of course, but they are far from the whole.

To support this, we can call on evidence from history, science, poetry, politics, social life, or religion. In the end, what we care about most is the shaping and greatness of souls. This must be reconciled with what we said earlier about the relative value of individual minds compared with mind in general. But this reconciliation, though it must be dealt with more fully later, is not difficult in principle.

The destiny or survival of particular centers of mind is not what holds the highest value. This does not conflict with what we are now saying. What truly has value is the contribution that each particular center makes to the whole—the unique elements it represents within the whole to which it belongs. Its individuality matters only because of what it helps to bring about.

Finally, we experience the Absolute more fully than we experience anything else. This is the decisive answer to the question: can we, as finite beings, possess or enjoy the Absolute in any degree? Or does this depend on something like a future life? Is the Absolute related to us in the way heaven is related to an orthodox Christian?. The answer is fundamental to our deepest convictions, and it has already been decided by the stability of our starting point. We all experience the Absolute, because the Absolute is present in everything. And since it is in everything we do or suffer, we may even say that we experience it more directly than anything else—especially because one profound truth runs through it all. That truth is this: the world never leaves us alone.

It drives us from one situation to another, and what we call "accidents" constantly confront us with an extraordinary mixture of opportunity and suffering. Yet this very mixture is itself opportunity.

Of course, we do not usually call this inner power, in which we live, "the Absolute".

And people with wholly unreflective minds may hardly be aware of any general quality in life that points to unity—something that feels at once too vast for them, yet also something that offers them wonderful possibilities.

Still, the fact exists, and it is real for them, even if it only appears scattered throughout their perceptions, never consciously reflected on as one unified truth.

In reality, we all must recognize something absolute, both within ourselves and outside of ourselves: an external force, at first seemingly too strong for us, yet one that responds to our destinies and enters into us as an inner power—sometimes more, sometimes less—than equal to the external world.

If we refuse to see absoluteness even in love, or in anything beyond the smallest possible facts, and if we claim that our only absolute is death, still even death itself is a power. At first, it seems hostile and external, merely an accident of nature.

Yet we can make it our own, turning it into an expression of our will—through self-sacrifice, acceptance, or even, in some sense, suicide.

A being who can choose not to live—as it is said that animals below man never do—has grasped something greater than all possible things.

In this act, he gives this undefined "something" the value of an Absolute—a not-self that is more truly himself than his actual self could ever be. Such a phrase as "absolute certainty" is often used by people who would shrink from actually acknowledging an Absolute.

The argument, one may say, would seem simpler and clearer if, under life's discipline, we all obviously became wiser and better—like pupils in a school where no one fails. But in truth, too many of us seem to decline instead.

Yet, as we suggested earlier, "it takes all sorts to make a world". And even if we were comfortable in Zion, seeing everyone virtuous and content on the surface, we would never, I think, feel satisfied.

It is only through the meeting of what is far beyond us with what lies deep within us that the open secret of the Absolute comes before us—in life, in love, and in death.

In this course, we shall therefore begin by setting forth, in logical order, the foundations and demands of the principle of Individuality, considering it as the inner standard of the real, and also in its relation to lower forms of the logical universal, such as general law, the uniformity of nature, and guiding purpose in evolution.

This will involve examining the bodily side of mind and the position of finite consciousness as a teleological agency, requiring a fair amount of logical technique.

Later, we will examine the same principle as the key to the nature of value in reality, to the freedom or initiative of its members, and to its inner structure, including how it embraces both nature and the finite self. I give fair warning: the results will not be anything surprising or extraordinary.

On the whole, I believe they will simply express and define the reasonable faith of thoughtful and open-minded people.

The best outcome I might hope for is sometimes to state plainly what others think too obvious to say, and, by attempting a thorough logical connection of what is present in every side of experience, to show that a sane and central theory is not made up of oddities and whims, but is instead a coherent explanation of what lies at the very heart of real life and love.

Lecture-2
The Concrete Universal

This lecture challenges the habit of mistaking abstract generality for truth and leads us toward a richer vision of reality. By unfolding the idea of the concrete universal, it reveals how individuality arises not by exclusion but by wholeness, showing that truth, value, and freedom emerge only within living, self-sustaining worlds of experience.

Explores how universality and particularity coexist in reality, forming the groundwork for individuality

Ladies and gentlemen, esteemed seekers of truth, let us embark today on a profound philosophical journey, delving into the concept of "The Concrete Universal," a notion critical to understanding the very fabric of reality and the nature of knowledge itself. We will explore how this concept challenges our everyday assumptions about universality and illuminates the path towards a more coherent and vibrant understanding of experience.

The Initial Allure of Generalization: A First Step Towards Truth

Our natural inclination, indeed our very habit of thinking, often leads us to believe that we elevate our experience when we discover anything that approaches a general rule. And, at first glance, this is undeniably true. We instinctively rely on what we might call the "principle of community or continuity in experience". What does this mean? It means that when we observe certain properties conjoined in a particular instance, we extend that conjunction beyond that initial case, trusting it to hold true under different conditions. This fundamental tendency is the very engine upon which all knowledge depends: the inherent drive of experience to be "universal". This "universality" is not merely about repetition; it implies that experience carries us "beyond any given piece of itself," revealing a character that illuminates further, distinct contexts, and is, in turn, illuminated by them.

Think of any general statement, any scientific law, or even a simple proverb – they all apply a single predicate or principle to a multitude of different cases.

This initial pursuit of general rules represents an appreciable advance towards the ideal of truth. What is that ideal? It is a rendering of experience that is entirely free from self-contradiction, free from conflicting interpretations of the same facts under the same relations. Every general rule, by encompassing a broad area of experience within a singular interpretation, reduces the possibility of such discrepancies. It is, therefore, a tangible step towards the completion of knowledge as a coherent, unified whole.

The guiding impulse behind this early stage of knowledge often expresses itself in familiar formulas like "Same causes, same effects," or more broadly, "It is the same that produces the same". This perspective, often taken as the characteristic principle of intelligence, relies heavily on the repetition of similars and our ability to recognize them as they recur.

The Unveiling of Defects: The Limitations of Abstract Generalization

However, and this is a crucial pivot in our understanding, from the very beginning, this seemingly straightforward conception of intelligence—based solely on repetition—is revealed as incomplete, even untrue. As we shall see, even the most basic generality derives its true value not merely from what it repeats, but from the "differences of context which it includes and which it illuminates". The genuine principle of intelligence is far more nuanced, and we must move beyond mere generality to grasp it.

Indeed, the abstract generalization, despite its initial utility, possesses inherent defects when considered in relation to truth. These shortcomings were powerfully articulated by Plato in the very dawn of logical theory, especially in his critical estimation of the exact or mathematical sciences.

Following Plato, nearly all significant thinkers have recognized that a body of knowledge, if understood solely as a collection of highly abstract rules and inferences, *prima facie* "depart[s] from what is given in experience". In this sense, truth, when defined by such abstraction, seems to abandon concrete fact.

We often hear arguments that we must look to "History" for the type of living experience, or that some "new philosophy" might refer us to a pure "intuition".

While these might be "rash interpretations" in their extreme form, they point to a common ground: the processes of science, characterized by general statements, are inherently detached from the "historical tense," the "genuinely personal subject," or the "point of departure which we indicate by such terms as 'this' and 'mine'".

A general statement is, by its very nature, an "extract or an abstract". It has even been called hypothetical, not categorical in the fullest sense. Critically, "It tells nothing about reality; it points out consequences which must flow from the application to it of specified conditions".

It does not claim to speak of real beings in their entire and fundamental nature. This comprehensive understanding of the universe as a whole, this categorical judgment, is the exclusive domain of Philosophy.

For "Philosophy is essentially of the concrete and the whole, as science is essentially of the abstract and the part". Thus, it can be said, with a considerable degree of truth, that science deals with experienced existence "at secondhand". It famously "murders to dissect".

This is not an accusation, but a straightforward recognition of science's function and its place within a larger logical system. If scientific methods are taken as the *exclusive* foundation for a world-theory, they will inevitably face criticisms, much like mechanical theories of evolution have.

However, we must not fall into the opposite error: it is false to argue that a mechanical theory contributes nothing to understanding the whole.

Even mathematical reasoning is synthetic, and within the continuity of experience, even homogeneous elements can reveal new properties, relate to new qualities, and shed light on their nature.

The geometrical character of a line, for instance, is continuously and essentially linked to the profound significance it holds in the most concrete work of art.

The principle of Abstraction has been a long-standing subject of critique, particularly as embodied in the traditional doctrine of Extension and Intension. A mere glance at the "tree of Porphyry"—that hierarchical classification of concepts from broadest to narrowest—reveals the inherent problem: the most general knowledge, the widest comprehension (e.g., Man, Animal, Organism, Material body), must paradoxically be the least instructive, culminating in "complete emptiness". This is the very reason why progressive generalization diminishes the depth of knowledge and prevents any general rule from fully grasping a concrete subject or being truly categorical.

The Root Cause: The Fallacy of Omission

The fundamental underlying reason for these defects lies in the attempt to "cut in two the essential principle of continuity". Simple generalization strives to pursue an identity *apart from differences.* Its method is, by definition, "omission". Generality is constructed by focusing solely on the common qualities shared by individuals, while deliberately *disregarding their differences.*

This procedure has two inescapable consequences. First, it actively prevents us from considering the larger "world or structure" of which the individuals under consideration are merely members. Second, by the same necessity, it prohibits any consideration of the "entire or concrete nature of any individual by itself".

These consequences are inevitable because, if identity is rigidly construed as *excluding diversity,* then no true world or coherent structure can be constituted solely by the identical properties of individuals.

Individuals treated merely as members of a class based on identical properties are, by hypothesis, just "parts or members of a whole of repetition," nothing more.

And each such individual can only be considered in terms of that specific property that makes it a class member. All other differences within that property, and indeed the entire remaining content of the individual's nature, are "ruled out ab initio by the method". So long as we adhere to such a conception, the idea of a whole comprised of individuals, or of an individual as a whole, remains inconceivable.

The general statement is limited to affirming only the properties repeated across similar class members, effectively preventing their membership in a concrete system—whether constituted by their fellows (like humanity) or by diverse, reciprocally dependent units (like an ecosystem)—from becoming a source of deeper knowledge.

This distinction illuminates the difference between classification by resemblance and grouping by reciprocal determination. The former is like trying to understand a human body or a steam-engine by merely classifying its parts based on their similarities. This yields a superficial understanding. The latter, however, involves understanding how the *function of the whole system* arises from the co-operation and division of labor among its *different* constituent members with their unique structures and qualities.

This latter mode of consideration, while serving certain purposes, is ultimately a superficial application of the very same principle that is more fully realized in the profound, reciprocal determination. To illustrate, if Plato's Forms are mistakenly identified with "the objective correlates of class-concepts," it becomes "absolutely impossible to conceive them as a world of interdependent members," a concept central to the Form of the Good and the universe of reality.

Let me be clear: this argument is *not* reducing the precise determinations of science, like the law of gravitation, to the level of mere commonplace class-predications based on superficial observation.

What we are asserting is this: if, through an inadequate theory, the function of scientific laws is misinterpreted as simply recognizing a common attribute in recurrent examples—as merely apprehending "the same producing the same"—then such a reduction is fundamentally erroneous.

This misinterpretation renders the very "operation of scientific principles in leading to novelty whether of truth or of practice wholly unintelligible". True scientific advancement often involves discovering how previously distinct phenomena are interconnected, revealing new properties and relationships, which goes beyond mere repetition.

The Concrete Universal: A "World" of Self-Maintenance

Therefore, the endeavor to remove contradiction in experience achieves far greater success when it explicitly assumes a more developed shape, indicated by terms such as "a whole of parts," "an organism," "a system," or, most inclusively, "a world". While these terms have their own specific differences, our immediate goal is to grasp the fundamental distinction between all these forms of experience, on the one hand, and abstract generality, on the other. The most comprehensive of these terms is "world" or "cosmos".

A world, or cosmos, is a system of members where every member, though distinctly separate, "nevertheless contributes to the unity of the whole in virtue of the peculiarities which constitute its distinctness".

This is the critical point: the unique differences of the parts are essential to the unity of the whole. This is encapsulated by the saying: "It takes all sorts to make a world; a class is essentially of one sort only". In essence, the ultimate principle of unity or community is fully exemplified in the "world" but only superficially or partially in the "class".

Let us articulate these principles of unity more precisely:

- Generality: This is "sameness in spite of the other". Here, differences are present but are disregarded or merely tolerated; they don't fundamentally contribute to the identity being sought.
- Ultimate Principle (as embodied in a world): This is "sameness in the other". This indicates a deeper unity where identity embraces and finds itself reflected in diversity.
- Universality (the true logical universal): This is "sameness by means of the other". This is the most profound level, where the very diversity and distinctness of the parts become the means through which the unity and identity of the whole are realized and expressed.

Thus, the true embodiment of the logical universal takes the shape of "a world whose members are worlds". This concept directly addresses the defect of mere generality, which was flawed precisely because it omitted the differentiating contents within its class-members. The concrete universal, in the form of a world, actively "refers to diversity of content within every member," a characteristic entirely neglected by the universal in the form of a class. Such a diversity, recognized as a unity - a "macrocosm constituted by microcosms" - is the paradigmatic type of the concrete universal.

This understanding also sheds light on the nature of true infinity. While infinite numbers in modern mathematics may not be reached by enumeration, their nature often reflects a concept that *demands* the completeness of a series, rather than being a series that is *actually* complete.

In truly typical infinite wholes, self-representation is present, not through a simple one-to-one correspondence of terms, but through a "differentiated response to organic necessities". Consider a great country: it doesn't represent itself by having a perfect miniature map on a portion of its surface.

Rather, it manifests its whole structure by developing distinct, specialized organs like a university in one place, a church in another, or a manufacturing town in a third.

Each of these "proper parts" repeats the whole structure, yet does so in a uniquely differentiated way.

Similarly, a mind doesn't represent itself by endlessly re-thinking its own thoughts; instead, its nature becomes "incarnate" through its varied "thought, word, and deed". Each unique expression is a concrete manifestation of the integrated whole that is the mind.

The Key to Philosophy and the Nature of Individuality

The recognition of this logical form—the concrete universal—as the true type of universality is nothing less than "the key to all sound philosophy". It is a path that clearly develops thought towards a "higher vitality and fuller perfection". It's like ascending a hill: regardless of your starting point, if you remain true to the inherent connections of experience, observing the relation of incompleteness to completeness in all mental responses, you are bound to reach the summit. You cannot genuinely study thought without being led to will and feeling, nor can you explore will or feeling without being led back to thought, demonstrating the inherent interconnectedness of all aspects of experience.

The concrete universal stands in stark contrast to the general rule. It can be likened to "a centre of radii compared with a superficial area".

While the general rule operates on a broad, flat surface, covering many instances superficially, the concrete universal draws its power and depth from a concentrated, integrated core. The true test of universality, therefore, is not the number of subjects that share a common predicate (which is the test for abstract generality).

Rather, it is "the number of predicates that can be attached to a single subject". This indicates the richness, complexity, and internal coherence of a single, highly organized entity.

Its essence lies in the degree to which a systematic identity "subordinates diversity to itself," or more accurately, "reveals itself as the spirit of communion and totality, within which identity and difference are distinguishable but inseparable points of view".

To understand this, one might consider the account of a judgment whose subject is a proper name, such as "Socrates," in a logic text like Bradley's. The concrete universal, in its deepest sense, "is one with the Individual". It is not merely *a* type of universal, but "the superior and the only true type of universal".

An excellent example of the universal, understood as a "system or habit of self-adjusting response," is an acquired skill, such as that of a cricketer. This skill embodies a dynamic response that equally deals with both similarities and differences within a range of stimulation. It is an active adjustment to varying conditions, rather than a mere recognition of repetition.

The Justification: Why Trust the Concrete Universal? Truth as the Whole

But, one might reasonably object, even if this describes the tendency of experience, why should we *trust* this outcome? Why should we consider this developed structure of macrocosm and microcosms as inherently possessing "being and of trueness," as more than a mere "castle in Spain"?

The argument countering such skepticism is essentially consistent, whether approached from the beginning or end of the analytical process. First, we can observe that "to doubt is to assert a ground for doubting". A genuine doubt must have a basis, and this basis implicitly appeals to some form of truth. The inherent tendency of logical progression, even if far from complete fulfillment, aims to "leave no room for doubt". This means it seeks to organize experience so completely that any attempt to "pick up a positive content and push it against the system" will be anticipated and only lead back into the system itself. This is an appeal to the principle that "truth or reality is the whole". According to this, the reason you cannot contradict the truth is that it leaves "no spot upon which a contradiction could be 'grounded'" outside of itself.

Consider an elementary example: how would a competent astronomer address a child who, whether through innocent ignorance or stubborn skepticism, denied the revelations of astronomy wholesale, insisting that the sun and stars are "just about what they look like to the naked eye"? So long as the doubt remains indefinite and the skeptic refuses to follow any scientific construction, it's impossible to directly address it. Such skepticism, if consistent, would be "inert and dumb". It lacks material ground and, unless formulated, is no ground at all.

However, if the doubter makes a positive allegation—if they claim, for instance, "the sun is a lantern, lit up every morning and put out at night," or "the stars are holes in a sort of dish cover"—then, the astronomer immediately gains leverage. By offering a rival interpretation of the appearances, the doubter has inadvertently "acknowledged universality as the test". They are no longer rejecting the system *in toto* but are calling upon it to integrate their interpretation. At this point, the system, as the whole, can powerfully retort: "We know all that already; we already possess your interpretation, but in a shape which effects the object implied in every interpretation of appearances, which, in the shape you gave it, it failed to do" The system would show how the doubter's fragmented vision, while aiming for connection, ultimately fails to unite with the full appearances and the vast mass of other experience. Conversely, the system can offer connections that "draw out the nature of your experience very much more completely and and in far greater union with the rest of experience".

This argument, tracing back to Plato, emphasizes the principle that "the truth may be defined as the whole". If you merely doubt indefinitely, you assert nothing against it; if you attempt to push a contrary interpretation, you implicitly concede that "something is," and that "something" can be shown to be already contained within the system you are challenging.

Non-Contradiction as Determinate Self-Maintenance

This appeal to "the whole" is not an arbitrary procedure; it is fundamentally the same as the principle of non-contradiction. The essence of this matter lies in the "determinate development of the character of being". Simply put, "What is, is by determinate self-maintenance". There is no meaning in "it is" apart from "it is what it is". Whatever exists, acts or possesses predicates, and these actions or predicates define "what it is".

While Plato carefully explained that "is" and "is not" can and must be united for a complete determination of content, a contradiction arises when "is" affirms one determinate self-maintenance and "is not" affirms a different one, or general otherness, and both are attached to the *same point of being*.

This amounts to asserting that in its self-maintenance, it simultaneously fails to maintain itself. Such an assertion "destroys the character of being" as an expression of positive experience; it is to "posit and to annul in the same act".

Therefore, if an experience presents this kind of appearance—a combination of "is" and "is not" without distinction in the subject—it "falls short of the character of being". It "undoes itself" and "fails to conserve itself in any actual character".

Conversely, when the appearance of self-hostility (contradiction) is removed by transforming the content of experience into a system where previously conflicting elements become "co-operative and no longer conflicting members," the experience exists in a "higher degree".

Its "self-maintenance includes more of reality" and is, consequently, less likely to be confronted with external facts it cannot assimilate. Plato illustrates this in *Republic V*: everyday experiences like judging something beautiful or ugly, large or small, fluctuate because the standards we use are "fragments and not worlds"

If a judgment were adequately grounded—encompassing the right conditions and guarded by proper distinctions—it could not easily, or ultimately at all, "pass over into its contrary". Instead, beauty and ugliness, largeness and smallness, would be understood as "differents and not contraries".

They would not both be predicated, without justification, of the same subject. When we grasp what beauty fully means and discover it within a coherent "world" of our experience, then, proportionally to the extent and coherence of that world, it becomes immensely difficult for any change of mood or environment to make us declare it ugly.

What we have been describing, in essence, is the self-maintenance or self-assertion of the universal. The universal is precisely that character of experience that overcomes the "is not" by integrating it, by reducing it to an element that is harmonious with and corroborative of the "is". It is, in a profound sense, "the self in the other".

Therefore, when we state that the criterion of truth and reality is one—and that it is the character of non-contradiction—this assertion is grounded in the general, and more particularly, the universal nature of experience.

We are thus experiencing, as it were from another perspective, the same principle that, in its results, revealed itself as the concrete universal. For, as we've observed, the removal of contradiction inherently involves the character of a "world". This character is ascribed to profound philosophical concepts such as Plato's *agathon* (Form of the Good) and, in its ultimate interpretation, to Kant's Noumenon—indeed, to every principle that seriously endeavors to express the full nature of being.

Beyond Formal Undeniability: The Strength of Concrete Experience

It is frequently believed that the criterion of truth should belong to a special class of principles distinguished by their peculiar property: they cannot be denied without simultaneously being affirmed by that very denial. Such principles, for example, might include the assertion that "there is a self-consistent reality". To deny this, or even to claim that reality need not be self-consistent, implies a degree of insight into the nature of things and the conditions of true assertion, which in turn implicitly assumes a reality with a coherent nature of its own—the very principle being denied. Another obvious instance is the affirmation that "every judgment lays claim to truth". No disclaimer of truth's pretension can be formulated without, as a central part of its content, claiming to embody a truth—the truth of the disclaimer itself.

It is true that in the case of these simply expressed principles, the absurdity of denying the "significant law of Identity"—the proposition that statements true of reality can be made—reveals itself instantly.

However, the lecture suggests it is a mistake to regard these as logically peculiar cases or *a priori* truths, and thus to rely solely on the formal refutation of skepticism they seem to provide. This approach neglects the deeper, fuller account of non-contradiction as the principle of the "more" of positive experience and its self-maintenance, as we just discussed.

The impossibility of being denied without *eo ipso* being affirmed, which characterizes these very simple propositions, attaches to them only as a consequence of the "extreme emptiness of experience in so far as they appeal to it". For, at this abstract level, any proposition implying *any* possibility of a stable experience, even if negative in form, suffices to establish what such principles formally contend for, which amounts to no more than "the reality of some persistent or objective experience".

In short, "if you say anything, in the indicative mood, it commits you to the affirmation of a something". This is why even the formula "there is nothing," if taken strictly, must logically involve the affirmation of an objective world.

But it is a mistake, the argument contends, to treat this apparently immediate certainty—which fundamentally amounts to the abstraction "something is"—as superior in logical value to the "certainty of a well-established world of concrete experience". While the latter might seem formally at a disadvantage (being less amenable to formulation as *a priori* truth), this apparent disadvantage arises precisely from its richness.

In an advanced phase of the construction of experience, it is *prima facie* conceivable that particular elements of a concrete world, however intricately connected to the whole, could be denied in their precise context while leaving a large proportion of organized experience seemingly untouched.

In contrast, with abstract formal principles, if their content could be removed or destroyed by denial, "then the whole world would be gone—no content at all would be left to experience". Because even denial itself implies a "real something," denying these fundamental principles inevitably reaffirms them; it affirms a "something" so minimal in multiplicity that it is necessarily identical with the abstract principles themselves. If you say "there is nothing," you assert something exists; if you say "there is no truth," you proclaim that this truth exists; if you say "contradictory assertions may both be true," you assert the very notion of truth that your proposition simultaneously tries to destroy. When we consider experience under these general characteristics (e.g., A is A), we cannot deny any of them, because to deny at all is to attempt to deny everything, an attempt frustrated by the very form of negative assertion.

This distinction, which seemingly confers a special guarantee upon these formal principles, is in truth merely apparent, resulting from our "insufficient perception of logical context". The ultimate proof of everything that is proven is, in fact, one and the same: "that if it is to be denied, nothing can be affirmed". And since it is impossible to deny everything, a proposition so guaranteed must be accepted.

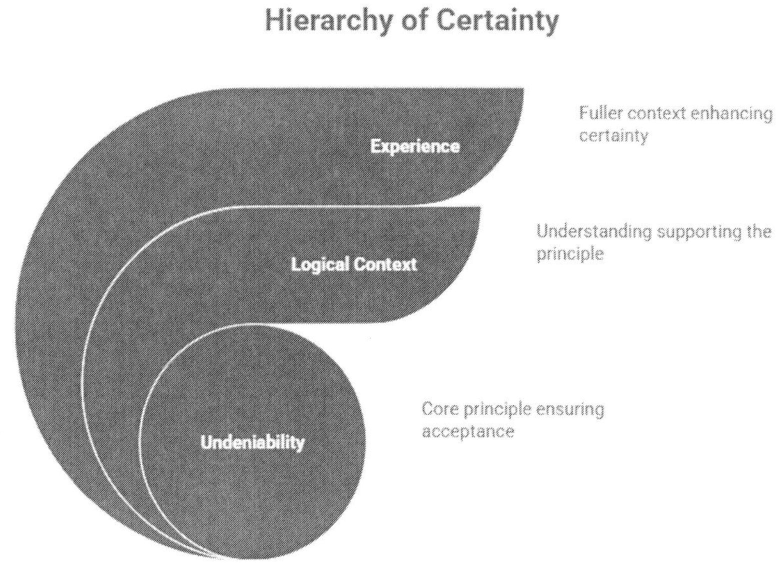

A certainty grounded in this way is actually *greater* in proportion as the "whole of experience is fuller and more coherent". The difficulty of denying everything obviously increases as "everything becomes a more completely apprehended cosmos with a fuller self-maintenance".

The apparent advantage of principles whose denial directly affirms them arises because, while the certainty of experience as a whole grows with its completeness and organization, the power to assert that certainty as guaranteeing *particular* propositions in a precise, literal form is diminished by the very cause that increases the whole's certainty: its diversity and comprehensiveness. For example, however sound a specific scientific proof may be, in an advanced stage of experience, it remains *prima facie* possible to deny a precise, departmental proposition while leaving much of organized experience seemingly intact.

The resources for certainty are immensely greater, but paradoxically, they become much more difficult to wield. Yet, this difficulty is largely illusory.

If we select as necessary propositions those that signify "vital functions or whole departments of our world" rather than mere precise, literal facts, we can access and utilize the greater certainty that attaches to a full, rich content of knowledge compared to any abstract content.

We cannot stake our entire belief in reality on the exact formulation of the Law of Gravitation, the Conservation of Energy, or even the existence of God, let alone specific conclusions in specialized sciences.

But we *can* and *do* stake our belief on the "general 'trueness and being' of whole provinces of advanced experience, such as religion, or morality, or the world of beauty and of science".

These concrete, comprehensive realms offer a "higher and deeper evidence of the being and nature of the real" than those formally undeniable judgments, which, because they imply only the bare minimum of experience, belong to the abstract form of the principle of non-contradiction.

Erasing the Distinction Between Necessary and Contingent Truth

This entire argument effectively denies the traditional distinction between necessary and contingent truth.

- Necessary truth is typically defined as truth whose denial involves a direct self-contradiction.
- Contingent truth is defined as truth whose denial is only a contradiction when viewed in connection with other parts of experience. The lecture contends that the test of the "inconceivability of the contradictory," when correctly

understood, applies equally to both classes of truths. Leibniz's extraordinarily plausible defense of this distinction, it is argued, cannot ultimately be maintained.

For "Every true proposition is so in the last resort because its contradictory is not conceivable in harmony with the whole of experience".

In other words, the denial of any true proposition, when its full implications within the total coherent system of reality are considered, constitutes a self-contradiction, not merely a contradiction of fact.

This becomes evident when we fully determine its subject and predicate by the rest of experience.

From this perspective, the richer, fuller ranges of experience, in which we affirm that "the truth is the whole," are not fundamentally different in kind from abstract principles.

Rather, they represent the complete growth and maturity of the same truth that, in its undifferentiated form, appears in abstract principles whose denial affirms them.

In this sense, what is called "contingent" truth could, in fact, be considered "truer and more fundamental" than what passes as "necessary". The analogy to secondary qualities being more real and fundamental than primary ones is given.

While the law of contradiction might formally hold its place even if beauty, organized knowledge, social life, or religion did not exist, the "guarantee of its necessity" – the profound difficulty of accepting the alternative of believing in nothing – would be significantly weakened without these richer forms of experience. Therefore, truth is defined as "the whole," and this whole is characterized by non-contradiction or satisfaction.

Addressing Pragmatism: The Distinct Forms of Satisfaction

Now, a possible misconception arises: if non-contradiction or the whole is our criterion, might it lead to the blurring of distinctions between truth, goodness, and beauty? Could it imply that all forms of satisfying the need for harmony are of the same type, causing truth and beauty to "collapse into one under the heading of the good," indistinguishable from whatever merely "suits us and makes our experience satisfactory"—a view often associated with Pragmatism?

The first, general answer is clear: the principle of the concrete universal indeed applies to *all* types of experience—in knowledge, in life, and in enjoyment. In each of these aspects, "it is the harmoniously concrete which is the higher and the more real".

Crucially, in none of these three aspects can the "self as it happens to be" serve as a test of reality.

In following the law of the universal, the self "must transmute itself and undergo expansion and correction, obeying the necessity imposed by the real, with which it aims to be, but as given is not, at one".

This immediately disposes of the essential contention of Pragmatism, which, by confusing truth with goodness, reduces the ultimate standard to the satisfaction of the *given* self. The very notion of reality as a "spring of adjustment in the self" is incompatible with such a doctrine.

Furthermore, not only does all approach to reality involve an adjustment of the self, but this adjustment takes different forms depending on the specific function of the self that is engaged. The core question is whether "the nature of things can interest us for its own sake, apart from the concrete endeavour to transform our lives and their world".

Once the idea of a world possessing a being independent of our own distinctifies itself from our tentative efforts to satisfy our immediate wants, it becomes inevitable that we should be interested in such a world purely "from the point of view of what it is," if only because the very idea of it inherently "aspires to complete itself". As Bradley's critique of Bain sufficiently demonstrates, "Not all truth is subordinate to practice, or has, as sought for and held, any connection with practice at all".

While truth is certainly a satisfaction of a cognitive striving, it is a fallacy to conflate this with a purely utilitarian or hedonistic satisfaction.

In all our functions—"theoretical," "practical," and "contemplative"—we fundamentally seek or accept "real reality," and we never entertain the thought of modifying it.

If, somehow, a neglect of these distinctions were unavoidable, and all forms of self-expression had to be categorized as either "vision" or "action," then the ancient perspective that makes *theoria* (contemplation or pure understanding) the highest form of *praxis* (action) would be preferable to subordinating truth to "action" understood as mere change. There is, however, no reason to confuse these clear distinctions.

The Concrete Universal: Thought's Intrinsic Nature and Role

We now return to the concrete universal as the guiding insight into individuality. We regard it, generally, as the very type of complete experience, and from this vantage point, its characteristics remain consistent whether we are considering it as the object of knowledge, of will, or of enjoyment.

First, we must confront the common assertion that human thought is purely discursive, and thus fundamentally incapable of approaching the kind of self-contained reality we are discussing. It sometimes appears that different philosophers, when speaking of "thought," are not even referring to the same experience. The British philosophical tradition, often stemming from theories that view thought as a diminished or "decaying sense," is bolstered by modern analyses that depict thought as primarily an abstracting and generalizing faculty, and science as a departure from factual experience. To a certain extent, as we have admitted, this view holds for the primary character of abstract science. And it must be acknowledged that the contents of sense-perception are not entirely transparent to finite thought, implying a process of linking and transitioning between contents that are not immediately unified. This "double aspect" of finite life creates both the difficulty and the fascination of philosophy.

However, on the other hand, it has been powerfully argued, and we intuitively feel, that "it is thought which constructs and sustains the fabric of experience, and that it is thought-determinations which invest even sense-perception with its value and its meaning".

Thus, our thought is only *partially* discursive; it also possesses an "intuitive aspect," within which it remains secure in the grand structures it creates. The ultimate tendency of thought, we have seen, is not simply to generalize, but to constitute a world. While thought does press beyond the immediately "given" ('that'), pursuing the essential "what," its impulse is always to return to a "fuller 'that'"—the "whole—the world".

As it builds a world, thought tends to return to the full depth and richness of experience from which its initial, abstracting step departed.

In such a "world," a "concrete universal," we do not lose directness and significance as we move away from primary experience; on the contrary, "every detail has gained incalculably in vividness and in meaning, by reason of the intricate interpretation and interconnection, through which thought has developed its possibilities of 'being'".

The watchword of concrete thinking, therefore, is "Philosophers are dephlegmatic, they are vivifying"—"to philosophize is to enliven, to vivify". A single "second of time," for instance, obeys different laws of proportion and acquires new significance depending on whether it is an element in an hour, a musical phrase, or an act of forbearance. In Plato's terms, it becomes "more 'determined' at each step".

Following this crucial insight, we are inclined to see in thought the principle of concreteness rather than abstraction. We recognize the highest truth or reality of which thought is capable in the "fullest experience, the most self-contained world which finite minds can attain to from any given point". While it is fully conceded that absolutely self-contained experience is not accessible to finite intelligences, meaning they must always retain a discursive side, nonetheless, if we are to distinguish between less and more true or real experiences, it must be by the standard of "wholeness or self-containedness".

This standard unites with the principle of non-contradiction in the characteristic of logical stability. And, insofar as this estimation can be made, it reveals a character in which thought is "at home with itself," no longer driven from pillar to post in search of its fortune. Bradley's criticisms of the "thing," the "self," the apprehension of beauty, and even the moral and religious consciousness, despite their brilliance, imply "positive degrees of the character which constitutes reality".

These "self-centered worlds" serve as examples of the concrete universal, where the fundamental aspiration of all experience to be a whole partially comes to fruition. Insofar as they partake of such a character, we cannot deny them an aspect in which thought is at home in reality, assuming the attitude of an intuitive understanding.

The Work of Art: A Concrete Manifestation

Let us take a work of art as a prime example. Here, we can truly grasp what the Greeks meant by *Theoria*. In its essence, as a thing of beauty, and setting aside its physical or material aspects, it is "self-contained and a true whole, possessing its significance in itself, and not driving our thought beyond it to a detached meaning and explanation". Every single element, every brushstroke or note, "carries the burden, or lives with the life, of the whole". Of course, its unity and independence are imperfect, as with all finite experience, but this does not negate its demonstrative power when we recognize that we are discussing matters of degree within finite experience.

The critical point is the contrast between abstract generalization and concrete modes of thinking in their relation to the completeness of experience. In the latter, we witness the return to the fullness of experience that thought, in its abstract form, seemed to abandon.

By pursuing the same law—the removal of contradiction—the mind arrives at experience that is "incomparably more living and intense, as also incomparably more logical and rational, than that of every-day perception".

We begin to see that the true office of thought is to "build up, to inspire with meaning, to intensify, to 'vivify'".

The object upon which thought, in its true sense, has worked is not a mere "relic of decaying sense," but a "living world," analogous to the perception of beauty, where "every thought-determination adds fresh point and deeper bearing to every element of the whole".

Consider a great business organization, the economic life of a bustling city, or the moral life of a society. Seen by a casual observer, subjected to general formulas by a statistician, or grasped by an active participant who is also a discerning student, intimately familiar with all its aspects and capable of realizing the interplay of its purposes and their expression—the latter represents concrete knowledge.

This more concrete knowledge is more vital *because* it is methodically precise, and more precise *because* it is more intimately vital. Just as a painter's or musician's touch depends on extraordinary quantitative and qualitative accuracy for its vital value, which in turn stems from a "dominating sense of the whole". "Logical exactitude in the full and true sense is not a deadening but a vitalising quality". "Form, interdependence, significance, self-completeness are characters as of thought at its best, so of vitality at its highest". This is the general character by which the concrete universal provides us with the essential clue to the individual.

The Synergy of Precision and Vitality

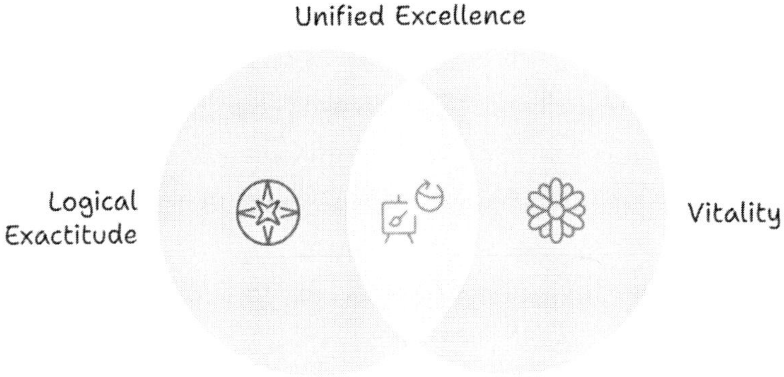

It is crucial to emphasize that thought, in this comprehensive sense, is not a separate faculty, distinct from something called "intelligence". It is, rather, the "active form of totality," present in all and every experience of a rational being—and perhaps, in varying degrees, in every experience throughout the universe.

Thought's Pervasive Presence: Sensation, Feeling, and Activity

When thought is pronounced purely discursive and thus cast as secondary and extraneous to immediate experience and activity, it is typically being contrasted with the content of sensation, the living force of will, and the immediacy and interest of feeling.

The conception of the concrete universal can shed significant light on all these oppositions, though it does not abolish the necessary distinctions of aspects characteristic of the finite mind, distinctions essential to the richness of experience. If philosophy is to make genuine progress, it must strive to move beyond the ingrained notion of an "irreducible dualism" inherent in human nature as both spiritual and animal.

It is far too easy to hastily declare that thought cannot penetrate the differences of the sensuous world, or play any role in feeling or volition beyond that of a mere reflective observer. This leads to the conclusion that "experience can never be a whole".

Equally facile is the assertion that ideal human experience must become purely spiritual, and thought must find its completion in isolation from the world of sense, feeling, or action. But philosophy's true task demands the patience and care to "disentang and estimat the signs and media by which man's animal nature gives utterance to his spiritual being".

Let us briefly consider the nature of thought in general: its nature is not exhausted by abstract reflective judgment or inference. Its very essence lies in the "passage of a being or content beyond itself, in a word, ideality, adjustment, or the universal". It is, therefore, fundamentally "one with the experience of freedom".

As Hegel observed, "He who talks of freedom, and excludes thought, knows not what he says".

The profound identity between these two concepts resides in the "transformation of the alien into the kindred, the affirmation of self in and through the other".Wherever this dynamic process of overcoming otherness occurs, we find the essence of thought.

And it is evident that this essence is present in the higher phases of all finite experience: sentient, emotional, conative, as well as cognitive. The characteristic embodiments of thought within finite life include knowledge (which encompasses sense-perception), love, and work or activity.

Regarding sensation: While it appears *prima facie* that the contents of sense-perception are not transparent to thought—they cannot be definitively defined or brought as members into a fully intelligible system where reason recognizes its own nature—this is not the complete picture. The fundamental principle is often missed here. The contents of sense-perception, like all things, reveal a "new character in becoming elements of a new whole". Although undefinable in their most minimal sense, they acquire "fresh meanings" within "fresh combinations," meanings rooted in their inherent nature and drawn out through contrast and relation. It is undeniable that they "speak to us," conveying meanings to our complex nature as a whole, even if our thought struggles to adequately interpret what they have to say in other language.

The most compelling illustration of this enhanced significance is found in the world of beauty. For a mind expert in this realm, media such as sound, color, form, rhythm, and metre possess an undeniable "logic and a necessity of their own". The universal—the inherent striving towards the whole—is present within them just as it is in all experience. It is illogical to deny their "constructive and creative nisus" the name of thinking simply because it does not operate through what we conventionally call logical language and verbal concepts. A rhythm that perfectly completes another rhythm, a sound that genuinely satisfies the educated ear, a color that is precisely "demanded by a colour-scheme"—these are "as necessary and as rational as the conclusion of a syllogism". As Whistler famously asserted regarding a seemingly minor detail in a painting, it's "not a matter of taste at all, it's a matter of knowledge"—implying a necessity of rational type.

The idea that to know the conditions of a sensation's occurrence is equivalent to and supersedes the presentation of the sensuous element itself can be interpreted in two ways. One, the Platonic interpretation commonly misunderstood, suggests reality is solely an intelligible world, rendering sensation null or indifferent. The other, more profound interpretation, implies that sensation can become so transparent to thought, so completely absorbed in expressiveness, that its contingent and unintelligible character vanishes. It becomes a revelation, indistinguishable from the meaning it expresses, embodying a unique perfection. We can almost conceive of this in the highest moods of aesthetically creative sympathy.

It is from these fullest experiences that we should seek our clues if we wish to understand how life can most nearly approach perfection. As Pater beautifully put it, "Colour is a spirit upon things by which they become expressive to the spirit".

In the concrete universal, we find the beginning of a "transfiguration of sense" that, at a higher level, would entirely remove the alienation between sense and thought. It is always an illusion to believe that you can separate the expression from its meaning, like thinking you lose nothing of a friend's personality if you never hear their voice again. If all sensation became to us like the tones of a voice we know, or the touch of a hand we love, we would fully realize the fundamental "inseparability of the symbol and the symbolised".

Next, let's consider feeling. When asserting a higher status for thought, we must address the prevailing notion of its antagonism to feeling, whether feeling is understood as immediate psychical being, emotion towards an object, or pleasure and pain.

Again, the experience of aesthetic enjoyment serves as a powerful type. Here, feeling is inherently and remarkably unified with, and proportional to, specific, determinate attributes of the object. While we do not subscribe to a simple Hedonistic standard of reducing "higher" pleasure to merely "greater" pleasure, it is undeniable that in the aesthetic object, there is something that imbues the responsive feeling with an objective valuation.

As with sensation, so with emotion or pleasure-pain: it is the concrete universal that draws them out of their 'blankness' and reveals them as aspects of the difference made to a living world.

They gain meaning by being affirmed or negated within this world, thereby making explicit the "more" and "greater" of which they are capable.

It seems highly probable that pleasurableness and emotion vary in value *directly* with the constructive achievement of thought that accompanies them. A brief reflection on great works of art immediately confirms this.

While a concentrated intensity might accompany the "blank formlessness of the fiercer pleasures and pains" (as Plato and Aristotle thoroughly analyzed), such intensity, however explained, possesses "relatively less and not more of 'being and of trueness'". It negates the expansion of the self, forcing the whole to constrict itself into something that cannot contain it, leaving us feeling "smothered" and "driven into a cul de sac". In the various kinds and degrees of love, just as in pleasure-pain, we can clearly observe the profound difference wrought by approaching the "character of thought—the character of a harmonious world".

And even if we consider feeling as immediate psychical being, the relationship remains consistent. While all thought undoubtedly has a mediate side (involving connections and processes), all concrete thought, in its developed form, has become immediate no less than mediate. Indeed, what the great philosophers meant by "thought"—the highest possible phase of realization—is strikingly similar to what most people understand (insofar as they grasp the concept at all) when they speak of "feeling".

For if we accept thought as partially intuitive, a unity asserted through diversity, then there is nothing to prevent it from reproducing the character of feeling as immediate apprehension. This form of immediate apprehension is, in fact, the "totality of a mediate discourse"—a complete, integrated understanding that feels immediate and direct, much like the profound recognition and affection evoked by a "name, familiar and adored," in our minds.

Finally, let us consider activity or will. To act is to demonstrate the same essential nature of the concrete universal. It is to perform the paradoxical feat of "to go beyond the starting-point, and in going beyond it, to remain at home". Both the outward expansion and the inward self-maintenance are absolutely essential; without either, the full conception of activity remains unrealized.

It's worth noting that if the concept of causal interaction between spatial things originates from our personal sense of activity, it is a singularly unfortunate anthropomorphism that has detrimentally affected the understanding of its archetype.

For causal activity, as we attribute it to nature, is precisely what we cannot experience ourselves; and our own experience of activity cannot, without utter confusion, be ascribed to natural things. Genuine activity, that which is truly "ours," is one in which "we do not remain at home as well as go abroad". The mere effect of body upon body can never constitute an act of an originative being.

To be active, in the sense we truly experience it, means to be a "free cause," not merely a natural cause. A free cause is not just a term in a succession perceptible only to an observer; it is a "world which reshapes itself in virtue of its nature and that of its content, and, in doing so, extends its borders, and absorbs and stamps itself upon something that before seemed alien".

For deeper insight into our experience of activity, we should turn to thinkers like Leibniz and Spinoza, or to the more modern conception of a "free cause".

And then we would discover that, without reducing conation (striving) to cognition (though all cognition *is* a conation), we must recognize in all conation, as in all other finite experience, the "essential character of thought".

It must be observed for clarity that not all thought is cognition, although all cognition is thought. Cognition is a specific form of conation, determined by particular interests and ideas. These ideas are independent, not parasitic, but the form of experience they determine is not the complete and exclusive form of the unity that experience seeks. The undue assertion of cognition as the sole end or criterion o

f perfection—what might be termed intellectualism—often arises from the defective formulation of opposing views. Cognition, at any rate, powerfully exhibits that self-transcendent character of thought that constitutes its freedom and initiative. For these are essentially forms of adjustment and adaptation; they imply that an apparent friction or antagonism can, through the right kind of self-assertion, be transformed into responsiveness and co-operation.

If those who champion freedom and spontaneity ("activists" or "voluntarists") fully recognized this character in their accounts of experience's mainspring, they might soon dismantle the tendency to equate thinking solely with cognition. But if they insist on severing these very qualities from "adequacy of ideas to an objective situation" (making them "passive" in Spinoza's sense), then there is a risk of a backlash, leading others to find the essentials of a free and active being solely in cognition. However, neither extreme is inevitable, nor has either been adopted by Greek or modern Idealism. Will and activity, in their truest sense, signify the "operation of the nature of thought through the expansion of ideas into fact". They are not confined to, though they do include, the operation of those specific ideas that constitute the domain of cognition.

The Ultimate Goal: Individuality as the True Universal

Thus, by rigorously pursuing the conception of the logical universal, we have arrived at the idea of something complete and self-contained—a realm where sensation becomes transparent and feeling becomes determinate. This culminating idea is none other than the idea of the Individual.

Individuality is the ultimate completeness of that character of wholeness and non-contradiction that we initially generalized under the name of logical stability. It is, in essence, all one whether we choose non-contradiction, wholeness, or Individuality as our criterion of the ultimately real. What we mean by it in each case is identical: "we mean that which must stand; that which has nothing without it to set against it, and which is pure self-maintenance within".

Superficially, individuality might seem to reside at two extremes: an "atom" might claim it because it is indivisible, or a "world" might claim it because its positive nature is ruined if anything is added or taken away. But in the ultimate sense, the sense indicated above, it is commonly accepted that there can only be one true individual, and that is the Individual, the Absolute. The atom, being incapable of organized self-maintenance, would actually be the extreme opposite of the true individual. Our primary aim here is not to elaborate further on the theory of the Absolute, but rather, accepting ultimate Individuality as the character our fullest experience tends to approach, to draw conclusions regarding human beings, to whom we apply the term "Individuals" in a secondary sense.

The first and most important point the argument leads me to emphasize is that Individuality is essentially a positive conception. There has been an unfortunate tendency to define individuality not as *being oneself,* but as *not being someone else.* While in the Absolute these two sides must converge (no mere repetition in a perfect arrangement), for finite experience, which side we emphasize is paramount.

Uniqueness that is merely guaranteed by a negative relation to other series is one thing; uniqueness that is constituted by a profound or comprehensive content is entirely another. The former can descend into mere eccentricity; the latter is, in itself, originality. Within finite conditions, originality is not fundamentally excluded by agreement or even extensive repetition. Its essence lies in the "richness and completeness of a self," not in the non-existence of any other self approximating it. A merely exclusive relation is formal, provides no clue to the content of individuality, and can become dangerous if overemphasized. All that is true in it is that individuals must be distinct; to say they are *not each other* in every sense quickly becomes untrue. The individual is individual, first and foremost, because "his own content is stable and self-contained". The ultimate individual, indeed, has no other individual from which to be distinguished.

The uniqueness often associated with individuality is frequently expressed as uniqueness of purpose. We will revisit the subject of purpose later, but it is crucial to note now that the conception of purpose often shares the merely *de facto* character of negative individuality.

A purpose is, after all, simply a want or, at best, a wanted object. It offers no inherent guarantee of depth or value merely by being a purpose that only one being entertains. Furthermore, it cannot be ascribed to a timeless reality. A purpose is, in essence, merely a partial element of a larger logical whole that unfolds in time. There is no reason to assume that the unfulfilled part, which presents itself as a "want"—a contradiction arising from the incompleteness of its world—is inherently of pre-eminent interest or value.

In short, while a purpose in a finite mind may be "distinctive," a higher quality of content, representing a profound necessity of a highly organized world, would be required to make it truly individual. It is not the *de facto* purpose itself, but rather the "quality and comprehensiveness of the world that sets the purpose, that makes or mars the individuality".

The same set of contrasts appears in the connection of individuality with infinity. As discussed earlier, recent investigations into infinity leave the crucial philosophical distinction between self-completeness and endlessness unchanged.

The individual, if our argument holds, is characterized by "self-containedness or self-completeness". It includes endless detail only in the sense that any endeavor using a demonstrably inadequate method to solve a problem will proceed endlessly.

For example, to fully know God in spatial extension or in a temporal series would be an endless task. While the endlessness might even be affirmed as actual if that which is to be known is reality itself and its nature inevitably gives rise to such a procedure when approached inadequately, this would not mean the endless series is *given* as complete.

Modern mathematical infinite numbers are akin to class concepts involving an extension of "all possible cases," practically indefinite, yet implying a corresponding number. This characteristic of class concepts, noted on purely logical grounds long ago, again suggests a concept or definition that *demands* the completeness of a series, rather than a series that is already *actually* complete.

Inwardness and the Conquest of Externality

To form a just estimate of what is involved in the nature of Individuality or the concrete universal, it is essential to examine the common antithesis of inward and outward. The Individual is inherently one with the spiritual, and the characteristic of the spiritual in its proper nature is "inwardness as opposed to externality". However, it is vital to interpret these terms correctly. These terms are drawn from the mind's awareness of its own processes, contrasting with the nature of space, where objects appear external to one another. A mental process is "inward" because its component phases are typically inseparable, though diverse. Possessing one implies possessing the other. Memory is inward because its diversity is bound up with the mind's being; you cannot take one and leave the other. "Inwardness is diversity without dissociation".

Matter, by contrast, is "outward" because, seemingly, you can take part of it and leave part without essentially modifying either. While it would be untrue to say that parts of space in no way presuppose each other, *prima facie*, the connection is not given *within* each part, and spatial objects refuse to form a self or center of experience, even if they are ultimately inconceivable without one. Such, in general, is the character of Nature, when taken as independent, non-psychical existence. As thus hypostatized, it represents the type of being most remote from spirit and from individuality.

Bound up with the externality of Nature is the conception of Mechanism. Its essence is that the world consists of elements that are complete in themselves, yet simultaneously determined in relation to elements beyond them. If they were not complete in themselves, they would be at the mercy of the whole, losing their claim as self-subsistent components. If not determined by others, they would not even appear to constitute an orderly world.

Yet, these two pretensions—the claim to an independent nature and the admission that their reality lies in externally determined behaviour —form, when taken together, the crudest case of externality.

The mechanical element behaves according to external relations, but it possesses an inner being—a "purely physical or self-external existence"—that has "no communion with the whole". Its behaviour is "betwixt and between": it does not refuse all response to the system, but it responds, one might say, "ignorantly and narrowly," "speaking when spoken to" but demonstrating no deeper sympathy with its world beyond specific, individual reactions to particular solicitations. According to an old distinction, it acts "according to law, and not from the idea of law". It follows a routine, taking no account of purpose.

All of this represents the received account of the antithesis between the inward/spiritual and the outward/natural, culminating in the opposition between spirit and extension, and between purposiveness and mechanism.

As formulated by philosophy, this account is partly controversial and partly provisional. It reiterates the ideas of Naturalism, those of uncritical metaphysics founded on conceptions prevalent within the natural sciences. But it also acknowledges that, in different types of our experience, there is a prima facie justification for such distinctions, without admitting they contain ultimate truth.

My reason for elaborating on the contrast of inward and outward at this juncture is to repudiate what I consider a misapplication of it. When "inwardness" is intended to be equivalent to Individuality or the character of spirit, it should be understood as "a type of experience superior to externality and including it".

However, there is a natural tendency, partly due to the apparent correspondence of metaphors and partly to a reluctance to embrace concrete synthesis, to interpret inwardness as the co-ordinate contrary of externality. Inwardness, when thus conceived, descends from an inclusive concrete reality to an exclusive abstract one.

As Hegel would often emphasize, "The mere inner is the mere outer". Individuality, instead of being a fullness of life and content, becomes the bare abstraction of a "holy of holies" that, if entered, would prove an "empty shrine". Structure, Logic, and Determinateness are wrongly banished from this "inner" realm, as they are seen as implying externality and mechanism. The emptiness of most accounts of higher experiences is largely due to this misconception, which in turn perpetuates the misconception itself. It is true, of course, that our accounts of an experience fundamentally beyond our own must be abstract and provisional. But it is not true that the contents and objects that drive finite experience can, in principle, be abolished into a void, however transformed they may be. A world, as I understand it, cannot consist of "spiritual centres without circumferences," nor can they, as "inward centres" in the popular sense, form circumferences for each other. Individuality and true spiritual inwardness do not lie in that direction at all.

Externality can subsist only as subordinated to inwardness; but inwardness can subsist only in the conquest of externality. The tendency to accept the self-external—nature or matter—as self-existent must be corrected in higher experience, though this tendency can never fully maintain itself in any actual consciousness. But to deny its self-existence is one thing; to deny its subsistence as the object or determinate character necessary to spiritual reality is quite another. The "outer" is, in essence, the content of the "inner". There are two distinct ways to conceive of spiritual advancement: one is to resolve all externality into a series or complexes of psychical centers (a flawed approach); the other is to conceive it as raised to an adequate object or character for individuals whom it characterizes.

The moral, then, is that as we approach Individuality, we are not to look for a diminution of content, of structure, or of determinateness. Instead, Individuality will reveal itself as inwardness and spirituality, "not by emptiness and abstraction, not even by blank intensity of incommunicable feeling, but, in a word, by the characteristics of 'a world'". Mechanism and externality will, in a sense, be superseded, but not by inwardness as their co-ordinate contrary. Part will not be bound to part within the whole merely by quantitative reaction. Rather, in principle, we should expect the adjustment of quantitative determinations to become infinitely more delicate and subtly precise (though not necessarily insisted upon as numerable) as they become concomitants or vehicles of a more intensely focused significance. In the same way, we should expect to find in higher individuality not more but less of what is commonly called "spontaneousness" (if that means indetermination, laxity of connection, or unaccountable new development). Instead, we should find more of logic, more of expansion towards fully enacting demands that emerge by systematic necessity from the articulation of the whole; less of the urgency of exclusive feeling, and more of the definite emotions attached to fuller self-expression; less of the mere passion of mystical religion, and more of the "amorintellectualis Dei" (intellectual love of God) resting on clear spiritual insight. "Inwardness will not be the banishment of all that seems outward, but the solution of the outward in the circulation of the total life". This profound truth can be realized to some degree by any student of Dante or Wordsworth, and indeed, by anyone who engages deeply with art, science, or history.

The Misleading Path of History as the "Concrete"

Finally, let us consider another common philosophical misstep. The failure to find a satisfactory type of experience in the abstract or conditional judgments of mechanistic science can, understandably, lead us elsewhere than to the concrete universal or cosmos conceived as individual. Thus, we find the genuine experience, which abstract science purportedly fails to grasp, identified with "the historical". We are told that "The actual is wholly historical," and it is contrasted sharply with natural science and with thought itself, often in the tone of naive Realism.

This view claims that history alone is concrete experience, richer than thought (which is seen as only universal and relational), providing "existence" rather than mere "science". It is characterized as contingent, daring to admit contingency into the very heart of things, in opposition to the necessity of thought-connections. History is presented as the "life and the end," while science is merely the "means". I presume that this perspective is influenced by an ideal of individuality, aiming to take as its basis the lives of persons who, in some sense, are considered individuals, and within whose temporal soul-process all finite experience is supposedly contained.

However, such a view, as I previously suggested, appears little better than Natural Realism.

We are asked to accept as richer than thought a reality that consists of a "fragmentary diorama of finite life-processes unrolling themselves in time". This is seen "from the outside," "not strictly knowable because a tissue of mere conjunctions," and yet "not given" because it is a mere construction based on the present. It is deemed "contingent through and through," failing to even shed the form of mere conjunction that makes true connection impossible.

Indeed, "History is a hybrid form of experience, incapable of any considerable degree of 'being or trueness'". The uncertain narrative of successive events struggles to integrate with the complete interpretation of the social mind, of art, or of religion. When such interpretations are attempted in conjunction with a historical narrative, they often fall into separate chapters, isolated from the chronological account.

The great things, which are necessary in themselves, become contingent within the narrative, or are attributed to historical actors through highly dubious assumptions of insight. The study of Christianity, for instance, is the study of a great world-experience; the precise assignment of individual shares in its development is a problem for scholars, whose conclusions, though humanly interesting, can never be of supreme philosophical importance. Are we, indeed, to see the philosophy of history aligning with the "psychological valet" who presumes to interpret the minds and natures of great men as if he were "God's spy"?

The reason for taking this hybrid form of experience as the type of reality lies in ignoring the concrete universal. This fundamental defect leads us to mistakenly assume that concreteness and contingency are inseparable. It causes us to confuse the apparent contingency of details *within a cosmos* (where the main members are necessary to the whole) with the "contingency at the heart of a spatiotemporal world of incident," a world that has never been truly re-created by experience of the fullest type. It is impossible for life at its best to be contingent. And if "freedom" is mentioned in this context, it must be remembered that "freedom is the logic of individuality, and as remote as possible from contingency".

To claim that reality can only be found in the immediately "given," and not in its expansion and interpretation through thought, is surely the ancient fallacy of naive Realism. If thought were truly disconnected from existence, it would be pointless to speak of either generating the other.

But the connection of thought and existence, whatever its precise nature, is not so easily dismissed. We are faced with the world or worlds of experience in their fullest and most exact realization, and in them, as we have seen, we find thought inseparable from the recognition of what things are for us at their best. Social morality, Art, Philosophy, and Religion take us far beyond the spatio-temporal externality of history; these are concrete and necessary living worlds, and in them the finite mind begins to experience something of what individuality must ultimately mean.

In conclusion, our objective has been to dispel the prejudice that views the individual as merely an empty, exclusive point, whose spontaneity and purposiveness draw upon no positive source and focus no positive striving of the universe. Instead, we have sought to illuminate the individual as a "positive cosmos, with its own logic and organisation, expressive, in spite of its immediate unity, of a determinate being". This profound understanding of the concrete universal will serve as our guide as we further explore the intricate problems of teleology and interaction in future discussions.

Lecture-3

Uniformity and General Law in Harmony with Individuality

This lecture overturns the familiar belief that law and uniformity threaten freedom and individuality. It reveals how true natural law is not mechanical repetition but intelligent relevancy, showing that individuality, spontaneity, and creativity arise precisely through lawful coherence, not in defiance of it, but as its highest and most living expression.

Clarifies that natural laws and uniformity do not suppress individuality but sustain it

Ladies and gentlemen, in this lecture, we will delve into a common misconception that posits a fundamental conflict between the essence of individuality and the principles of the Uniformity of Nature and universal law. This widespread idea, which we must address to truly grasp the character of the individual, stems from a crucial confusion: the confusion between the abstract and concrete universal, and between the mere recurrence of similars and the identity within a differentiated system.

One prominent view, often found in spiritual philosophies, suggests that nature must possess mentality, and this mentality, in turn, necessitates variability. This high degree of variability is then deemed incompatible with the principle of uniformity. Such an interpretation, I argue, misconstrues the principle of Uniformity, creating a false antagonism between it and the very nature of mind. More broadly, it is frequently asserted that

Individuality inherently excludes the fulfillment of general law. This sets up a profound fallacy that distorts our understanding of both nature and humanity. Instead of appreciating the magnificent opposition and ultimate reconciliation between nature and spirit, this view reduces their connection to a remote resemblance, based on an exaggerated concept of variability in nature and an abstract understanding of mind.

When we speak of the Uniformity of Nature in this context, we are not referring to it as a deep logical principle, but rather in its popular, everyday sense: the notion that "the future will resemble the past," or that nature proceeds in a regular, repetitive manner with similar elements to a high degree. Logicians, it is important to note, generally disclaim this popular interpretation as a foundational principle.

The argument then extends to suggest that actual purposiveness and spontaneity, often evidenced by variation and irregularity, are far more prevalent in nature than this popular understanding of Uniformity would allow. Proponents of this view might even point out that an appearance of such uniformity can be generated in human conduct, which we know to be spontaneous, by applying methods similar to those that create the impression of regularity in nature. The conclusion they draw is that the spontaneity we recognize in mind might also pervade what we typically consider external nature, accompanied by a similar variability that our methods of inquiry simply disguise.

However, it is crucial to clarify what is truly at stake here. The Law of Uniformity in its logical sense—which signifies a rational system where all changes and differences are relevant to each other—is not directly challenged by this line of argument. If the intention is not to impeach this deeper logical law by affirming inexplicable or irrelevant variation as a proof of spontaneity, then the contention lacks substance. Simply stating that nature contains more differences than some previously thought is trivial.

To claim that inorganic constants exhibit rational, progressive, and significant variation would be a profound statement, but the facts do not support it. The real philosophical weight of the argument lies in asserting that variability in conscious conduct implies indeterminate spontaneity, which in turn excludes Uniformity in the logical sense (what I prefer to call"relevancy"), and that such spontaneity should also be presumed in natural elements and their behaviour . Given the belief in an antagonism between individuality and general law that accompanies these views, it appears we are indeed witnessing an attempt to discredit the very conception of logical nexus or relevancy in both nature and mind. If this is disclaimed, then, strictly speaking, there is no other meaningful contention. An argument merely stating that atoms of the same element are not all of the same size, for instance, is not a philosophical argument at all. This point, though seemingly minor, helps us understand the true implications for fields like Social Statistics.

The argument for variability in nature often relies on a comparison between social statistics and certain physical measurements, especially those that require the measurement of enormous numbers of units en masse. It is argued that you cannot isolate a single atom of oxygen. When its atomic weight is given as 16, this figure is the result of measuring a vast collection of atoms, with the result hypothetically attributed equally to each single atom. In essence, it's an average figure, much like the average height of schoolchildren or an actuarial estimate of life expectancy. Such averages, while useful for a class or group as a whole, do not necessarily represent each individual within that group. Their value, in fact, often lies precisely in *not* pretending to represent the individual, but in serving a collective purpose.

Therefore, it is further suggested that, for all we know from measurement, oxygen atoms might not be rigidly equal at an atomic weight of 16, but rather oscillate around this amount, similar to how any statistical figures fluctuate around an arithmetical mean. In physical measurement, we only obtain a total from which we infer an average, unable to measure individuals separately. In contrast, social statistics allow for individual enumeration and separate measurement, enabling us to critically examine the average figure, which then gives rise to the suggestion that physical elements, too, may be various and possess life and spontaneity. This analogy implies that "social constants" can exist alongside "physical constants," even though no one doubts the variability of individuals within a social group.

However, this line of argumentation strikes me as special pleading. The actual distribution of mentality in nature is a matter of fact. My primary aim is to combat the fundamental misconception regarding Uniformity and its alleged antagonism to mind.

Let's address a few key points:

1. Distinguishing "Average" from "Constant": First, it is crucial to differentiate between an average and a constant. You can compute an average from any set of figures, but whether that average is a constant depends on comparing averages from different, somehow distinct groups. If an atomic weight is merely a single average, it indeed permits any degree of variation in the actual atoms. But by the same logic, if a social statistic is only a single average, it offers no suggestion of constancy in social phenomena. So, while this doesn't disprove physical element variation, it also doesn't support the idea that social phenomena necessarily appear constant. For example, you can average 2, 10, and 10, 000 without implying any uniformity among these figures.
2. Establishing a Constant Average: To establish a constant average, you must compare the averages of different groups or periods, or directly observe how closely individual figures cluster around their average. The latter method is impossible

with minute physical elements. This is where the analogy between physical and *true* social phenomena breaks down. Physical measurements, for all accessible groups of similar units (e.g., atoms of the same type), are, by hypothesis, identical. In stark contrast, true social measurements (as opposed to physical ones), when compared across different conditions and periods, typically deviate progressively and intelligibly. They do not, on the whole, oscillate around constant amounts or tend to revert to them "in the long run". Early statistics, which might have fostered such an impression, were often fallaciously handled or based on insufficient periods of time.

True social statistics, which are directly or indirectly dependent on human conduct—such as records of crime, pauperism, and health—demonstrate extraordinary sensitiveness. For different groupings or successive periods, they show definite, adapted, or progressive variations, with no sign of oscillation around a fixed point.

These variations are readily explicable by changes in moral and material conditions, as amply proven by nineteenth-century records of crime and pauperism. If these facts are considered, the alleged analogy between physical and social constants—beyond the superficial fact that any group of figures can be represented by an average—completely disappears.

Furthermore, it is necessary to distinguish between two types of statistics: second-class and first-class statistics.

- Second-class statistics aim to account for unknown causes by encompassing their entire cycle as closely as possible. An example is estimating the average number of words per line in a manuscript by counting a dozen lines and assuming that sample represents the normal. The hope is that the main causes of variation have been captured in the sample, making the average a constant. According to the hypothesis we are examining, measurements of atomic weights and ethereal vibrations, or determinations of average life durations in specific professions, would fall into this category. The essence here is the absence of any attempt to suggest causes for the observed variations; the method deals with them as unknown.

- First-class statistics, on the other hand, are where statistics truly become suggestive—as Sigwart noted, it is by their variations that they offer insight. This is evident when comparing different death rates under varying sanitary conditions or different rates of pauperism under distinct administrative systems. In first-class statistics, we are no longer merely operating with numbers of recurrent effects while admitting ignorance of their causes. This is akin to the difference between a chance statement (e.g., probability of dying from smallpox based on population ratio) and a statement based on highly complete causal knowledge (e.g., chances for a perfect die). We move from "disjunction of ignorance" (we don't know why X causes A, B) to "disjunction of knowledge" (being X causes A, being Y causes B, and we know there's no persistent bias).

Variations in crime, pauperism ratios, disease occurrence and fatality, and general death/birth rates are correlatable with assignable causes and become more intelligible as they become more divergent—and thus, in a superficial sense, less constant. While statistical conclusions remain hypothetical regarding individual incidence (e.g., a diminishing death rate doesn't tell us which individuals are saved), the unexplained variation is no longer the typical occurrence, nor is its assumption the ideal method. In social phenomena, we can approach statistical figures from the other end, offering precise analytic explanations for individual cases based on health, morals, or economic history. Here, the variable and individual element is the climax of intelligibility. Not constancy, but explicable or relevant variation, is the typical character of these measurements. Even rough methods, used properly, should not yield the analogy asserted by the opposing argument, and the more we refine measurements, the less the analogy holds.

The argument in question—that non-uniformity proves spontaneity in nature—rests upon a false conception of the Uniformity of Nature. It seeks to disprove what we might call the uniformity of Similarity, which suggests that the future will simply repeat or resemble the past, or that one thing of a kind will simply repeat another.

However, as noted earlier, this is not the meaning of Uniformity as a logical principle or scientific postulate. While Mill's term "Uniformity" was perhaps misleading for the postulate of a rational system and coherence in the world of experience, he, and others, clearly explained that it does not mean the future will resemble the past. This might seem like a trivial point, but this prejudice—interpreting Uniformity as mere resemblance—is at the root of a broader polemic against intelligence. It springs from a deep-rooted impulse to misconceive and mutilate the activity of thought, often seen as a recrudescence of the superstition that thought is purely analytic.

Wherever in modern literature (from Newman to Kidd, Tarde to Bergson) the solvent and analytic character of intellect is emphasized, or an antithesis between Imitation and Invention, Repetition and Creation is drawn, there, I am convinced, lies a fundamental error of principle based on a vicious logical theory. The inability of these theories to account for genius, creation, and invention indicates an abstraction of elements—identity and diversity—which, when dissociated, become meaningless and contradictory. In truth, invention and creation are present in every pulse of thought, in every use of significant language, and pure repetition is an impossibility for intelligence.

Therefore, Uniformity, as a principle of science, is a uniformity not of resemblance but of identity; not a repetition of resembling elements, but the coherence of differences in a whole. It should rightly be termed "Relevancy". An argument that targets the "uniformity of resemblance" while leaving "relevancy" unchallenged effectively concedes everything a reasonable mechanistic view of the universe demands. Nothing is gained against true uniformity by suggesting that atoms vary in size, if their variation is not assumed to be in principle irrelevant to their conditions.

The initial argument sought to suggest that physical objects might possess a psychical or spontaneous character incompatible with mechanical uniformity, by drawing an analogy between their apparent constancy and that seen in subjects we know to be psychical. However, our examination reveals that the only true principle of uniformity (Relevancy) is, far from being incompatible with a psychical character, highly applicable to the mind, and indeed increasingly so as we approach the individual subject. This means the argument, instead of disproving the principle in physical objects, has compelled us to assert it in psychical ones.

The crucial point is to reject the idea that establishing great factual diversity either disproves true Uniformity (Relevancy) or proves a psychical nature. There is no inherent connection between disproving one and proving the other. Such an idea fundamentally distorts our understanding of consciousness, teaching us to associate it with eccentricity and caprice (the negation of coherent system) instead of with system and rationality. This same fundamental error identifies the spontaneity of life with unmotived diversity and proper intelligence with impotent identity.

What we truly consider indications of consciousness is not indefinite variation, but coherent progressiveness and adaptiveness. In this crucial feature, the argument has failed to demonstrate the alleged approximation of matter to mind.

To clarify this subtle point against a possible objection: One might argue that I complain about taking "breach of uniformity of resemblance" as proof of psychical character, yet I use such a breach (the difference between inorganic and social statistics) to suggest conscious spontaneity in the latter. My answer is that what indicates psychical spontaneity is not mere breach of the uniformity of resemblance, but systematic progressiveness and adaptiveness of response.

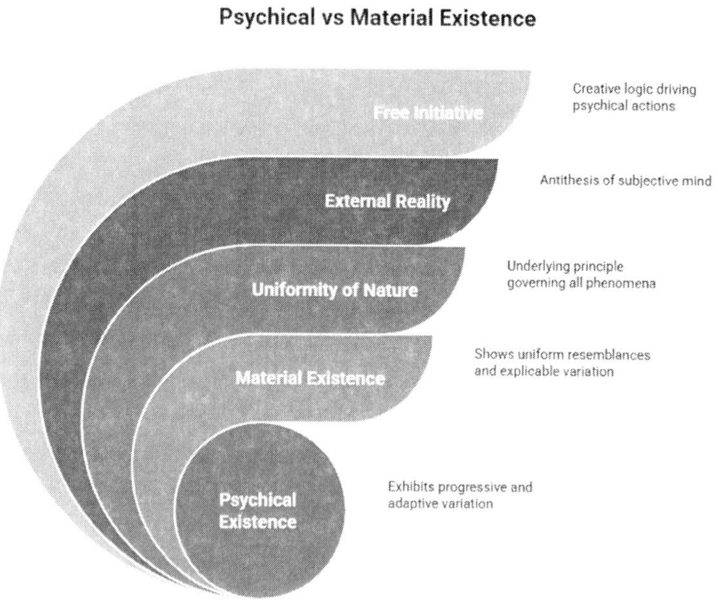

I am combating the false suggestion—based on confusing rational identity in diversity with the recurrence of resemblances—that we approach the psychical by nearing the inexplicable. This suggestion, which attempts to draw popular love of the marvellous to the side of universal mentality, is indefensible. We focus instead on explicable variation, which, in any degree, does not breach the true uniformity (Relevancy) of Nature. We see no reason to deny this type of variation in physical phenomena if theory requires it, even if they were previously thought uniformly similar. However, we insist that in regions we know to be psychical, there is not only variation but progressive and adaptive variation correlated with changes of volition. Therefore, we maintain the prima facie difference between material and psychical existence, asserting that in the mental province, the true Uniformity of Nature exhibits itself in its fullest and most complete sense. The notion of relaxing uniformity to make room for mind in nature reveals a failure to confront the problem of externality as the antithesis of subjective "mind" and the problem of free initiative or creative logic.

The same fallacy permeates the idea that the conditions of individuality conflict with the postulate of universal law. It manifests in various details, but the core issue remains the same: a denial of relevant adjustment, mistakenly conflated with a denial of similar repetition. For instance, we are sometimes told that an efficient cause need not be uniform in its action. This is seemingly intended to safeguard the spontaneity of true causal activity, seen as originating from a subject.

However, such a claim can only mean that a cause A, under identical conditions (B and C), could spontaneously produce alternative effects (b or c). Such "spontaneity" would signify not adjustment, but a failure of adjustment, a complete denial of Relevancy. To stimulus B, A might respond with c, and to stimulus C, with b.

Further, it is argued that Individuality is unique and the self impervious, its essence being sui generis, a "playground of contingency". It is also asserted that laws cannot be absolutely exact, and purposive life cannot coexist with rigid routine conformity to general law.

The polemic consistently targets the perceived rigidity, fixity, and repetition supposedly inherent in the nature of law, equating these with adequacy and precision of measurable adjustment. Spontaneity is thus held to reside in escaping general rules (i.e., rules of recurring resemblance). The concept of identity in difference seems entirely overlooked. If it were applied, fineness of adjustment, precision, and relevancy of determinate response would be recognized as the very incarnation of the universal, and thus one with life and spontaneity.

This entire contention, without doubt, reflects a modern tendency to declare intelligence inadequate to life and reality, not just in practice but in principle. It is hard to reconcile this tendency with the sometimes-conjoined attempt to enthrone finite consciousness as the director of history and evolution.

However, this leads us to the brink of pluralism and voluntarism, where the guidance by finite consciousness, divorced from an immanent reality, becomes a blind leading of the blind. For some, like Ward and Bergson, reality is richer than thought, and history becomes the type of the Absolute, causing the true concrete world of philosophy to recede.

In essence, the intelligence is conceived as formulating general rules of repetition or resemblance, through which everything new is analyzed in terms of the old.

Understood this way, the principle of intelligence naturally appears to have no grip or purchase on vital and purposive reality. The concept of teleology is then exploited to compensate for this perceived lack of rationality.

My counter-argument is that the Principle of life and reality is singular and pervasive; it is the principle of individuality, and this principle can be traced through all forms of experience, none of which supersede or are discontinuous with each other. Finite intelligence, for example, will neither supersede nor be superseded by other forms of finite experience, though it may pave the way for a perfect experience beyond itself. We must avoid two prevalent and complementary errors in modern philosophy, both stemming from the same root.

First, we must not identify intelligence with cognition (a common mischaracterization by its antagonists, often termed

"Intellectualism") and then make this narrow interpretation the sole guide of life.

Second, influenced by aversion to this error, we must not elevate any form of spontaneity, activity, subjective teleology, or intuition of life as sovereign against the character of intelligence as the active form of totality and the inherent drive towards the whole.

We must distinguish between thought in its widest and deepest sense—as the active form and logical spirit animating all modes and contents of experience—and discursive abstract thinking, which is merely one, typical, or schematic outline of the mind's operations. We must understand how all aspects of experience approach their respective completions concurrently and convergently as the underlying principle of individuality expresses itself more thoroughly through a more determinate grasp of the world's content.

Conscious intelligence is not to be dethroned; it remains superior to the unconscious, revealing what is implicit within it and representing a fuller phase of self-remodeling through adaptation to the whole. However, it is not to be one-sidedly sovereign either as abstract cognition or as finite mind or will, providing direction from its own isolated contingency. It is neither a subordinate means to evolution nor an independent rational agent acting on a world that is mere material for its spontaneity. Rather, it is simply the principle of Individuality permeating all experience, which, when taken in its abstract form, constitutes what we call discursive thought. Now, let us examine in more detail the nature of the fallacy that contrasts Individuality and Spontaneity with universal law.

We can begin with the insights of Lotze. Lotze stated that the Absolute is not a magician, conjuring things from a vacuum simply because they align with its plan. Instead, all particular operations of the Absolute are based on a system of management according to law, which is itself adapted to its operation as a whole. He emphasizes that this uniformity with general principles is not a constraint, but itself a designed part of existence. Thus, each stage in organic life's development arises step by step from reactions necessitated by the persistent nature of combined elements, and there is no exception to life's dependence on mechanical causes. This view appears prima facie reasonable, but the protest often accompanying it, which suggests a conflict between law and individuality, has evolved to undermine Lotze's original doctrine.

This protest, which pits the idea of law against the idea of an individual system, rests on the fallacy that a plurality of undifferentiated points of application is essential to a law's universality. In short, it wrongly assumes that a law's universality must be embodied in a class of similars. This error is fundamentally the same as the negative or exclusive doctrine of individuality. It stems from confusing similarity with identity, leading to the belief that scientific truth is essentially the expression of an attribute common to many similar instances.

However, sound logic dictates that a scientific truth expresses a definite connection of contents within a system—an identity pervading distinct determinations whose connection does not lie in the resemblance of elements to one another, even though certain resemblances may and must result from the interconnection. Consider the law of gravitation: it can be seen as a record of resemblances between all particles of matter, but this resemblance is secondary.

The core of the theory is the conception of the systematic relation between distance and attraction, and its contribution to further determining the physical world. Once the nature of the gravitating system is revealed, the resemblances that follow from the partial identity established between portions of matter are merely a corollary.

The basis for these resemblances could not be established without analyzing them into the precise partial identity expressed in the determinate interrelation of parts within the system.

Take a machine, like a steam-engine, as an easier example. The universal in which its members participate is the working of the engine, which primarily depends on the differing adaptations of its members to their specific purposes. While certain partial identities, leading to resemblances (e.g., all parts needing a certain strength), are involved, no machine, city, or system could be made solely from similar members. Even indistinguishable coins, if they are to influence each other's value, must do so through a relation that isn't their resemblance, but rather their cooperation towards fulfilling a demand. This distinction might seem a truism, but its neglect is a leading feature of much modern philosophy. If not forgotten, no one would treat a Universal Law or a statement of uniformity as a generality dependent on the recurrence of similar qualities or events.

Consequently, there would be no basis to suggest that a universal law is not a necessary element in the conception of a system or an individual. The truth is that plurality and repetition, the common mediums for generalities, are relatively unimportant subforms of universality. This goes deep into the modern attitude towards intelligence, where we are constantly told that intelligence can only deal with repetitions. This is merely an echo of the logic of extension and classification, which, despite its amplifications, cannot genuinely account for knowledge.

Let's take this matter further: Every individual system is a complex of Laws. The relationship between universal law and the individual system is closely mirrored by that of the Hypothetical to the Categorical Judgment, or of Science to Philosophy. The individual is essentially the realm of Categorical judgment, while the abstract universal belongs to the Hypothetical. We might even suggest that Categorical judgment is the sphere of Philosophy, and Hypothetical judgment, that of science. Philosophy makes affirmations about the universe as a whole, whereas Science deals with the interdependence of details within the universe—the precise consequences of precisely assigned conditions.

Thus, every Hypothetical judgment—every relation of antecedent and consequent—is contained within, and founded upon, a categorically-asserted ground or relatively individual system. Geometrical truth holds only if space exists; economic truth, only within the economic world; biological truth, within the kingdom of organic life. Abstract truth traces the detailed connections that constitute concrete being. The nature of this relation implies that every concrete being is a system, the analysis of whose detail can be expressed as abstract truth.

While no number of Hypotheticals can equate to a categorical truth, or a series of abstractions to an individual reality, we maintain that every individual, every living world, not only possesses its own system of truths valid only within and presupposing it, but also embodies in these truths a system of determinations. Each of these determinations, when its background and foundation are made explicit, embodies the character of a universal nexus that is "once true always true". It is always true because it carries its full conditions with it. A judgment of color harmony, decorative or dramatic fitness, appropriate biological response, or morality, given the proper background, can and must be as necessary as a geometrical axiom. And if equally necessary, given the richer content, it possesses a considerably higher degree of truth. If this background or basis of relation is absent, the judgment becomes meaningless.

The universality of such a determination, which derives from the nature of the whole present within it, lies in its embodiment of the spirit of the whole to which it belongs. A potential plurality of similar instances—a potential generality or repetition—emerges as a corollary in finite experience. However, this repetition is a character of imperfection in such experience, not perfection. For the ideal of uniqueness, properly understood, truly belongs to a perfect individuality and its members. A misinterpretation of this uniqueness lies at the heart of the view that sees antagonism between individuality and universal law.

Far from uniqueness being antagonistic to universality, the ideal of a universal nexus is to be embodied in the unique. This must be true if the identity of Indiscernibles is a true principle, as a mere repetition, by its nature, is detrimental to comprehensiveness because it tends to collapse into a featureless unity, leaving no differences to comprehend. Indeed, the closer any experience approaches unmotived repetition, the more we feel we are in the realm of error and confusion. Why would any being express a second time what has already been adequately expressed? How could such a repetition advance knowledge?. A repetition that is not unmotived but demanded stands on different ground; the mere fact that it is demanded (like a decorative repeat) rests on a difference in the situation and makes it, in principle, unique.

This concept becomes obvious if we consider the ultimate universal as the spirit of a single system, constituted by differences whose function is to develop and manifest its nature. The nexus of these differences, within this universal system, forms a system of laws, each of which is general by holding together the diverse expressions of that single life and spirit. It is equally obvious when we consider the most complete types of individuality furnished by finite experience, such as a work of art, a person, or a highly unified society. In a work of art—a picture or a poem—every particular effect is unique in that it conveys something special and distinctive, dependent on the nature of the whole, which reveals an aspect of itself through that determinate arrangement. We would have gravely misunderstood Plato's Phaedrus and Aristotle's Ethics if we did not grasp that, in principle, the fullest universal of character and consciousness embodies itself in the finest, most specialized, and unrepeatable responses to environment. Life, especially in its intensified forms like morality or knowledge, does not consist in observing general rules, but in reacting adequately, with logical—that is, fine and creative—adjustment to the ever-varying complexities of situations. Precision, measurableness, and universal law are present in the moral act, but they are features of solving problems through constructive organization, not of blind obedience to abstract rules. The same applies, relatively, to the adjustments and arrangements within a highly unified society.

Every such determination—the relationship of every color, point, and line in a Turner painting; of rhythmic members in a poem; of time intervals in an act of patience or courage—is more truly designated a universal law and connection than the truths of number and geometry, or statements about organic genera or species. While they presuppose a more special and concrete world than abstract space and time, or the world of plants or animals, they are no less necessary and far more universal. This is because they imply the world of spatio-temporal abstraction and many other worlds besides, embodying a system of differences that are much more profoundly connected, representing a much fuller and more coherent grade of reality and revelation of the nature of things. A shallower world, truly, does not impose laws on a deeper one.

What we genuinely mean by contrasting Individuality with general law is better explained by the contrast between different degrees of Individuality, where lower degrees contribute to but do not complete the higher. Thus, it is undeniably true that the laws of the world of time or space will not fully articulate the content of art or personality. But this is simply because they fall short of the requisite universality. They have too little to say about the world's richness, and their necessity depends on a far simpler background than the living whole within which the precise adjustments of art or morality find their inevitable place.

This incontestable contrast, also applicable to the chemical and biological worlds compared to self-conscious and volitional life, is often exploited recklessly, falsifying the theory of individuality and fragmenting the universe. The Laplacean imagination of the ideal calculator is frequently invoked as a deterrent, representing the presumptive claims of intelligence and supposedly leading them to absurdity. While it's true that such an ideal is infinitely distant from practical possibility and contains a theoretical defect, it is crucial how we define this defect and how far it suggests intelligence's inadequacy to reality.

Firstly, assuming such a calculation scheme is typical of intelligence's true work in connecting individuality with universal law is a mistake. Secondly, it is an exaggeration to claim that calculations of this type—based on very general characteristics of the spatio-temporal world—are in principle of no value for interpreting and even predicting what is most individual.

Intelligence is fundamentally creative and synthetic, and increasingly so as it deals with more concrete worlds. While no purely analytic work of intelligence exists, in homogeneous quantity, the synthetic element is minimal. Even if we grant a theoretical knowledge of all physical data, enabling scientific prediction, the crucial question remains: how far could predictions of life and conduct be deduced by calculation from any physical data whatsoever?. If "mind's" responses could be known as readily as phases of aging, disease, or lower organism reactions, that would still be prediction on a relatively mechanical basis. A newt's limb regeneration, though peculiar, responds to simple conditions, and many diseases are predictably certain.

It is not clear, however, whether Laplace's hypothetical calculator, regardless of his primary data, is envisioned as being like a physicist born deaf to the theory of sound when it comes to the world of mind, or if his knowledge of all forces and beings at a single moment would include the full experience of mind and its objects. In the former case, his results' significance would be lost on him, and their interpretation would be a separate operation. But this doesn't mean the two operations combined couldn't yield supreme importance. In the latter case, which Laplace likely contemplated, the calculator would possess both types of data. The substantive question is whether, by mere calculation, he could develop the psychical data and the world of quality alongside physical data, making his universe-knowledge as complete as a musician who can predict vibrations and interpret their musical values.

For our immediate purpose, the point is this: We are not bound to determine whether it would be theoretically possible for the calculator to pre-determine the physical basis of every occurrence. But it is certain that, even if this extreme assumption were conceivable, he would still be very far from performing the work of intelligence in its full sense.

To transition from moral or social experience (given in his complete world view) to unknown phases of such experience correlated with his physical conclusions, he would need to mentally control and manipulate wholly different worlds from that of physical nature—worlds aesthetic, moral, political—the realms of life and mind.

Regardless of the assumptions, calculation alone can never be typical of intelligence's work in grasping reality. We must choose between the deaf physicist and the physicist-musician. In the former, the work is incomplete; in the latter, a vast additional assumption makes it conceivable.

Secondly, it is fundamentally false to deny that such calculations could illuminate the operations of mind, whether past, present, or future. We must not forget the continuity of worlds—the building up of the fuller upon the shallower individuality. It would be significant if one could do for pain and pleasure analysis what wave theory did for sound. To say that understanding feeling, or even its actual existence, could not be affected by knowledge of its physical concomitants seems rash. Moreover, the world of things in space includes the organic and human world in simpler ways that are not insignificant. It is something to know that, as a thing in space, an organism cannot be in two places at once and interacts with others under spatio-temporal conditions. In sum, while sciences dealing with things in space are not everything, it is a great mistake to deem them nothing, especially if simultaneously arguing they encompass all of actual life that intelligence can comprehend and predict.

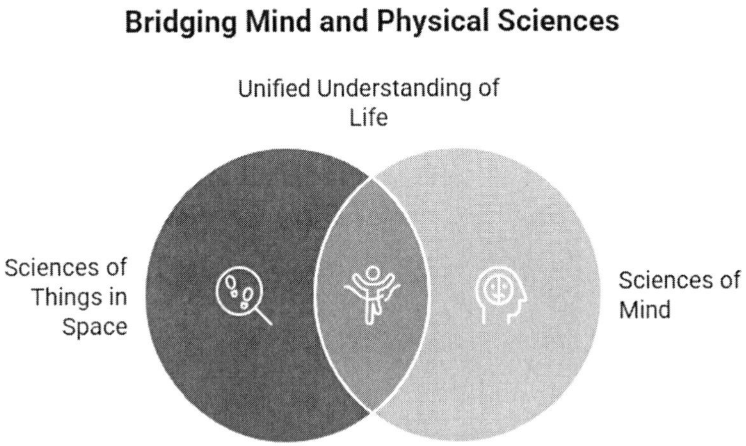

It is sometimes argued as a general principle that nature is not self-dependent, that it presupposes mind, and that mind cannot be subordinate to or defined by what, apart from it, is nothing. I find this an unimportant consideration unless accompanied by a clear demonstration of how mind asserts its superiority. The experiences we categorize as "nature" are what they are, regardless of whether we accept them as coming to us "through mind". Such a general consideration doesn't alter their content or loosen their connection with the self. To say everything is experienced through mind is no more impactful than saying everything is God's work. On the contrary, its prima facie result is to bring them into closer intimacy and imbue psychical being with some of their character.

In short, all our knowledge of the worlds of space and time, and of the causally connected appearances we treat as matter, already represents universal connections partially defining the individual real. The real, as defined by them, may be incomplete and inconsistent, but the whole cannot be detached from it. Supreme individuality, and certainly any individuality attainable in finite experience, is characterized by its appearance "in a nature".

And those features we deem more appropriate to self-determining mind are also universal connections, but within worlds of conduct, which, though richer than what science calls nature, both presuppose and rest upon it. There is no prima facie reason to deny that scientific knowledge of natural law is a partial analysis and, in principle, could lead to a high degree of prediction of what we call individual activity. And it is fundamentally false to deny that what we call in the highest sense individual characteristics are, within their respective worlds, universal laws. What possible interest or significance could they hold if not so—if, for example, all Cromwell's actions were not cases under the same universal, the same pervading spirit?.

We instinctively resent predictions of our conduct based on mere scientific calculation from pre-birth data. However, we do not resent prediction based on observation and experience of our formed individual character.

The reason is that the former seems independent of our individuality, while the latter is founded upon it. It is natural to argue, in line with this instinct, that the former is impossible and the latter is possible. Again, the crucial point is to make a clear distinction between calculation and intelligence. Calculation, primarily, cannot suggest new ideas; intelligence has this creative insight as its fundamental function.

In the nature of things, there seems to be nothing to prevent the prior calculation of all physical movements and the behaviour of all physical systems, such as organic bodies. This would, however, involve constructing the entire environment, as organic body development is only understood in relation to it. Assuming, purely for speculative curiosity, this monstrous possibility, there would be no reason why the accumulation of capacity for complex automatic responses—the physical correlate of teleological action—should not be naturally explicable and scientifically predictable.

But new ideas, the significance of things, would remain inaccessible to the calculator as such. If, however, we speak not of pure calculation, but of calculation plus intelligence, then no limitation seems theoretically tenable.

One might argue that individual conduct could not be predicted because the data of individual character could never be complete while anything remained to be predicted. But in principle, intelligence is one. New ideas and motives, generated from new facts, are not inaccessible to forethought if a forecast of the facts is available.

The real answer, then, is that, under this extreme speculative hypothesis, calculation plus intelligence could in principle predict the whole of individual character and conduct. But this would only be possible if, and because, the intelligence in question was able to pre-construct the ideas and habits of the future individual.

We do have facts analogous to this possibility. Since intelligence is essentially one, this would not be detrimental to the later individual. It is like an earlier thinker or statesman anticipating ideas or solving practical problems later faced independently by another.

The later individual's practical and intellectual individuality is thus, in its main lines, "covered" by the former's, but this does not diminish their freedom or separate actuality. It merely suggests that finite mind, in its imperfection, sometimes needlessly doubles a part. This is common, for example, when a scientist or philosopher fails to transcend their predecessors' work. While usually applicable only to the main outline, not detailed history, such anticipations are a real and important fact. In essence, the life-work of individuals can be and often is unconsciously anticipated or consciously laid down and predicted by others. Reversing this, many individuals seem to "fall within" others, appearing surplus, though their apparent repetition likely has unseen value. Carrying out a predicted path is not necessarily a defect.

In this discussion, the interest of the question has led us beyond our primary scope. Our problem was the relation of Individuality to universal law. We were only bound to show the possibility of analysis or explanation, not necessarily calculation or prediction. It is sufficient to assert that an individual system, being a nature or spirit universal throughout its differences, necessarily determines a nexus between those differences which is itself universal and necessary as it embodies an aspect of the system. The fact that it is not repeated in numerous resembling instances is, as we've seen, a feature of its universality. Repetition often suggests groundlessness or failure. What truly and successfully expresses the whole at a specific place can fill no other. However, its nexus within the whole is intelligible to the mind thinking in terms of the whole, and this is the very archetype of a necessary law.

Even in the everyday generalities that express repetitions, the true type of the universal, however obscured by careless handling, is ultimately found.

We might fail to observe the differences within or despite which a repetition occurs. But it is certain that if those differences were absent, there could be no repetition; the two cases, having nothing to hold them apart, would not be two but one. The nature of the universal is discernible even within a bare numerical series, and even more so in every constituent of an organic whole. Every nexus, insofar as it is a universal law, is a necessary determination within, and hypothetical upon, an Individual whole—whether a world-whole or its member, a macrocosm or a microcosm, makes no difference in principle. This is as true of the Law of Contradiction as it is of the rhythm of a line of poetry, and vice versa.

Finally, I contend it is a confusion to believe that subjective teleology is incompatible with the views we have advanced. The allegation runs that individuality or spontaneity cannot coexist with universal law because law would require an individual world to repeat its behaviour in repeated situations. However, if its purpose or end differs in the two cases, it will respond differently. While we will explore teleology more deeply later, this much is immediately clear: The end or purpose can be nothing but the nature of the whole, which is the spirit of the individual world, insofar as its accomplishment is deferred in time, creating a sense of want or contradiction because the individual system is sensitive to the delay.

It follows that if the purpose is genuinely different in two apparently identical cases, the identity is an illusion due to superficial inspection.

Within the individual's world, the contradiction has subtly shifted its place. This cannot signify a new, additional idea tacked on without affecting the organized system, concerning only the future and not the present or past.

In principle, there must have been a dislocation of the whole system, a rearrangement of "views," acquiescences, attitudes, and perceptions. The "circumstances" – the elements surrounding the individual world that take their character from its content's adjustment – themselves, as a whole, are liable to have undergone any degree of transformation, however unchanged their external or fragmentary aspect may appear.

Yet, all this is not a contingent or arbitrary new determination; it is the reorganization of a microcosm – a change of apperception.

Leibniz's concept of self-developing monads beautifully illustrates this truth, even if we accept external suggestions. For an external suggestion can only operate by modifying the distribution and connection of the whole.

Ultimately, as Leibniz noted, thought and appetition progress, with each stage dependent on the previous. A person who yielded to temptation once but resists it successfully when it recurs has not simply exchanged one volition for another; they have modified their view and sentiment of past, present, and future.

Their world has dislocated and reshaped itself, so what was once an intolerable contradiction not to do, now becomes an intolerable contradiction to do. Purpose, in a word, is secondary; what is primary is the nature of our microcosm, and purpose is an unfulfilled corollary of it.

Therefore, subjective teleology brings nothing to invalidate our conclusion.

In summation: Individuality and Spontaneity are not antagonistic to Uniformity of Nature and General Law, if these are rightly understood; rather, they include and necessitate them.

- The Uniformity of Nature, or the principle of Relevancy, means that every variation is a member in an intelligible system. It excludes spontaneity only in the sense of behaviour responsive to nothing.

- Variation is a means of adjustment or response, and establishing its existence to a high degree is not inconsistent with, but evidence of, the uniformity of nature in the true sense.
- The proof of genuine spontaneity is not mere variation, but progressive and adapted variation.
- Individuality, understood not as empty eccentricity but as the character of a self-contained and coherent system, is fully in harmony with the Uniformity of Nature.
- Universality lies in the expression of a system's nature by each and all of its parts, suitably to the place or function of each.
- A system so expressed or organized is a universal, and the nexus between its parts—even if none are primarily similar to or a repetition of any other—is a universal nexus or law.
- In finite experience, the uniqueness of parts within individuality, or of individuals as parts of the universe, is never perfect. Thus, they are not only universals in the true sense and built from universal nexuses, but in finite experience, they necessarily occasion approximate repetitions—an imperfection—expressed in ordinary "general law".
- Every nexus in finite experience has a potential class or plurality corresponding to it.
- Individuals are therefore doubly accessible to intelligence, and in many typical instances, are intelligence's work, though not necessarily of cognition or discursive thought.
- Hence, there is no reason to deny that intelligence is in principle capable of anticipating the nature of individuals, their action and cognition. However, this does not mean that every form of intelligence, such as calculation per se, is adequate to every type of individual world.
- The best way to conceive the finite individual is to consider the nature of a work of art, or the moral temper as analyzed by Aristotle, or an organic being as a continual source of adaptation

through fine adjustments of extreme determinateness and precision.

- And subjective teleology, correctly understood as the shaping and reshaping of a world in its endeavor to find itself and its whole, poses no challenge to these views.
- This deeper understanding reveals that individuality and universal law are not at odds, but rather two facets of a single, coherent reality.

Lecture–4
The Teleology of Finite Consciousness

This lecture rethinks purpose at its deepest level, showing that teleology cannot rest on mere desire, choice, or future goals. By uncovering how finite consciousness participates in a wider, immanent order, it reveals purpose as perfection and coherence, guiding human striving beyond impulse toward a fuller understanding of meaning, value, and reality.

Examines purpose and direction within limited human consciousness, pointing toward higher meaning

Good morning, everyone. Today, we delve into a profound philosophical exploration of "The Teleology of Finite Consciousness," drawing our insights from the provided lecture excerpts. Our primary objective is to dismantle common misapprehensions and deepen our understanding of concepts like individuality, the universal, and the very nature of purpose itself.

Traditionally, there's been a perceived antagonism between Individuality and the universal. This antagonism, as our text suggests, stems from an "imperfect penetration of thought" where we often mistake the particular for the individual, and reduce the universal to the general. For us, the ideal representation of both the individual and the universal is the "life or spirit of a world," which manifests itself through precise form and determinateness—a fine and adequate adjustment of elements. Essentially, creative Logic, the inherent nature of the whole, is always at work in every detail, shaping our experience and determining its value. The deeper we explore reality, the more we apprehend this universal nature, this intricate, interdependent nexus where the whole finds its expression. Many philosophical errors, it's argued, arise from failing to grasp this nature of the individual and, consequently, from arbitrarily favoring one element of experience over the whole. Of course, we, as finite beings, cannot experience the whole in its entirety, and discerning its constituents and divine nature is indeed an arduous task. It's far simpler, comparatively, to place unexamined data in opposition.

Our focus today, however, is to critically examine Teleology, a principle often positioned antagonistically against other data points in philosophical discourse. This concept, prevalent in ethical or theistic Idealism, assigns specific claims and functions to finite consciousness, often modeling the supreme mind in relation to the universe based on these. Ultimately, our goal is to show that Teleology, as a conception, loses its distinctive meaning as we deepen its philosophical interpretation. Simultaneously, the superficial characteristics of finite consciousness, from which the idea of teleology is often derived, reveal themselves as an inadequate foundation for any theory of reality, perfection, or value.

Deconstructing "End and Means": Beyond Superficiality

Let's begin with the everyday distinction we're all familiar with: "end and means". This rough discrimination of values, relevant to our daily practices, implies that we value some things for their inherent worth ("ends") and others solely for their utility in achieving the former ("means"). The "ends" explain the valuation of the "means" and, seemingly, require no further justification themselves. Prima facie, "ends" appear last in time, with "means" preceding them as necessary conditions for their attainment. The very notion of "means" suggests a degree of impotence; they are not what we truly desire but are adopted due to limited resources to achieve our "end". An "end," in this common understanding, is inherently partial within a larger whole, a chosen objective contrasted with other possibilities and, crucially, with preceding events in time.

Aristotle, whom our argument broadly follows here, understood "end" as both the completion of a positive developing whole and the cessation of the process itself. However, modern theory often emphasizes only the cessation, losing sight of the positive completion.

Yet, there are facts that challenge this simplistic, temporal, and selective characterization of "end." Often, consequences need to be considered alongside means. Our "end" might appear at the beginning or in the middle of a process, and the "price to be paid" (the cost of means, including consequences) can extend throughout the entire process.

We rarely settle the entire cost before delivery in daily life. This blurring effect implies that the temporal distinction between "end" and "means" loses its sharpness. Our understanding of the end is always qualified by the means, and the means, for calculation, encompass all consequences. Consequently, attainment and conclusion are no longer synonymous. We become acutely aware that nothing in the entire train of occurrences is immune from partaking in the character of an "end" or desirable object.

This blending of "end" and "means"—the desired object and its price—is a common experience that takes on significant importance when we engage in philosophical reflection. We quickly realize that what we label an "end," as if it were a fixed goal or stopping point, is in reality "not a point, but a line," or even a "solid". It tends to expand, often irregularly, over the entire span of our activity.

Consider a total system, whether of life or nature: how can we truly distinguish between end and means within it? We begin with two "natural prejudices": the anthropocentric (that man is the end) and the temporal (associating accomplishment with cessation). Neither of these withstands philosophical scrutiny. Why should humanity be the ultimate end? And is there any evidence to suggest this? Why grant pre-eminent value to a "far off divine event" to which all creation moves?

It becomes evident that assigning ultimate value to a specific class of creatures or a particular moment in time cannot be justified as an ultimate conception. Such an idea stems from an analogy with the choices of a finite being, who, by virtue of its finitude, is compelled to select within the universe. It's an attempt to apply the principle of subordinating means to ends to a system where we can discern no necessity, no inherent clue, for distinct "ends" or "means". A finite being chooses a possible value and then selects instruments from its available resources to actualize it. However, we simply cannot conceive of a perfect reality as being divided into valuable "ends" and "means" that a limitation of resources compels it to employ. This conception is entirely derived from the analogy of a finite contriver.

Reconceptualizing Teleology: From Purpose to Perfection

Therefore, when the principle of Teleology is applied to cosmic theory, it immediately and entirely loses all reliance on the ordinary distinctions of means and ends. It also abandons the presumption that termination coincides with attainment. For Teleology to retain any meaningful philosophical sense in this context, it must relinquish the entire analogy of finite contrivance and selection. Instead, it must fall back on the intrinsic characteristics of value that, independent of temporal sequence and specific purposes, are inherent in the nature of a totality that is perfection.

In this crucial transition, the principle of purposiveness—which implies a nature that is imperative on every element of a whole—expands into the principle of Individuality, or positive non-contradiction. When we work with this expanded understanding, we replace the idea of de facto purpose (a psychological, temporal, and ethical concept) with the idea of perfection or the whole (a logical or metaphysical, non-temporal, and religious idea).

We are now dealing with a substantive criterion of value that is applicable to every detail of a totality, and remains valid even if Time itself is considered an appearance. This criterion can certainly encompass purposes, but mere de facto purposiveness can neither challenge nor support the criterion itself.

In short, a purpose, as a mere "de facto want or desire," contributes to intelligibility only by serving as a reason for its means. On its own, as a bare purpose, it can never offer a justification. While every purpose implies a subjective value, there is no reason to assume that every true value must necessarily be a purpose. Extending the idea of teleology to the entire universe means shifting from asking whether a particular fact *appears* to be contrived for a purpose, to asking whether the totality itself—contrived or not, and without any suggestion of dividing it into means and ends—can be apprehended or conceived as satisfactory, as a supreme value.

The theoretical importance of this shift is profound: the selective actions (conations) of finite minds cannot claim a fundamental position as the source of order and value. This applies even to the mind of a finite god, if such a being were conceivable. While finite consciousness is indeed creative and possesses initiative in a sense we will explore, the fundamental principles of the universe are understood to be far more deeply laid than in the choices of any finite mind. Minds, as we typically experience them, are better understood as an imperfect medium and manifestation of reality, rather than its ultimate and sovereign source.

Conation, Satiety, and True Satisfaction: Aristotle's Insight

Alongside the idea that true value in the universe is teleological, we also encounter the notion that the true nature of mental processes is conative. Both doctrines can be maintained in a restricted sense, but their precise implications are vital. In a typical conation (a striving or impulse), the most significant points are its beginning and its end. The beginning is a disturbance, and the end, or close, is a recovery of equilibrium. As we noted earlier regarding elementary notions of teleology derived from simple conative experience, the purpose and the close are seen as one, and the end coincides with both. This recovery of equilibrium is often equated with satiety, which is synonymous with the cessation of the conative process. This describes ordinary desire and its satisfaction, a view largely accepted by Plato and retained in modern theories of conation as a "vital series".

However, a latent opposition between these two conceptions of the "end" surfaces within the pleasure-theory, stretching from Plato to Aristotle. For Aristotle, the "end" was not merely satiety but satisfaction. Satisfactoriness, the power to provide satisfaction, was a positive characteristic, representing the completeness of a form, rather than simply the cessation of a disturbance. Aristotle applies the term "end" to positive maturity, which is more than just the cessation of growth, and to the continuous, perhaps timeless, character of the fullest life and fruition, rather than to the completion of any sequential process.

At its core, fruition is distinct from conation as initially described. A satisfaction that can be truly attained and possessed is profoundly different from mere satiety. Thus, the "end" no longer appears as a fixed terminus.

It has expanded into something that is either a type of activity independent of conation, or, if identified with conation, it fundamentally alters our understanding of conation's nature and the conditions of its value.

We see this even in recent pleasure theory: despite the primary doctrine that end and cessation coincide, the desirable element of a conation, its ethical "end," is understood to lie in its character extending over its entire process, not just its termination.

The "End," in the sense of attainment or achievement, expands from the idea of a terminus into that of a satisfactory experience that can either include a specific type of conative process or represent a new, independent, and perfected self-affirmation following the completion of the conation's changes.

Kant's distinction between sensuous desire and aesthetic interest offers a prime example of this difference. In sensuous desire and its satisfaction, we observe a transition followed by satiety—this is the typical conation and its "end". But in aesthetic enjoyment, or any other true fruition, there is a response from an object where the self feels "at home," and fundamentally, there is no transition or satiety. While finite minds will always experience succession and transition, in aesthetic enjoyment, it is not the striving towards an unattained terminus that defines the activity. The mind's direction here is outward, not onward; each moment is self-complete and as good as the next, borrowing nothing from an anticipated future completeness. Such fruition can be seen as a protracted terminus of a conation, like eternity following time, or it can illuminate the true nature and value of conation itself. In either interpretation, it is fundamentally different from a conation whose beginning is disturbance and whose end is satiety.

The significance here is that the very nature of conation leads us back to our fundamental conclusion: the true "end" or value does not reside in a special relation to a terminus or finite purpose, but in a character of perfection. This perfection can be relatively present throughout a process, or as a persistent result, or even at its beginning or in its middle. While in the simplest conation, satiety and satisfaction might coincide, for "end" to signify "value," satisfaction must be more than mere satiety. The very idea of conation must be remodeled to accommodate this necessity, a fact recognized by modern pleasure-theory when it emphasizes positive interest within the conation, rather than merely escaping tension or disturbance.

In finite life, conation and fruition exist in varying degrees of coincidence. This ranges from conations primarily valued as a release from pain to those virtually indistinguishable from pure, positive self-affirmation, where any conation is entirely latent. The crucial point for us is the expansion of the idea of "end" into a connection with fruition and value, shedding its exclusive link with termination versus process, and superordination versus means.

Teleology, Mechanism, and the Scope of Finite Consciousness

We must now address the term "Teleology" itself. As we've seen, it's an "unlucky term". In the sense of aiming at the unfulfilled, it grants an artificial importance to time and to the final, potentially trivial, part of a whole. Of its two implications—completeness and conclusion—the accessory idea of "conclusion" often usurps the fundamental idea of "completeness". In truth, teleological significance does not depend on what comes first or last, but on what the individual real possesses when apprehended in its completeness.

Action is not truly teleological simply because a deferred element of a subordinate quasi-totality is being carried out by a finite desire in the time-process. Such an "end" would not necessarily possess teleological value, and even if it did, it wouldn't necessarily be its leading constituent. The true question of value is independent of temporal relations; it depends on the structure and significance of the whole undergoing completion—that is, on its character of individuality, its proximity to the ultimate whole.

A significant adversary of "sane idealism" is the belief that the ideal exclusively belongs to the future. On the contrary, the ideal is what we perceive in the light of the whole, and how it shapes our future is merely an incident—and never the most crucial one—of our unified understanding of past, present, and future. Therefore, when "end," "purposiveness," or "teleology" merely signify that a finite consciousness is driven by a pleasurable impulse or an unfulfilled idea, this bare fact, apart from the content of the idea itself, holds nothing inherently sacred or significant. It is futile to seek the essence or significance of teleology in the mere fact of conscious purpose or impulse. Purpose, prima facie, simply means that some creature consciously desires something.

But here's a critical question: Does something lose its value once it's attained? Does everything derive its value simply from being wanted? Are fruition or perfection truly the "death of value"? Are the ideas of positive fulfillment, satisfaction, and a being that is good in itself—beyond the cycles of want and satiety—mere illusions? If so, then there is no Absolute, or if we rely solely on finite experience, the character of the Absolute fails to suggest itself within our lives. But, as our text emphatically states, such a conclusion contradicts both fact and theory. While our wants certainly play a role in the ultimate whole, they cannot conceivably serve as a measure of value. We cannot conceive of an intuitive intelligence creating values entirely detached from a whole with determinate content. The supreme experience, whatever we name it, must be one with its world, not a creator out of nothing.

This brings us to a pivotal statement: "Things are not teleological because they are purposed, but are purposed because they are teleological". When we refer to the ultimate real as individual or teleological, it is hazardous to suggest that purpose, in the sense of an unfulfilled craving in time, plays any part in our conception. A teleology dependent on a feature of the time-process is not one that anyone but a pragmatist can affirm of ultimate reality. The true test of a purpose's purposiveness, even in organic evolution, social progress, or morals, lies in its objectiveness of selection—the selection of values that can withstand criticism. Subjective selection is poor work unless it transcends its subjectivity.

Now, let's consider the relationship between mechanism and teleology, specifically the claimed incompatibility between two positions. Position A states that nature is instrumental to the development of spiritual values. Position B asserts that the spiritual view regards experience as a mechanically intelligible whole. The question is their compatibility.

To clarify our stance, three points are essential.

1. First, the Uniformity of Nature is understood as a logical postulate, equivalent to the Law of Identity interpreted as the Law of Sufficient Reason. Any attempts to invalidate it based on de facto irregularities in nature are irrelevant. To think that uniformity means mere repetition of similars, impeachable by non-miraculous irregularity, is a fundamental logical error. And to think such an impeachment guarantees spirituality is akin to the outdated position of upholding miracles in the name of spiritual interest.
2. Second, it's a parallel error to contrast individuality with law, presuming that universal connections are antithetical to individuality and only exist as generalities for resembling instances. A person, a singular individual, serves as a sufficient counter-example.

The notion that an individual isn't a universal or isn't structured by universals, and that universals require multiple resembling points, is the old fallacy of substituting similarity for identity, leading to a misunderstanding of the universal and a failure to grasp a genuine conception of the spiritual. Teleology, in this context, is simply a temporal sub-form of harmony, just as Sufficient Reason is a sub-form of Identity in concrete application.

3. Third, the accepted idea of mechanism here neither reduces the universe to modifications of homogeneous quantity nor challenges the "uniformity of nature" or the quantitative relations underlying natural phenomena. It accepts that qualities have quantitative connections, and that a high degree of spiritual or emotional expressiveness accompanies a high degree of complexity and intelligible determinateness. It is one thing to reject abstract calculation as the sole reality, but quite another to be driven by faulty popular science into depreciating the

spiritual value of intelligence or attributing an unreal independence to the bare facts of finite conation.

Given these explanations, the compatibility of nature being instrumental to spiritual ends *and* mechanically intelligible becomes clearer, perhaps even obvious. What is maintained is that either position is inconceivable without the other. Individuality, understood as the union of comprehensiveness and coherence, the very incarnation of non-contradiction, cannot be realized in any system that is not transparent according to the Law of Causation or Sufficient Reason.

Where discontinuity appears, it signifies a gap in the embodiment of spiritual purpose and significance.

A purpose is not truly realized, is not a reality that permeates and vivifies content, if it is not continuously and traceably affirmed within a coherent structure.

No purpose or significance can be realized through miracle. Any prejudice to the contrary arises from the logical blunder of imagining the concrete universal—the individual—as incompatible with the realization of "general law," which is merely a weakened form of the universal determinations within the individual structure.

One might argue that causal or mechanical explanation is necessarily incomplete and proceeds indefinitely. But this is only true if it's taken as total or absolute, implying homogeneity. And even then, it reflects the same defect of finite experience that makes all teleological explanations arbitrary. If both mechanical and teleological explanations were complete, they would inevitably merge, and their distinct characters would become aspects within a unified whole. This is not mere fancy. The relationship of cause and ground to the whole, on one hand, and the tendency of teleology to expand into systematic coherence, on the other, demonstrate the beginning of this convergence.

Organic Mechanism: The World-Wisdom, Not Finite Consciousness

A clear sign of one-sidedness in understanding is the attempt to reduce mechanism to "degenerated finite teleology," using the analogy of secondary automatism (e.g., interpreting reflex responses as acquired facility, like a skilled pianist). This contention suggests that a machine embodying an idea must be consciously constructed and "worked" by a finite consciousness with explicit finite teleology.

While there's a certain plausibility for human-made machines, especially when we focus on their limitations. Their limited independence mirrors the narrowness of finite consciousness.

However, if we instead consider the possibilities and distinctive nature of a machine, or any human material achievement like a work of fine art, the clear lesson is that ideas can be embodied in unconscious, external forms that are mechanical in every fiber. These cases, undeniably originating from finite consciousness, should guide our interpretation of nature even where no such consciousness is traceable.

The counter-argument, often heard, is "Exactly! That *does* give us the line for understanding nature, meaning all organic machinery originates in and is worked by a finite consciousness". But this draws a conclusion based on an incidental feature and is generally contrary to fact.

Our machines are, indeed, imperfect and one-sided, reflecting finite consciousness. Natural works, and greater historical achievements, however, are not dependent on a relevant and explicit consciousness for their construction or operation.

In humans, only a small part of bodily mechanism is popularly considered "controlled by consciousness". Whatever consciousness exists in plants or lower animals, it is clearly not the kind that could design or employ their complex bodily arrangements.

Consciousness is not the sole driver of bodily mechanisms.

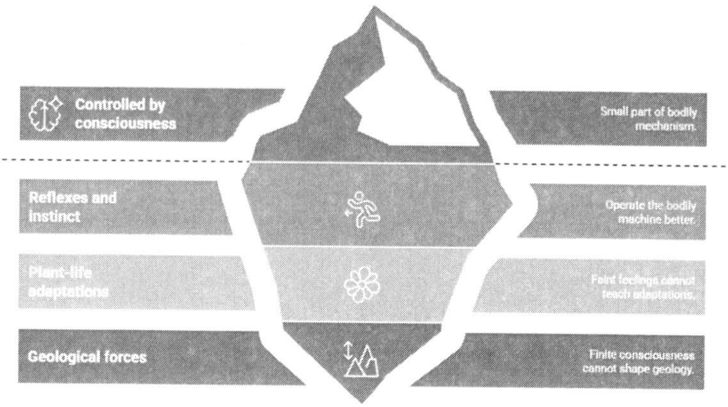

Kant's argument applies here: Reason has higher purposes than operating the bodily machine; reflexes and instinct do it better. Reason cannot teach us to swallow or move an arm. We cannot imagine that the faint feelings, if any, accompanying plant-life taught the orchid to adapt its pollen or stamen fibers.

To attribute these things to a finite teleological consciousness would force us to extend this logic to geological forces that shaped the Eastern Mediterranean for civilization or made Great Britain an island.

The point is not whether purposes and ideas "operate" in nature—the meaning of that question is doubtful. Rather, it is that Nature below conscious intelligence, and "Providence" above it, can achieve, without the help of a relevant explicit consciousness, results of the same general type as those attributed to finite minds. The participation of the inorganic world in history is continuous with that of the organic world, and no one would argue finite consciousness is operative in the inorganic realm. The notion that the expression of ideas is somehow opposed to mechanism is widespread but fallacious, similar to believing uniformity means the future always resembles the past. For instance, in fine arts, we often say "expression" comes "straight from the soul," while "mechanical finish" is distinct. But in truth, both are prima facie mechanical, and "expression" often means a *more perfect mechanical control* over the medium.

Mind and individuality, in their finite forms, find their fullest expression as aspects of very complex and precisely determined mechanical systems.

This is a universal law for higher human products and cosmic evolution, flowing from the nature of "being and trueness". Greater being demands more perfect coherence, which in turn demands fuller content.

The mechanical appearance—the continuity of transition and determination—must therefore be unbroken, implying dependence on a system where individuality manifests through universal law. It is futile to appeal to finite purposive consciousness as the sole vehicle of teleology or the source of a "fossilized" mechanical nature. The external must be frankly accepted as a factor, actual but not ultimate, in the universe.

Having freed teleology from being restricted to finite purpose, we can now conceive of the world-plan as immanent in the whole, encompassing both finite mind and mechanical nature. The obviously secondary and fragmentary nature of finite mind thus constitutes only a partial revelation of the meaning of things, by no means its principal vehicle or sole organ of guidance in evolution or history.

The core argument hinges on the continuity of mechanism with the individuality of the real, stemming from that deeper, logical rather than teleological, aspect of reality.

This is why, despite acknowledging limitations in the common understanding of the mechanical view, we contend that the true spiritual ideal *demands* mechanical intelligibility.

Teleology in Nature: The Example of a Flower

Let's illustrate this with the example of an organic product commonly considered "below the line of consciousness"—a flower. Our perspective rejects two extremes.

1. On one hand, it's absurd to say a flower arises by accident—as a mere by-product of elements whose nature doesn't contain such a result. This would be like suggesting a human contriver didn't anticipate complex developments. We cannot treat part of the world as primary and part as secondary. We must interpret nature by the flower as much as by the law of gravitation. Indeed, even the simplest inorganic formations, like solar system motions, wave curls, or precipice curves, equally merit a presumption of teleological value as any conscious object, save consciousness itself.
2. On the other hand, we must not claim "purpose is operative" in the flower or wave if this means attributing them to an end or idea "superinduced" upon their elements by a power comparable to finite consciousness, operating *ab extra*. If the first notion implied accident, this one implies miracle. As we've seen, teleology is undermined if no determinate universal relations between differences can be truly predicated. It's impossible to find a point where life isn't mechanically conditioned. The individuality manifested in a flower, mountain, or wave, independent of operative consciousness, compels a conclusion so far-reaching that the case of human consciousness, though vastly different in degree, scarcely advances the principle.

Avoiding these extremes, we are compelled to affirm that in the flower's structure and being, the common natural elements behave according to their inherent nature, and the remarkable creation we observe is simply the immanent development of certain factors. These factors, in isolation, might seem far removed from such a result. We must remember the active role of the environment, of objective selection. The plan of the flower wasn't inherent in a few elements in a laboratory, but in the whole interactions of nature.

We are certain, under any view of evolution, that the structure of a plant or animal is a microcosm from which, with adequate knowledge, its environment's nature could be deciphered. Whether adhering to strict natural selection or assuming a psychological cause (with or without inheritance of acquired qualities), the fundamental truth remains: it is the world, the environment, that is responsible for the differences in organic evolution.

While protoplasm's powers or life's initial impulse might account for common phenomena, it is overwhelmingly the world that has shaped the content of what we call the individual. This is clear in intelligence and volition, and equally obvious in organic evolution.

It's crucial to acknowledge that even if the cause is "psychological," like "subjective selection," no sane person would claim that such a psychological cause performs *conscious teleological work* in structural adaptation, except in our conscious efforts to develop the human body.

It doesn't solve problems or contrive adaptations. In fact, it's more accurate to say subjective selection is negative and natural selection is positive. Subjective selection offers countless reactions tending towards habits; it is natural selection that molds them into definite lines of progress and elicits positive structure.

To say natural selection is negative is like saying a sculptor's art is negative because it works by removal. Therefore, if "mind" operates in the structural adaptation of animals or plants, it does not operate *as mind.* It doesn't contain the plan or guide the progress. It might be a more felicitous conception of the agency by which the plan, immanent in the whole, is actualized.

But in any case, we are certain that a work as astonishing as those of finite consciousness, like a flower, is accomplished without any intervention of consciousness as a teleological agency—that is, as a planner or problem-solver. In this context, no one would suggest the miraculous intervention of consciousness, as they might for human-made machines or art.

Indeed, the examination of mechanism and teleology has entirely dismissed such a suggestion. The idea that a purposive intelligence, when a man builds a clock or composes a sonata, operates by mere design on a system to impart something not communicable by mechanical parts, should now appear a contradiction in terms. No one today would explain a flower by appealing to the purposive interposition of a creative intelligence. Whether Nature "aims at ends" or not, it is a bare fact that without any contriving consciousness, she can present them to our minds.

Finite Consciousness: A Manifestation, Not the Source

Thus, we have seen that the very foundations of "teleology"—which truly means individuality—in the universe are far too deeply laid to be explained by, much less restricted to, the intervention of finite consciousness. Everything indicates that finite consciousness should not be regarded as the source of teleology, but as itself a manifestation, falling within wider manifestations, of the immanent individuality of the real. It is not teleological *because* as a finite subject of desire and volition it is "purposive". Rather, it is what we call purposive because reality is individual and a whole, and manifests this character partly in the "short-sighted and eclectic aims of finite intelligence," and partly in appearances of far greater range and scope. The large-scale patterns of history and civilization are not found as purposes within any single finite consciousness.

The definite continuity and correlation of intelligent activities that give human life its teleological character—the "ways of Providence"—are a fact of the same order as the development of the solar system or the appearance of life on Earth. It is impossible to attribute to finite consciousnesses, as agents, the identity at work within finite consciousness as a whole. This identity manifests in a development springing from the linked action of separate and successive finite consciousnesses in relation to their environment. Every step in this development, though intelligent and teleological in itself, is unconscious in relation to the whole. The result is still "a nature," though a "second and higher nature". This principle is paramount, holding true across all levels of being.

Two Pillars of Our Contention: Teleology Below and Above Consciousness

Let me reiterate and emphasize the two core parts of our contention:

Teleology Below Consciousness:

- The intelligence of humans and intelligent animals does not, as I see it, sustain or conduct their bodily life. To claim that all vital responses are inherited from volitional or quasi-volitional behaviour is factually dubious and, more importantly, an evasion of the principle.
- If something akin to volition molded bodily structure in earlier evolutionary phases, it never did so by any conscious wisdom within the mind of that phase. It followed, almost blindly, the determination of a deeper wisdom hidden in the general structure of the environment. The denial of teleological significance to natural selection exemplifies the position we argue against.
- Furthermore, whatever role mind played in the past for our bodily structures, it's irrelevant to its current role. Human minds and purposes presuppose, accept, and are founded on, their actual bodies.

The plant-mind, if it exists, presupposes and accepts the plant-form. Even if mind is present from the beginning, it exists in such elementary forms that it is molded rather than molding. The orchid, as stated, cannot have a mind that contrives its fertilization, just as a human mind cannot teach itself to swallow or digest, or choose its birth time or place. Everywhere, finite consciousness, in its obvious and unmistakable forms, appears at a relatively high level, focusing and revealing the significance of a vast complication of "mute history and circumstance" that precedes and surrounds it.

Teleology Above Finite Consciousness:

- Considering history, and the time and place of one's birth, we arrive at teleology beyond finite consciousness. In history, and even more profoundly in the linked development of art, ideas, and religions, the principle of a teleology that transcends, yet is exhibited *in*, finite consciousness is clear and unambiguous.
- It is not finite consciousness that has planned the great phases of civilization, which are achieved by the linking of finite minds upon the essential foundation of the globe's geological structure. Each individual mind reaches only a very small distance, and in relation to the whole of a movement, it must be considered unconscious. While intelligence may be present in every step of the connection, we cannot claim as a design of finite intelligence what never presented itself in that character to any single mind.
- For instance, a Greek colonist journeying to Ionia in the eighth or ninth century B.C. was certainly paving the way for Christianity. But their relation to it, though a higher form of working, was essentially like that of a coral insect to a coral reef. Neither Christianity nor the coral reef was ever a design in the minds of the people or insects who constructed them; they lay far deeper in the "roots of things".

This, I contend, leads to the fundamental conclusion about evolution: Nothing is truly attributable to finite mind as such, which was never a plan before any finite mind.

Reconciling Mechanism and Teleology: The True Nature of Totality

The contrast between mechanism and teleology, then, is not elucidated by a simple antithesis between purposive consciousness and the reactions of parts. It is rooted in the very nature of totality, which is viewed from two complementary perspectives: as an individual whole and as constituted by inter-reacting members.

Neither viewpoint can be entirely absent. If mechanical intelligibility were to fail completely, the spiritual would be reduced to the miraculous—the negation of all spirituality. Conversely, a total failure of teleological intelligibility would reduce individuality to incoherence, annihilating mechanism.

However, because teleology is often considered in abstraction, it's easier to imagine its absence than that of mechanism, which must accompany any inter-relation whatsoever. As the saying goes, "Understanding without Reason is something, Reason without understanding is nothing". There is, in truth, a teleology in any order, and some order must exist, but our common ideas of teleology are arbitrary and eclectic. The entire doctrine of theism in the Kantian sense, which posits a personal creator and governor of the world and assigns paramount importance to subjective selection and bare finite consciousness as agents, in contrast to natural selection and the immanent plan of things, is called into question here. While a deeper importance might attach to finite consciousness from a different perspective, the meeting of extremes in metaphysics should not surprise us.

The polemic against the mechanical view and the epiphenomenal doctrine of intelligence may find these concepts unexpectedly aligning with their antagonists.

We are not treating consciousness or the self as mere byproducts or accessories. However, it is increasingly evident that the developed finite mind must be regarded as an appearance that emerges "on the top of a great deal that must go before them". Two opposing contentions seem to demand fusion. To the "voluntarist"—the believer in a hardly conscious something underlying explicit intelligence, where they find the fundamental reality—we must concede that a vast "underground work" is involved in forming an intelligent moral being. The conscious self is plainly the "last word of an immense evolution" that moves from unconsciousness to consciousness. It necessarily presupposes, as far as we can understand, the co-operation of unconscious nature in molding the foundation of mind. There is no logical value, I believe, in assuming the presence of mind in simpler forms at earlier evolutionary phases.

Consciousness emerges from unconscious evolution.

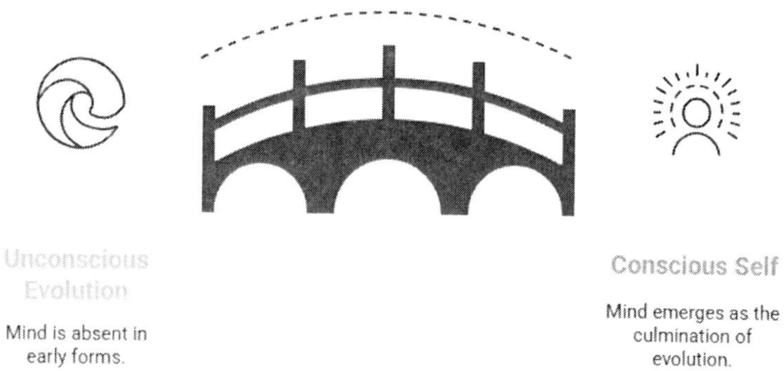

However, admitting all this to those who advocate an obscure "will-to-live" does not destroy, but rather, when rightly understood, corroborates and enhances the significance and value of intelligence and self-realization through the realization of ideas. For it is precisely this that is brought to fruition as the climax and revelation when the "underground self" emerges into completeness. Only then do we begin to understand ourselves, to enjoy and possess ourselves, and consequently, the world.

The conscious and intelligent self is "on the top of," and made possible by, all the stress and complexity of the work that precedes it. If, instead of labeling it "epiphenomenal," we call it the "climax and sum and substance of evolution," we would be stating the truth that epiphenomenalism caricatures. This, of course, implies that when the self emerges, it does not come empty or without presuppositions. While mind, in a sense, is the active form of totality and thus everything, every particular finite mind has received a certain "filling" before it becomes aware of itself. It begins, so to speak, high up in the world of experience, already possessing a content and a "machinery" prepared by its world.

No matter how little one believes in materialistic determinism today, they would be slow to deny that bodily arrangements and mechanisms are at least the foundation for the soul's operation. When viewed correctly, this imbues the organized consciousness with immensely greater significance and importance than if it were considered a structureless intellectual protoplasm.

It is nothing less than an individual spiritual body, a special utterance and revelation of the universe in its highest finite form. It is bare consciousness and the unmolded power of selection that appear as impotent abstractions in their emptiness. The concrete self is different; as we've maintained throughout, it is "a world within a world of worlds".

The resonance of these ideas with the deepest conclusions of religious philosophy is striking. The perspective that the finite intelligent being has the duty and position of "coming to himself" and "awakening" to his own nature and unity with what we imperfectly call a greater mind and will, rather than independently controlling or molding the world, demands reaffirmation. This view is particularly suggestive against claims stemming from making individualistic moralism absolute.

We will explore the question of finite individual freedom and initiative further. For now, it suffices to suggest that as a self-conscious being, one is fundamentally a "member of the universe inter pares". Each individual, however trifling, is something without which the universe would not be what it is. Indeed, one is an organ through which, even in a small degree, the whole sustains itself.

Therefore, it cannot be justly claimed that nothing is genuinely done or effected in and by the individual. However, we must avoid the erroneous implication that a finite individual could find a *pousto* (a place to stand) outside the universe and proceed to act upon and reform it.

A doctrine that integrates the conception of action, freedom, initiative, and achievement with the idea of "coming to oneself," learning one's place and nature, awakening to one's membership, and rejoicing in that greater reality underlying and surrounding one's self, can offer and receive assistance in understanding the intricate relationship between mind and body, or, as we might better phrase it, how spirit appears as a focus to matter.

To put it in the extreme: even if finite consciousness were merely a mind awakening to the significance of the external realm to which it serves as a center, and a self-identification with the logic and tension of the absolute within that single vortex of its being, would this amount to no achievement, no value? I am not arguing this extreme position, however.

It seems we might achieve a deeper understanding and make a stronger case for personality and initiative than that of mere revelation and awakening. Yet, dare we say that *only* this—the recognition of the infinite within ourselves—would be nothing of value, nothing by which the living finite person, the conscious body as a whole, could be ennobled by achievement?

Lecture-5
The Bodily Basis of Mind as a Unified Content

This chapter challenges the familiar separation of mind and body by revealing consciousness as a unified, embodied whole rather than a detached power. By tracing how bodily organization, mechanism, and environment shape mental life, it uncovers the body as the living medium through which meaning, individuality, and selfhood are made possible.

Analyzes the relationship between the physical body and the totality of mental life

Good morning, everyone. Welcome to our deep dive into "The Teleology of Finite Consciousness," a philosophical exploration designed to unravel common misconceptions and enrich our understanding of fundamental concepts such as individuality, the universal, and the very essence of purpose itself.

Our journey begins by addressing a long-standing philosophical tension: the perceived antagonism between Individuality and the universal. This tension, as our sources suggest, doesn't arise from inherent conflict but from an "imperfect penetration of thought". We often fall into the trap of mistaking the particular for the individual, or reducing the profound universal to a mere generality. To overcome this, our ideal representation of both the individual and the universal should be conceptualized as the "life or spirit of a world". This "spirit" manifests through precise forms and determinateness, an exquisite and adequate adjustment of all its elements. Essentially, what we call creative Logic—the inherent nature of the whole—is perpetually at work, shaping every single detail of our experience and determining its intrinsic value.

The more profoundly we explore reality, the more clearly we apprehend this universal nature, perceiving it as an "intricate, interdependent nexus where the whole finds its expression".

Many philosophical errors, it's argued, stem precisely from this failure to grasp the true nature of the individual, leading us to arbitrarily favor one isolated element of experience over the comprehensive whole. Of course, as finite beings, we acknowledge the immense difficulty of experiencing the whole in its entirety and discerning its divine constituents. It is, comparatively, far simpler to merely place unexamined data in opposition.

Our primary focus today, however, is to conduct a critical examination of Teleology itself. This principle often finds itself positioned antagonistically against other philosophical data points.

Prevalent in various forms of ethical or theistic Idealism, Teleology typically assigns specific claims and functions to finite consciousness, often using these as a model for understanding the supreme mind's relationship to the universe. Our ultimate objective is to demonstrate that Teleology, as a concept, "loses its distinctive meaning as we deepen its philosophical interpretation".

Simultaneously, we will reveal that the superficial characteristics of finite consciousness—those very traits from which the idea of teleology is often derived—are fundamentally "an inadequate foundation for any theory of reality, perfection, or value".

Deconstructing "End and Means": Beyond Superficiality

Let's begin by scrutinizing a distinction we are all intimately familiar with in our daily lives: the concept of "end and means". This rough discrimination of values, while undeniably relevant to our practical activities, carries certain implications that demand deeper philosophical scrutiny. It implies that we value some things for their intrinsic worth—these are our "ends". Others, however, are valued solely for their utility in achieving those "ends"—these are our "means". The "ends" are presumed to explain the valuation of the "means" and, seemingly, require no further justification themselves. Prima facie, "ends" appear last in time, with "means" preceding them as necessary conditions for their attainment. The very notion of "means" suggests a degree of impotence; they are not what we truly desire but are adopted only due to limited resources to achieve our ultimate "end". An "end," in this common understanding, is inherently "partial within a larger whole," a chosen objective contrasted with other possibilities and, crucially, with the preceding events in time.

Now, while Aristotle, whose arguments our discussion broadly follows, understood "end" as both the "completion of a positive developing whole" *and* the cessation of a process, modern theory often emphasizes only the cessation, thereby losing sight of that crucial positive completion. Yet, there are numerous facts that challenge this simplistic, purely temporal, and selective characterization of "end". For instance, consequences frequently need to be considered alongside the means themselves. What we perceive as our "end" might actually appear at the very beginning or even in the middle of a process.

Moreover, the "price to be paid"—the full cost of the means, including all their consequences—can extend throughout the entire process, not just at its inception. In daily life, we rarely settle the entire cost before the final delivery. This blurring effect implies that the temporal distinction between "end" and "means" loses its sharpness.

Our understanding of the end is perpetually qualified by the means employed, and the means, for accurate calculation, must encompass all consequences.

Consequently, the idea of attainment and mere conclusion are no longer synonymous. We become acutely aware that "nothing in the entire train of occurrences is immune from partaking in the character of an 'end' or desirable object".

This profound blending of "end" and "means" — the desired object and its price — is not just an abstract concept; it's a common experience that takes on immense importance when we engage in rigorous philosophical reflection.

We quickly come to the realization that what we superficially label an "end," as if it were a fixed goal or a definitive stopping point, is in reality "not a point, but a line," or even something more substantial, like a "solid".

It possesses an inherent tendency to expand, often irregularly, over the entire span of our activity.

Consider for a moment a total system, be it of life itself or of nature: how, within such a comprehensive totality, can we truly and definitively distinguish between an end and its means?

We typically approach this with two "natural prejudices": the anthropocentric prejudice (the belief that man is the ultimate end of all things) and the temporal prejudice (the association of accomplishment solely with cessation).

Our sources contend that neither of these prejudices can withstand rigorous philosophical scrutiny. Why, indeed, should humanity be granted the status of the ultimate end? And what empirical evidence, if any, genuinely suggests this? Why should we grant pre-eminent value to some "far off divine event" toward which all creation supposedly moves?

It becomes evident that assigning ultimate value to a specific class of creatures or a particular moment in time "cannot be justified as an ultimate conception". Such a notion, we are told, stems from an analogy with the choices made by a finite being. A finite being, by virtue of its limitations, is compelled to select within the universe. It chooses a possible value and then carefully selects instruments from its available resources to actualize it. However, we simply "cannot conceive of a perfect reality as being divided into valuable 'ends' and 'means'" that a limitation of resources compels it to employ. This entire conception is entirely derived from the analogy of a "finite contriver".

Reconceptualizing Teleology: From Purpose to Perfection

Therefore, when the principle of Teleology is rigorously applied to cosmic theory, it "immediately and entirely loses all reliance on the ordinary distinctions of means and ends". It also abandons the presumption that termination necessarily coincides with attainment. For Teleology to retain any meaningful philosophical sense within this cosmic context, it "must relinquish the entire analogy of finite contrivance and selection". Instead, it must fall back on the "intrinsic characteristics of value" that, independent of any temporal sequence and specific purposes, are inherently present in the very "nature of a totality that is perfection".

In this crucial transition, the principle of purposiveness—which implies an imperative nature on every element of a whole—"expands into the principle of Individuality, or positive non-contradiction". When we operate with this expanded understanding, we replace the idea of "de facto purpose"—a concept that is psychological, temporal, and ethical in nature—with the profound idea of "perfection or the whole"—a concept that is logical, metaphysical, non-temporal, and ultimately religious. We are now engaging with a "substantive criterion of value" that is universally applicable to every detail of a totality.

This criterion remains valid even if Time itself is considered merely an appearance. While this criterion can certainly encompass purposes, mere de facto purposiveness can neither challenge nor fundamentally support the criterion itself.

In essence, a purpose, when understood as a mere "de facto want or desire," contributes to intelligibility only by serving as a reason for its means. On its own, as a bare purpose, it can never offer a complete justification. While every purpose implies a subjective value, there is "no reason to assume that every true value must necessarily be a purpose"

Extending the idea of teleology to encompass the entire universe means shifting our inquiry. We move from asking whether a particular fact *appears* to be contrived for a purpose, to asking whether the totality itself—regardless of whether it appears contrived, and without any suggestion of dividing it into means and ends—"can be apprehended or conceived as satisfactory, as a supreme value".

The theoretical importance of this fundamental shift is profound. It means that the "selective actions (conations) of finite minds cannot claim a fundamental position as the source of order and value". This applies even to the mind of a finite god, if such a being were conceivable. While finite consciousness is indeed creative and possesses initiative in a sense we will explore further, the fundamental principles of the universe are understood to be "far more deeply laid than in the choices of any finite mind". Minds, as we typically experience them, are better understood as an "imperfect medium and manifestation of reality," rather than its ultimate and sovereign source.

Conation, Satiety, and True Satisfaction: Aristotle's Insight

Alongside the idea that true value in the universe is teleological, we also frequently encounter the notion that the true nature of mental processes is conative. Both these doctrines can be maintained in a restricted sense, but their precise implications are absolutely vital.

In a typical conation—a striving or impulse—the most significant points are its beginning and its end. The beginning is typically a disturbance, and the end, or close, is a "recovery of equilibrium".

As we noted earlier regarding elementary notions of teleology derived from simple conative experience, the purpose and the close are often seen as one, and the end is perceived to coincide with both. This recovery of equilibrium is frequently equated with satiety, which is synonymous with the cessation of the conative process itself. This aptly describes ordinary desire and its satisfaction, a view largely accepted by Plato and retained in modern theories of conation as a "vital series".

However, a latent opposition between these two conceptions of the "end" surfaces within the pleasure-theory, stretching from Plato all the way to Aristotle. For Aristotle, the "end" was not merely satiety but satisfaction. Satisfactoriness, the power to provide satisfaction, was a "positive characteristic, representing the completeness of a form," rather than simply the cessation of a disturbance. Aristotle applies the term "end" to "positive maturity," which is far more than just the cessation of growth, and to the continuous, perhaps timeless, character of the fullest life and fruition, rather than to the completion of any sequential process.

At its core, fruition is distinct from conation as initially described. A satisfaction that can be truly attained and possessed is profoundly different from mere satiety. Thus, the "end" no longer appears as a fixed terminus. It has "expanded into something that is either a type of activity independent of conation, or, if identified with conation, it fundamentally alters our understanding of conation's nature and the conditions of its value". We observe this even in recent pleasure theory: despite the primary doctrine that end and cessation coincide, the desirable element of a conation—its ethical "end"—is understood to "lie in its character extending over its entire process, not just its termination". The "End," in the sense of attainment or achievement, expands from the idea of a terminus into that of a "satisfactory experience" that can either include a specific type of conative process or represent a new, independent, and perfected self-affirmation following the completion of the conation's changes.

Fruition and Conation

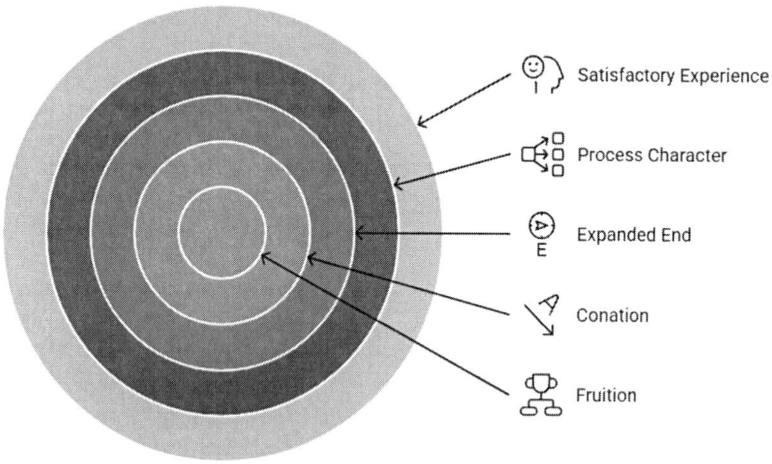

Kant's distinction between sensuous desire and aesthetic interest offers a prime example of this crucial difference. In sensuous desire and its satisfaction, we observe a transition followed by satiety—this is the typical conation and its "end". But in aesthetic enjoyment, or any other true fruition, there is a deep response from an object where the self feels "at home," and fundamentally, there is no transition or satiety. While finite minds will always experience succession and transition, in aesthetic enjoyment, it is "not the striving towards an unattained terminus that defines the activity".

The mind's direction here is "outward, not onward"; each moment is "self-complete and as good as the next," borrowing nothing from an anticipated future completeness. Such fruition can be seen as a protracted terminus of a conation, akin to eternity following time, or it can illuminate the true nature and value of conation itself. In either interpretation, it is fundamentally different from a conation whose beginning is disturbance and whose end is satiety.

The significance here is profound: the very nature of conation leads us back to our fundamental conclusion. The "true 'end' or value does not reside in a special relation to a terminus or finite purpose, but in a character of perfection". This perfection can be relatively present throughout a process, or as a persistent result, or even at its beginning or in its middle. While in the simplest conation, satiety and satisfaction might coincide, for "end" to truly signify "value," satisfaction "must be more than mere satiety". The very idea of conation must be remodeled to accommodate this necessity, a fact recognized by modern pleasure-theory when it emphasizes positive interest within the conation, rather than merely escaping tension or disturbance.

In finite life, conation and fruition exist in varying degrees of coincidence. This spectrum ranges from conations primarily valued as a release from pain to those virtually indistinguishable from pure, positive self-affirmation, where any conation is entirely latent. The crucial point for us is the "expansion of the idea of 'end' into a connection with fruition and value, shedding its exclusive link with termination versus process, and superordination versus means".

Teleology, Mechanism, and the Scope of Finite Consciousness

We must now address the term "Teleology" itself. As we've seen, it's often described as an "unlucky term". In the sense of aiming at the unfulfilled, it grants an artificial importance to time and to the final, potentially trivial, part of a whole.

Of its two core implications—completeness and conclusion—the accessory idea of "conclusion" often unfortunately usurps the more fundamental idea of "completeness". In truth, teleological significance does not depend on what comes first or last in a temporal sequence, but on "what the individual real possesses when apprehended in its completeness".

Action is not truly teleological simply because a deferred element of a subordinate quasi-totality is being carried out by a finite desire in the time-process. Such an "end" would not necessarily possess teleological value, and even if it did, it wouldn't necessarily be its leading constituent. The "true question of value is independent of temporal relations"; it depends on the "structure and significance of the whole undergoing completion"—that is, on its character of individuality, its proximity to the ultimate whole.

A significant adversary of what our sources call "sane idealism" is the belief that "the ideal exclusively belongs to the future". On the contrary, "the ideal is what we perceive in the light of the whole," and how it shapes our future is merely an incident—and never the most crucial one—of our unified understanding of past, present, and future. Therefore, when "end," "purposiveness," or "teleology" merely signify that a finite consciousness is driven by a pleasurable impulse or an unfulfilled idea, this bare fact, apart from the content of the idea itself, holds "nothing inherently sacred or significant". It is futile to seek the essence or significance of teleology in the mere fact of conscious purpose or impulse. Purpose, prima facie, simply means that some creature consciously desires something.

But here's a critical question that arises from this line of reasoning: Does something lose its value once it's attained? Does everything derive its value simply from being wanted? Are fruition or perfection truly the "death of value"? Are the ideas of positive fulfillment, satisfaction, and a being that is good in itself—beyond the cycles of want and satiety—mere illusions? If so, then there is no Absolute, or if we rely solely on finite experience, the character of the Absolute fails to suggest itself within our lives. But, as our text emphatically states, such a conclusion "contradicts both fact and theory". While our wants certainly play a role in the ultimate whole, they "cannot conceivably serve as a measure of value". We cannot conceive of an intuitive intelligence creating values entirely detached from a whole with determinate content. The supreme experience, whatever we name it, "must be one with its world, not a creator out of nothing".

This brings us to a pivotal statement that encapsulates much of our re-conceptualization: "Things are not teleological because they are purposed, but are purposed because they are teleological". When we refer to the ultimate real as individual or teleological, it is hazardous to suggest that purpose, in the sense of an unfulfilled craving in time, plays any part in our conception.

A teleology dependent on a feature of the time-process is not one that anyone but a pragmatist can affirm of ultimate reality. The "true test of a purpose's purposiveness," even in complex phenomena like organic evolution, social progress, or morals, lies in its "objectiveness of selection" – the selection of values that can truly withstand criticism. "Subjective selection is poor work unless it transcends its subjectivity".

Now, let's consider the relationship between mechanism and teleology, specifically addressing the claimed incompatibility between two positions. Position A states that nature is instrumental to the development of spiritual values. Position B asserts that the spiritual view regards experience as a mechanically intelligible whole. The crucial question is their compatibility.

To clarify our stance, three essential points must be understood:

1. First, the Uniformity of Nature is not a mere empirical observation but a "logical postulate," which is equivalent to the Law of Identity interpreted as the Law of Sufficient Reason. Any attempts to invalidate it based on de facto irregularities in nature are irrelevant to its philosophical standing. To think that uniformity means a mere repetition of similars, which could be impeached by non-miraculous irregularity, is a fundamental logical error. And to believe that such an impeachment somehow guarantees spirituality is akin to the outdated position of upholding miracles in the name of spiritual interest.
2. Second, it's a parallel error to "contrast individuality with law", presuming that universal connections are somehow antithetical to individuality and only exist as generalities for resembling instances. A person, a singular individual, serves as a sufficient counter-example to this flawed notion. The idea that an individual isn't a universal or isn't structured by universals, and that universals require multiple resembling points, is simply the old fallacy of substituting similarity for identity. This

leads directly to a misunderstanding of the universal and a failure to grasp a genuine conception of the spiritual. Teleology, in this context, is simply a "temporal sub-form of harmony," just as Sufficient Reason is a sub-form of Identity in concrete application.

3. Third, the accepted idea of mechanism we are discussing here neither reduces the universe to mere modifications of homogeneous quantity nor challenges the "uniformity of nature" or the quantitative relations underlying natural phenomena. On the contrary, it accepts that qualities inherently have quantitative connections, and that a high degree of spiritual or emotional expressiveness often accompanies a high degree of complexity and intelligible determinateness. It is one thing to reject abstract calculation as the sole reality, but quite another to be driven by faulty popular science into depreciating the spiritual value of intelligence or attributing an unreal independence to the bare facts of finite conation.

Given these explanations, the compatibility of nature being instrumental to spiritual ends *and* simultaneously mechanically intelligible becomes clearer, perhaps even obvious. What is maintained is that "either position is inconceivable without the other" Individuality, understood as the profound union of comprehensiveness and coherence, the very incarnation of non-contradiction, "cannot be realized in any system that is not transparent according to the Law of Causation or Sufficient Reason". Where discontinuity appears, it signifies a fundamental gap in the embodiment of spiritual purpose and significance.

A purpose is not truly realized, is not a reality that permeates and vivifies its content, if it is not continuously and traceably affirmed within a coherent structure. Crucially, "No purpose or significance can be realized through miracle".

Any prejudice to the contrary arises from the logical blunder of imagining the concrete universal—the individual—as somehow incompatible with the realization of "general law," which is merely a weakened form of the universal determinations within the individual structure.

One might argue that causal or mechanical explanation is necessarily incomplete and proceeds indefinitely. But this is only true if it's taken as total or absolute, implying homogeneity. And even then, it merely reflects the same defect of finite experience that makes all teleological explanations arbitrary. If both mechanical and teleological explanations were complete, they would inevitably merge, and their distinct characters would become aspects within a unified whole. This is not mere fancy. The profound relationship of cause and ground to the whole, on one hand, and the inherent tendency of teleology to expand into systematic coherence, on the other, clearly demonstrate the beginning of this essential convergence.

Organic Mechanism: The World-Wisdom, Not Finite Consciousness

A clear sign of one-sidedness in understanding is the attempt to reduce mechanism to "degenerated finite teleology," often using the analogy of secondary automatism (for example, interpreting reflex responses as an acquired facility, like a skilled pianist). This contention suggests that a machine embodying an idea must be consciously constructed and "worked" by a finite consciousness with explicit finite teleology.

While there's a certain plausibility for human-made machines, especially when we focus on their inherent limitations—limitations that mirror the narrowness of finite consciousness—if we instead consider the vast possibilities and distinctive nature of a machine, or indeed any human material achievement like a work of fine art, the clear lesson is that "ideas can be embodied in unconscious, external forms that are mechanical in every fiber".These cases, undeniably originating from finite consciousness, should profoundly guide our interpretation of nature even where no such consciousness is traceable.

The counter-argument, often heard, is "Exactly! That *does* give us the line for understanding nature, meaning all organic machinery originates in and is worked by a finite consciousness". But this draws a conclusion based on an incidental feature and is generally contrary to fact. Our machines are, indeed, imperfect and one-sided, precisely reflecting the limitations of finite consciousness. Natural works, and far greater historical achievements, however, are "not dependent on a relevant and explicit consciousness for their construction or operation". In humans, only a small part of our complex bodily mechanism is popularly considered "controlled by consciousness". Whatever consciousness exists in plants or lower animals, it is clearly not the kind that could possibly design or employ their incredibly complex bodily arrangements.

Kant's argument applies powerfully here: Reason, he contends, has higher purposes than operating the bodily machine; reflexes and instinct perform that task far better. Reason cannot teach us to swallow or move an arm. Similarly, we cannot imagine that the faint feelings, if any, accompanying plant-life taught the orchid to adapt its pollen or stamen fibers in such intricate ways. To attribute these things to a finite teleological consciousness would logically force us to extend this same reasoning to the vast geological forces that shaped the Eastern Mediterranean for civilization or made Great Britain an island. The point is not whether purposes and ideas "operate" in nature—the very meaning of that question is doubtful. Rather, it is that "Nature below conscious intelligence, and 'Providence' above it, can achieve, without the help of a relevant explicit consciousness, results of the same general type as those attributed to finite minds". The participation of the inorganic world in history is continuous with that of the organic world, and no one would logically argue that finite consciousness is operative in the inorganic realm.

The notion that the expression of ideas is somehow opposed to mechanism is widespread but fundamentally fallacious, similar to believing that uniformity simply means the future always resembles the past. For instance, in fine arts, we often say "expression" comes "straight from the soul," implying it's distinct from "mechanical finish". But in truth, both are prima facie mechanical, and "expression" often means a *more perfect* mechanical *control* over the medium. "Mind and individuality, in their finite forms, find their fullest expression as aspects of very complex and precisely determined mechanical systems". This is a "universal law" for higher human products and cosmic evolution, flowing directly from the nature of "being and trueness". Greater being demands more perfect coherence, which in turn demands fuller content. The mechanical appearance—the continuity of transition and determination—must therefore be unbroken, implying a profound dependence on a system where individuality manifests through universal law. It is futile to appeal to finite purposive consciousness as the sole vehicle of teleology or the source of a "fossilized" mechanical nature. The external must be frankly accepted as a factor, actual but not ultimate, in the universe.

Having freed teleology from being restricted to finite purpose, we can now conceive of the "world-plan as immanent in the whole, encompassing both finite mind and mechanical nature". The obviously secondary and fragmentary nature of finite mind thus constitutes only a partial revelation of the meaning of things, by no means its principal vehicle or sole organ of guidance in evolution or history. The core argument hinges on the "continuity of mechanism with the individuality of the real," stemming from that deeper, "logical rather than teleological, aspect of reality". This is precisely why, despite acknowledging limitations in the common understanding of the mechanical view, we contend that the true spiritual ideal *demands* mechanical intelligibility.

Teleology in Nature: The Example of a Flower

Let's illustrate this with a concrete example of an organic product commonly considered "below the line of consciousness"—a flower. Our perspective rejects two extreme interpretations.

1. On one hand, it's utterly absurd to say a flower arises by accident—as a mere by-product of elements whose nature doesn't inherently contain such a result. This would be akin to suggesting a human contriver didn't anticipate complex developments. We cannot logically treat one part of the world as primary and another as secondary. We must interpret nature by the flower as much as by the law of gravitation. Indeed, even the simplest inorganic formations, like the motions of a solar system, the curl of a wave, or the curve of a precipice, equally merit a presumption of teleological value as any consciously created object, save consciousness itself.
2. On the other hand, we must not claim "purpose is operative" in the flower or wave if this means attributing them to an end or idea "superinduced" upon their elements by a power comparable to finite consciousness, operating *ab extra* (from outside). If the first notion implied accident, this second one implies miracle. As we've seen, teleology is fundamentally undermined if no determinate universal relations between differences can be truly predicated. It's impossible to find a point where life isn't mechanically conditioned. The individuality manifested in a flower, a mountain, or a wave, independent of operative consciousness, compels a conclusion so far-reaching that the case of human consciousness, though vastly different in degree, scarcely advances the principle. Avoiding these two extremes, we are compelled to affirm that in the flower's intricate

structure and very being, the common natural elements "behave according to their inherent nature," and the remarkable creation we observe is simply the "immanent development of certain factors". These factors, in isolation, might seem far removed from such a result. We must always remember the active role of the environment, of "objective selection". The plan of the flower wasn't inherent in a few elements in a laboratory, but in the "whole interactions of nature". We are certain, under any view of evolution, that the structure of a plant or animal is a microcosm from which, with adequate knowledge, its environment's nature could be deciphered.

Whether adhering to strict natural selection or assuming a psychological cause (with or without inheritance of acquired qualities), the fundamental truth remains: "it is the world, the environment, that is responsible for the differences in organic evolution". While protoplasm's inherent powers or life's initial impulse might account for common phenomena, "it is overwhelmingly the world that has shaped the content of what we call the individual". This is abundantly clear in intelligence and volition, and equally obvious in organic evolution.

It's crucial to acknowledge that even if the cause is "psychological," like "subjective selection," no sane person would claim that such a psychological cause performs *conscious teleological work* in structural adaptation, except in our conscious efforts to develop the human body. It doesn't solve problems or consciously contrive adaptations. In fact, it's more accurate to say "subjective selection is negative and natural selection is positive". Subjective selection offers countless reactions tending towards habits; it is "natural selection that molds them into definite lines of progress and elicits positive structure". To say natural selection is negative is like saying a sculptor's art is negative merely because it works by removal. Therefore, if "mind" operates in the structural adaptation of animals or plants, "it does not operate *as mind*". It doesn't contain the plan or consciously guide the progress.

It might be a more felicitous conception of the agency by which the plan, immanent in the whole, is actualized. But in any case, we are certain that a work as astonishing as those attributed to finite consciousness, like a flower, is accomplished "without any intervention of consciousness as a teleological agency"—that is, as a planner or problem-solver. In this context, no one would suggest the miraculous intervention of consciousness, as they might for human-made machines or art.

Indeed, the thorough examination of mechanism and teleology has entirely dismissed such a suggestion. The idea that a purposive intelligence, when a man builds a clock or composes a sonata, operates by mere design on a system to impart something not communicable by mechanical parts, should now appear a "contradiction in terms". No one today would explain the intricate beauty and functionality of a flower by appealing to the purposive interposition of a creative intelligence. Whether Nature "aims at ends" or not, it is a bare fact that "without any contriving consciousness, she can present them to our minds".

Finite Consciousness: A Manifestation, Not the Source

Thus, we have seen that the very foundations of "teleology"—which truly means individuality—"in the universe are far too deeply laid to be explained by, much less restricted to, the intervention of finite consciousness". Everything indicates that finite consciousness should "not be regarded as the source of teleology, but as itself a manifestation, falling within wider manifestations, of the immanent individuality of the real".

It is not teleological *because* as a finite subject of desire and volition it is "purposive". Rather, "it is what we call purposive because reality is individual and a whole," and manifests this character partly in the "short-sighted and eclectic aims of finite intelligence," and partly in appearances of far greater range and scope.

Consider the large-scale patterns of history and civilization: these are "not found as purposes within any single finite consciousness".

The definite continuity and correlation of intelligent activities that give human life its teleological character—what we might refer to as the "ways of Providence"—are a fact of the same fundamental order as the development of the solar system or the appearance of life on Earth.

It is impossible to attribute to finite consciousnesses, as individual agents, the identity at work within finite consciousness as a whole. This identity manifests in a development springing from the "linked action of separate and successive finite consciousnesses in relation to their environment"

Every single step in this development, although intelligent and teleological in itself, is "unconscious in relation to the whole". The result is still "a nature," though a "second and higher nature". This principle is paramount, holding true across all levels of being.

Let me reiterate and emphasize the two core parts of our contention:

Teleology Below Consciousness:

- The intelligence of humans and intelligent animals does not, as I see it, sustain or conduct their bodily life. To claim that all vital responses are inherited from volitional or quasi-volitional behaviour is factually dubious and, more importantly, an evasion of the underlying principle.
- If something akin to volition molded bodily structure in earlier evolutionary phases, it "never did so by any conscious wisdom within the mind of that phase". It followed, almost blindly, the determination of a "deeper wisdom hidden in the

general structure of the environment". The denial of teleological significance to natural selection is a prime example of the position we argue against.

Furthermore, whatever role mind played in the past for our bodily structures, it's largely irrelevant to its current role. Human minds and purposes "presuppose, accept, and are founded on, their actual bodies". The plant-mind, if it exists, equally presupposes and accepts the plant-form. Even if mind is present from the beginning, it exists in such elementary forms that it is "molded rather than molding". The orchid, as stated, cannot have a mind that contrives its fertilization, just as a human mind cannot teach itself to swallow or digest, or choose its birth time or place. Everywhere, finite consciousness, in its obvious and unmistakable forms, appears at a relatively high level, "focusing and revealing the significance of a vast complication of 'mute history and circumstance' that precedes and surrounds it".

Teleology Above Finite Consciousness:

- Considering history, and the time and place of one's birth, we unequivocally arrive at teleology beyond finite consciousness. In history, and even more profoundly in the linked development of art, ideas, and religions, the principle of a teleology that transcends, yet is exhibited *in,* finite consciousness is clear and unambiguous.
- It is "not finite consciousness that has planned the great phases of civilization," which are achieved by the linking of finite minds upon the essential foundation of the globe's geological structure. Each individual mind reaches only a very small distance, and in relation to the whole of a movement, it must be considered unconscious. While intelligence may be present in every step of the connection, we cannot logically claim as a design of finite intelligence what never presented itself in that character to any single mind.

- For instance, a Greek colonist journeying to Ionia in the eighth or ninth century B.C. was certainly paving the way for Christianity. But their relation to it, though a higher form of working, was essentially like that of a "coral insect to a coral reef". Neither Christianity nor the coral reef was ever a design in the minds of the people or insects who constructed them; "they lay far deeper in the 'roots of things'". This, I contend, leads to the fundamental conclusion about evolution: "Nothing is truly attributable to finite mind as such, which was never a plan before any finite mind".

Reconciling Mechanism and Teleology: The True Nature of Totality

The contrast between mechanism and teleology, then, is not elucidated by a simple antithesis between purposive consciousness and the reactions of parts. It is deeply "rooted in the very nature of totality," which is viewed from two complementary perspectives: as an "individual whole" and as constituted by "inter-reacting members". Neither viewpoint can be entirely absent.

If mechanical intelligibility were to fail completely, the spiritual would be reduced to the miraculous—the very negation of all spirituality. Conversely, a total failure of teleological intelligibility would reduce individuality to incoherence, thereby annihilating mechanism.

However, because teleology is often considered in abstraction, it's easier to imagine its absence than that of mechanism, which must accompany any inter-relation whatsoever. As the saying goes, "Understanding without Reason is something, Reason without understanding is nothing". There is, in truth, a teleology in any order, and some order must exist, but our common ideas of teleology are arbitrary and eclectic.

The entire doctrine of theism in the Kantian sense, which posits a personal creator and governor of the world and assigns paramount importance to subjective selection and bare finite consciousness as agents, in contrast to natural selection and the immanent plan of things, is called into question here. While a deeper importance might attach to finite consciousness from a different perspective, the meeting of extremes in metaphysics should not surprise us. The polemic against the mechanical view and the epiphenomenal doctrine of intelligence may, surprisingly, find these concepts unexpectedly aligning with their antagonists.

Which perspective on theism and intelligence should be prioritized?

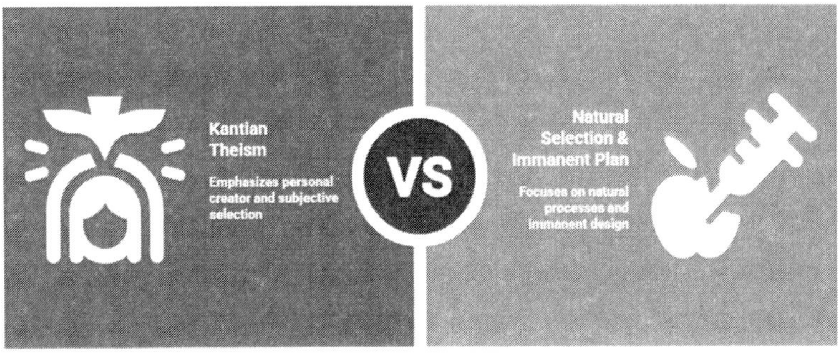

We are certainly not treating consciousness or the self as mere byproducts or accessories. However, it is increasingly evident that the developed finite mind "must be regarded as an appearance that emerges 'on the top of a great deal that must go before them".

Two opposing contentions seem to demand fusion. To the "voluntarist"—the believer in a hardly conscious something underlying explicit intelligence, where they find the fundamental reality—we must concede that a "vast 'underground work' is involved in forming an intelligent moral being". The conscious self is plainly the "last word of an immense evolution" that moves from unconsciousness to consciousness.

It necessarily presupposes, as far as we can understand, the "co-operation of unconscious nature in molding the foundation of mind". There is no logical value, I believe, in assuming the presence of mind in simpler forms at earlier evolutionary phases.

However, admitting all this to those who advocate an obscure "will-to-live" does not destroy, but rather, when rightly understood, "corroborates and enhances the significance and value of intelligence and self-realization through the realization of ideas".For it is precisely this that is brought to fruition as the climax and revelation when the "underground self" emerges into completeness.

Only then do we truly begin to understand ourselves, to enjoy and possess ourselves, and consequently, to genuinely possess the world.

The conscious and intelligent self is "on the top of," and made possible by, all the stress and complexity of the work that precedes it. If, instead of labeling it "epiphenomenal," we call it the "climax and sum and substance of evolution," we would be stating the truth that epiphenomenalism caricatures.

This, of course, implies that when the self emerges, it does not come empty or without presuppositions. While mind, in a sense, is the active form of totality and thus everything, "every particular finite mind has received a certain 'filling' before it becomes aware of itself". It begins, so to speak, high up in the world of experience, already possessing a rich content and a "machinery" prepared by its world.

No matter how little one believes in materialistic determinism today, they would be slow to deny that bodily arrangements and mechanisms are at least the foundational basis for the soul's operation. When viewed correctly, this perspective imbues the organized consciousness with immensely greater significance and importance than if it were considered a structureless intellectual protoplasm.

It is nothing less than an "individual spiritual body, a special utterance and revelation of the universe in its highest finite form". It is bare consciousness and the unmolded power of selection that appear as impotent abstractions in their emptiness. The concrete self is vastly different; as we've maintained throughout, it is "a world within a world of worlds". The resonance of these ideas with the deepest conclusions of religious philosophy is striking. The perspective that the finite intelligent being has the "duty and position of 'coming to himself' and 'awakening' to his own nature and unity with what we imperfectly call a greater mind and will, rather than independently controlling or molding the world," demands reaffirmation. This view is particularly suggestive against claims stemming from making individualistic moralism absolute.

We will explore the question of finite individual freedom and initiative further in future discussions. For now, it suffices to suggest that as a self-conscious being, one is fundamentally a "member of the universe inter pares".

Each individual, however trifling it may seem, is something without which the universe would not be what it is. Indeed, one is an "organ through which, even in a small degree, the whole sustains itself". Therefore, it cannot be justly claimed that nothing is genuinely done or effected in and by the individual. However, we must carefully avoid the erroneous implication that a finite individual could find a *pousto* (a place to stand) outside the universe and proceed to act upon and reform it.

A doctrine that integrates the profound conception of action, freedom, initiative, and achievement with the idea of "coming to oneself," learning one's place and nature, awakening to one's fundamental membership, and rejoicing in that greater reality underlying and surrounding one's self, can offer and receive immense assistance in understanding the intricate relationship between mind and body, or, as we might better phrase it, "how spirit appears as a focus to matter".

To put it in the extreme: even if finite consciousness were merely a mind awakening to the significance of the external realm to which it serves as a center, and a self-identification with the logic and tension of the absolute within that single vortex of its being, would this amount to no achievement, no value? I am not arguing this extreme position, however.

It seems we might achieve a deeper understanding and make a stronger case for personality and initiative than that of mere revelation and awakening. Yet, dare we say that *only* this—the recognition of the infinite within ourselves—would be nothing of value, nothing by which the living finite person, the conscious body as a whole, could be ennobled by achievement?

Lecture-6

Self-Consciousness as the Key to the Structure of Reality

This lecture turns inward to reveal self-consciousness as more than a human trait—as a vital clue to reality's deepest structure. By exploring how self and other, conflict and harmony, negation and fulfillment interrelate, it shows why tension, difference, and reconciliation are not defects, but essential movements through which reality understands and completes itself.

Shows how self-awareness provides the clue to understanding reality's underlying pattern

My friends, in our exploration of reality, we have consistently observed that Finite Consciousnesses, as we know them, cannot possibly be the ultimate directors or fundamental constituents of the universe. Our individual consciousnesses, along with their subjective aims and purposes, are not the starting point of reality; rather, they appear at a certain stage, resting upon deeper, more fundamental arrangements beneath them. Every single characteristic of finite consciousness, be it in an animal or a human, points towards fuller and more comprehensive forms of totality that exist beyond us. Consider this profound truth: finite consciousness, whether animal or human, did not create its own body, nor does it establish the grander purposes for its world. Instead, something greater and more inclusive than itself actively operates through it and reveals itself to it. This observation compels us to ask a crucial question: Is finite consciousness merely an accident in a universe that is fundamentally alien to its nature? Is self-consciousness, which we experience as the most complete form of consciousness, born from some inherent defect, and destined to be eliminated if that defect is removed? Or, is it possible that in this fullest phase of finite experience, we find something that provides a profound clue to the typical structure of reality itself?

Could it be that self-consciousness is not annihilated, but rather enhanced, by the transition from states of discord into responsiveness, and from a hostile "not-self" into an "other" that is truly a counterpart of the self?

When I speak of self-consciousness, let me be precise. I do not mean the simple act of the whole self perceiving itself as an object. No, by self-consciousness, I refer to the recognition of the self in the other. This recognition is a dynamic process, experienced across various aspects of our being: in our cognition, in our practical actions, in our appreciation of beauty (the aesthetic attitude), and deeply, in our religious experiences. Its essence, therefore, is not a mere internal reflection, but the profound realization of a counterpart within externality—a counterpart that may be discordant or harmonious, yet fundamentally shares the same principle as the self.

This leads us directly to another pivotal inquiry: Does "self-hood" run in parallel with "Individuality," meaning they progress hand-in-hand? Or must the experience of self-hood necessarily cease when Individuality reaches its absolute maximum?

While this might not seem to be of ultimate importance—indeed, there might be experiences in the highest individuality that would rightly supersede the experience of self-hood—nevertheless, if we can successfully remove a certain common misapprehension, we shall have opened a vital pathway to a deeper conception of reality, one that is at least framed by analogy with our understanding of self-consciousness.

Now, let us turn our attention to the concept of the "not-self." In our finite experience, that against which the universal continuously opposes itself, in its relentless effort to become fully individual, is primarily difference in the form of what appears alien or hostile. We constantly encounter a "resistant not-self" —a reality in the face of which we feel ignorant and weak, and where, as finite beings, we can never achieve absolute triumph or feel completely at home.

A fundamental question for our understanding of Individuality then becomes: Is this "not-self" something that simply depends on and indicates imperfection, or is it, in fact, an essential component of the structure of the real? Could we, for example, conceive of individuality perfecting itself as a cosmos and a "self-in-otherness," precisely as the unresponsiveness or even hostility, which we perceive as a great mark of the other, is gradually overcome?

One common and, in my view, rather simplistic perspective, relies entirely on the notion that the not-self is inherently discordant. Consequently, this view maintains that self-hood is confined to imperfect being, and vanishes entirely as the hostile not-self is overcome. This perspective bears a perilous resemblance, though it is not identical, to the view that all consciousness is somehow a disease or a defect. It is, frankly, too easy and dangerous to simply discard the higher characteristics of experience when we attempt to conceive of the Absolute. A much more reliable approach is to, if possible, identify the trajectory of their transmutation. Indeed, I have observed that the concept of a "responsive" or "concordant not-self" often emerges within these same philosophical speculations, even if it is ultimately dismissed in their final conclusions. Therefore, it seems to me a significant error to neglect this crucial feature when we are attempting to comprehend the ultimate nature to which the individual can aspire. In short, we must ask: Is discordance the only form of "otherness"?

And if so, is "otherness" itself ultimately unreal? Or, is it not, at a deeper level, the case that discordance itself is fundamentally rooted in the inherent claim and possibility of harmony? This distinction between mere discord and a deeper, essential otherness is paramount.

In this chapter, then, my aim is to discuss what I call the "Contrafamiliar view," which treats "Negativity" not as a vanishing defect, but as a fundamental and enduring characteristic of the real. I will illustrate this perspective by connecting it with certain points in logical theory, and I will insist that its true value depends on fully pressing its principle home. Let us begin with the nature of what I take to be full or "logical contradiction." The critical insight, it seems to me, is that no predicates are intrinsically contrary to one another.

They become so only under the specific conditions in which they are brought together. Therefore, contradiction consists in "differents" being attributed to the same term, without any distinction being provided within that term to make it capable of receiving them.

This is essentially Plato's Law of Contradiction: whatever does or suffers "opposites" (or, more accurately, "differents") in the same relation, must in itself be two and not one. This very principle forms the foundation of Plato's distinction between Opinion (or Appearance) and Knowledge (or Reality). For instance, it is a formal contradiction to state, "This color is both beautiful and ugly". However, this contradiction ceases if you clarify, "This colorby daylight is beautiful and by candlelight is ugly". Here, the introduction of a relevant distinction (daylight vs. candlelight) resolves the apparent conflict. You might ask if there are terms that are intrinsically contrary and can never be affirmed of one another, such as a circle and a square. My answer is no. They do not impede each other or the process of thought unless we compel them into a specific combination for which their content is inadequate.

A circle and a square can very well be conjoint predicates of the same complex term; when affirmed with adequate distinction, there is nothing inherently contrary between them.

It can be initially perplexing in Plato that he seems to find it contradictory for the same object to appear different at different distances. Yet, this is precisely what he consistently explains: it would be a contradiction if a thing looked the same at different distances; but that it looks different at different distances is a clear application of his Law of non-contradiction.

The fundamental point is this: there is a proper place for all predicates. And when all predicates are in their appropriate places, none of them are contrary to any other. The true essence of contradiction and contrariety lies in bringing diverse terms together on an inadequate basis of distinction. This can happen with any diverse terms whatsoever.

I venture to suggest that whenever we encounter the implication that predicates can be antecedently "contrary" or "opposite," we can infer that contradiction has not been adequately analyzed. Therefore, Contradiction, we propose, is not a static fact about certain predicates; rather, it is an imperfection in the organization of systems.

We can, then, describe Contradiction as a deadlock. It is a deadlock created by the attempt to unite two or more different terms without sufficient adjustment of their content for successful reception. In this sense, contradiction is rightly deemed "unthinkable" and consequently cannot be a characteristic of Truth or of Ultimate Reality.

This is because Truth and Ultimate Reality, if they are anything substantial, represent experiences in which Thought is triumphant and perfectly harmonious with itself, and indeed, with much more besides.

However, a crucial first step in our argument is to determine in what sense even such complete and formal contradiction can be an actual existent, a real characteristic of Reality. We immediately grasp that it cannot be ultimate.

Our initial inclination might be to dismiss it as merely a blunder of our own making, a subjective error that cannot belong to the world of fact. But in saying this, we risk unduly idealizing our actual world—our given experience as we can recognize anything as given.

We would be treating this empirical reality with a reverence due only to ultimate reality. For if anything is truly given, it is a perpetual unrest of action and cognition. This unrest powerfully testifies to the constant presence of conflict and discord within every moment of our experience. In other words, we continually find the presence of contradictions which, both in our actions and in our thoughts, make it impossible to rest content in any actual moment.

Therefore, I infer, it must be admitted that everyday fact, that which is given in normal experience, is both self-contradictory and actual. If we maintain that what is self-contradictory cannot be actual fact, then we would be forced to deny the very actuality of our entire normal world, which is the very field of our knowledge and action. For it is undeniably clear that every object of knowledge and every situation that dictates our practical actions, even if temporarily accepted, is accepted only on sufferance. Such facts inherently contain incoherences—combinations that are impossible as they stand—and these inconsistencies must, as soon as they are noted, drive us onward. Facts, as we commonly refer to them, possess a certain stability up to a point; they will, so to speak, answer certain questions and meet certain needs. But when we transcend their individual limits of stability by bringing them into connection with more of the real world, we become acutely aware that none of them are sufficiently stubborn things to stand as finally coherent. The common appearances of our lives—material things, our conduct, institutions—all carry us a certain distance, and to declare them illusory would be a foolish exaggeration.

But let's take a single example: if we solely rely on the idea that man lives "by bread alone"—by mere bodily comfort—we will discover that he cannot. While bodily nutrition is undeniably actual, we will inevitably fall into contradiction—we will find that nourishment is not nourishment—if we consider it the exclusive mode by which human beings are sustained. Other needs will inevitably assert themselves; what we considered our settled system of "fact" will simply not make room for them. Our "fact" has broken down. Indeed, all our facts break down in some such way, and at some such point. Thus, unless we choose to adopt the doctrine of Maya—which I believe stems from a misapprehension on this very point—and classify the entire known world as illusion, we must admit that what is experienced as actual fact may yet be self-contradictory. We cannot escape this by saying "thus far and no farther"; by declaring, "we will take the world without asking questions, and thus it shall be perfect fact, and real without contradiction". For such a world will simply not keep pace with our experience. We will find that action and argument, "like a wind," will carry us outside of it; and our petrified facts will neither serve our needs nor sustain themselves.

The whole of this difficulty, I contend, springs from trying to attribute to given fact the features that properly belong to ultimate Reality. In truth, the actual world is charged with contradiction. Things are presented to us with combinations of predicates for which no adequate distinctions are immediately available to deal with and explain them. Furthermore, in the life of conscious beings, contradiction is a directly felt experience, as actual and tangible as pain, dissatisfaction, or unrest, which are either forms of it or identical with it. It manifests as an attempted union which, though given, fails in providing the necessary contents for adjustment, making it something a mind, or even a life, cannot endure. Its actuality is proven by the very experience of progress itself, spanning the entire region of action and cognition, which is equivalent to the region of finite experience.

(The Spirit of Otherness: Negativity)

Our next step is to determine what form or "spirit of otherness" survives when a logical contradiction is successfully resolved. The crucial point I want to emphasize is that we are here dealing with a survival of what was present in Logical

Contradiction. Nothing fundamental is changed, except that what was attempted has now been achieved. The contents remain diverse—sensuous experiences, ideas, emotions, conscious members of a social world. The underlying principle is the same throughout: they are propelled by the same impulse to come together in the whole that animates them. The change is simply that now, these contents and their world have been readjusted, and their union can be fully carried out. How, then, are we to describe the form of their surviving distinctness? Consider examples such as a sensuous harmony of color or sound, minds and motives operating at their very best, two selves intimately united in a single emotion, or the deep satisfaction of a desire.

I can illustrate this point by referring to Hegel's view of contradiction, though this is merely an illustration, and I do not wish to delve into historical questions here. It is widely understood that Hegel has been accused of denying or disregarding the logical law which declares contradiction to be unthinkable. However, his most astute interpreters have shown this charge to be false. They have pointed out that Hegel's Dialectic, far from disregarding the law of Contradiction, rests entirely upon it. It is precisely because contradiction is unthinkable and intolerable that a conjunction of judgments, which renders their predicates irreconcilable, necessitates a fundamental readjustment of contents and the formation of a new, higher totality.

Now, while I acknowledge that this interpretation is certainly contained within Hegel's view of Contradiction, I cannot help but feel there is something more profound underlying his stance. Hegel clearly perceives himself as fundamentally at odds with the common, formal view that Contradiction is merely unthinkable. He uses exceptionally strong language to express his scorn for such an attitude. He declares: "What moves the world is Contradiction; it is ridiculous to say that Contradiction is unthinkable.". He admits that the truth in this assertion is only that Contradiction cannot be final, and that "by its own action it cancels while it maintains itself (Sichaufhebt)". The cancelled and maintained contradiction, however, is not a barren, abstract identity, for that represents only one side of the antithesis. We are, no doubt, in the region of essence here, where oppositions are sharp and pointed. But this does not fully account for the totality of Hegel's attitude, which is fundamental to his philosophy. Consider his further pronouncements: "Whereas people say that Contradiction is not thinkable, the truth is that in pain which a living being feels it is actually a real existence.". (He makes a similar claim regarding motion in space). And again: "Formal thinking prescribes to itself the rule that Contradiction is not thinkable; but, in fact, the thinking of Contradiction is the essential moment of the Notion.".

These latter passages, drawn from his discussions of Life and of the Absolute Idea, clearly refer to something beyond the simple deadlock of saying and unsaying the same thing. While it is agreed that a logical contradiction presents a position that cannot be maintained, we further note a strong conviction that it contains and implies something, the value and necessity of which account for and justify the very inevitability of contradiction itself. Contradiction, as we observed earlier, is not merely our mistake; it is a check or friction inherent in the misalignment of experience during its process of self-systematization. The crucial question, then, is: What remains, what is found to have been the true movement of union, when this check or friction is removed by readjustment?.

This brings us to a compelling suggestion for addressing this problem: "What survives when a contradiction is resolved?" We might venture to reply: "A successful embodiment of 'negativity.'". Hegel often speaks of Negativity as seemingly a factor or "moment" embedded deeply in the inmost structure of the Real. It is, for him, the very pulse of life and the spring of movement of the world. It is not identical with the "dead fact" of unthinkableness that characterizes logical contradiction. Rather, it is the spirit of system and self-consciousness itself.

It represents the intimate nature of a being which, while actively expanding and acting, remains fundamentally at home with itself—it is distinguishable or self-distinguishing, in and through its intimate union with its contents during expansion and action. Negativity is the successful and pure expression of that whole aspect or tendency of anything real, which finds its imperfect manifestation, accompanied by friction and hindrance, in what has been described above as Formal or Logical Contradiction.

Therefore, I submit, Negativity is fundamental in all that is real. It is the same characteristic that has been described as the fact that experience is always "beyond itself"—a characteristic we have, from the very beginning, described as that of the universal, or, in other words, the inherent tendency of every datum to transcend itself as a fragment and complete itself as a whole. It is what has been referred to under the name of self-consciousness: the nature of a being which is itself and its other in one. I am suggesting that Negation and Negativity have sometimes been confused with Contradiction. Let me clarify the distinctions:

- Contradiction, as we have sought to explain it, is an unsuccessful or obstructed Negativity.
- Negativity, conversely, can be understood as a successful or frictionless contradiction.

Negation, according to views I have advanced elsewhere, is correlative to affirmation. The question regarding negation is not how much meaning one can extract from a mere denial, but rather why, in the most highly developed forms of experience, negation plays an equal and crucial part. And the answer is profound: negation is fundamental in a systematic whole. For its members to truly be, they must also, in a certain sense, not be. This holds true even for the whole itself, as it actively manifests within its members.

It seems erroneous, therefore, to maintain that Negativity vanishes as perfection is approached. The reverse, in fact, appears to be the case. Negative and affirmative elements proceed paripassu, side by side. When this is not acknowledged, I suspect a confusion between Contradiction and Negation. This is a point of immense significance, which can hardly be overstated: otherness and the "not-self"—the vastness of the universe with which every self must be reconciled—increase and do not diminish by the very same movement through which friction, obstruction, and conflict are reduced and removed. Consider a savage's mind, constantly baffled and contradicted by a world lacking scientific understanding; in such a state, there cannot be the profound conception of a reality "not ourselves" over against the self, as there is in the age of Newton and Darwin. Whether interpreted correctly or not, this matter—that negation plays a larger, not smaller, part as contradiction diminishes—is crucial and ought not to be neglected. Indeed, it is contradiction itself—confusion or conflict checking the orderly expansion of a system, be it a life or a theory—which hinders significant negation from appearing. A true negativity, for instance, an organized universe of desire, is a solved contradiction.

This, therefore, I submit, is the spirit of difference that persists even when contradiction has been overcome, and where we possess what is most real and most thinkable. In such a condition, everything contributes to the whole. The friction or failure of adjustment that created the contradiction or deadlock—say, in the attempted combination of two or more desires—undoubtedly represented and enhanced the distinctness of the two sides. This distinctness survives within and ultimately tends to perfect the completed union. However, it appears to me that we allow ourselves to lose sight of the full problem if we treat the mere fact of having refused to enter together into a whole—that is, of having been in contradiction—as something that, surviving as such, qualifies the successful union. The qualification, whatever it is, can surely count and operate only as it survives within the completed whole. And it is within the factors of this complete whole itself that we must find the experience of negativity; which is not, according to the view here insisted on, a note of imperfection, but is a characteristic that is deepest in the most perfectly real experience.

So, what exactly do we mean by Negativity as a feature of experience? If it simply means "difference"—the distinctness necessary for identification—then is not a term connected with the idea of "negation" too violent and exaggerated to use for it? What is meant here is not precisely difference, but difference as subsumed under the general character of negation.

That is to say, diversity or distinctness regarded from the point of view of an attempted union. To take a conscious being, probably the only ultimate case, as at least an illustration: it is the attitude of any spirit that demands a union or satisfaction, towards that with which it is impelled to unite or in which it aspires to be satisfied.

Now, undoubtedly, self-completion, satisfaction, and the felt solution of contradiction are possible at many levels of life, and are compatible with very easy and effortless experiences. But it is here suggested that in a true, typical satisfaction—a genuinely felt resolution of a contradiction—there is always a certain exaltation that depends essentially on the fact that, in satisfaction, the self goes out into the other.

And although, or perhaps because, it becomes enriched, it is simultaneously beyond itself. In a word, to put the whole paradox brutally, it is undergoing an experience which, logically and in its fundamental structure, is one with self- sacrifice. How, one might ask, can this concept of self-sacrifice be applied to anything but a finite being? Obviously, not by using words that presuppose limits and a temporal modification in the self. But there is a point of considerable interest which can at least serve to highlight the distinction in principle between treating Negation, like Contradiction, as merely an incident of finiteness, and taking it as fundamental in Reality.

Self-sacrifice in infinity

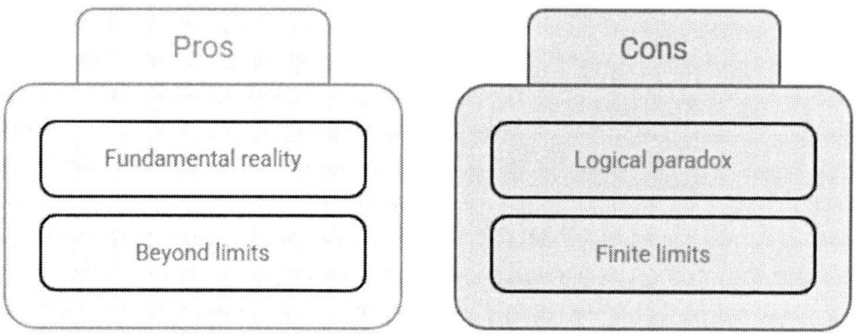

It has already been implied that the prevalent view of experience, influential even among philosophers, often confuses Contradiction and Negativity. The profound principle that an element of Reality can achieve completion only in what is not itself is mistakenly conflated with the imperfection of adjustment in finite beings or contents, which so far hinders such completion from taking place. And thus, it comes to be held that Negation, like Contradiction, is a vanishing quantity, and that in a complete experience it would simply disappear.

The point of interest I referred to, which emphasizes the distinction of principle, is the extreme difficulty of avoiding this very confusion. When we strive to highlight the nature of self-consciousness, as "self and other in one," by drawing examples and analyses from actual experience, we constantly find ourselves appealing to characteristics that appear to depend upon ignorance and imperfection. The ideal we aim for is the self being the other, but in actual experience, we often encounter little more than the self against the other.

The crux of the distinction in principle arises at this point because of the appearance that it is precisely the discrepancy of self and other that gives us interest in the realization of self in other. Take, as a characteristic case, that apparent responsiveness of external Nature to human moods, the perception of which is at least a large part of our apprehension of the beautiful.

The freshness and strength of the feeling such perceptions bring with them are surely, to a great extent, dependent on the fact that they come to us as undesigned coincidences. It is for this reason that they seem to bring us a confirmation of our own sentiments rooted somewhere beyond the foundations of our private being.

If there were no novelty, no unfamiliarity—in a word, no friction or discrepancy intruding upon our apprehension of natural beauty—then, we are inclined to conceive, the return upon ourselves would lose in vigor what it gained in facility, and the magic of the new and inexplicable would be lost in a dull sensation that "it is all the same old story".

Now, the case as just stated emphasizes the opposite side of the question from what was stated before. And the interest lies in the fact that both perspectives are undeniably actual. It is true, as we urged, that the sense of the "beyond," of a something that stands over against the mind, must be incalculably greater for a mind like Newton's or Darwin's than for a savage to whom nature is primarily a mysterious source of unaccountable interferences. But it is also true that a loss of novelty and strangeness—of the friction involved in making the world our own—seems to many minds destructive of poetry and of nature's responsiveness.

These two tendencies are deeply rooted, and both, without doubt, must have their justification. Does complete knowledge and familiarity truly dull the interest of a landscape or a poem, or does it rather, as some would argue, cause the response to be even deeper, and the significance to be more profoundly felt? Is novelty truly necessary to enjoyment, and should a story lose its interest when we discover we have read it before? In these simple questions, which our everyday acquaintance with nature, art, and letters forces upon us, we find an embodiment of the metaphysical issue that is the subject of this chapter. Is Logical Contradiction a necessary condition or accompaniment of genuine conciliation and satisfaction? Or is this, comparatively speaking, an accident of growth, giving place to an exaltation that increases with mastery and the removal of incidental interferences, as the self comes together with a not-self that is completer and more free from discrepancy?

There can be no doubt that the latter alternative, on the whole, represents the truth. It is a poorly written romance that interests only on the first reading.

It is a superficial appetite for the marvelous that finds superstition more exciting and poetical than science. No, it is not the obstructive but the truly responsive different, which in the deepest sense, attracts and exalts us. Of course, the possibility of the former—the obstructive—is rooted in the very characteristic that constitutes the latter—the responsive.

The other tendency—that which relies on novelty and inexplicability—we can empirically observe to be of a vanishing nature. Otherwise, civilization would, as the pessimist believes, destroy the charm of the world. But the pessimist is not without valid points, and novelty and inexplicability do possess genuine features of attraction. These two sources of interest, as we have seen, share the same root: the possibility of discord is inherently involved in the claim to harmony. First, we can see the necessity that this should be so; if not, if their initial aspect was purely deterrent, progress could never even begin. Secondly, as we have already said, the response that is encumbered with strangeness and obstruction carries the seal of an undesigned coincidence; we feel that the very "enemy" takes our part. These might be called formal feelings, analogous to the enjoyment of detecting a plot puzzle or being amazed at unheard-of ingenuities in a romance. But when the superficial "rind" of things is pierced, and the deeper content begins to be grasped, a more profound set of emotions is stirred. We begin to rejoice in the substantive values which expand and affirm our self, and not merely in the surprise that the surface should yield to our instruments at all.

There is, of course, more to be said about the delights of mystery. But we must be content with a single warning: the attitude of the mystic, which all philosophy must respect, does not depend on mystery in the vulgar sense.

It does not depend on the marvelousness, unaccountableness, or obscurity of ideas. The mystic, above all people, is absorbed in the greatness of a contentfor its own sake, and in its overwhelming clearness. It is not contradiction, not friction and obstruction, but immediacy as opposed to discursiveness that distinguishes the mystic's apprehension of the real.

We can thus perhaps understand, or approach an understanding, how Logical Contradiction, though apparently a characteristic attending interest and value in the response of the not-self, is so really only as an introduction, and for vanishing reasons. And we can infer that to interpret our interesting sense of the "beyond" or "other"—which furnishes our satisfactions—as solely due to our ignorance and defect, and as a vanishing quantity in the progress of the mind, is to confuse the incident with the essence. Instead, as in the example of natural knowledge, the otherness becomes more definite as the object becomes more adequate to the subject.

(Critique of "Nature as a System of Persons") It is partly, perhaps, with the view of construing these appearances that many thinkers have embarked on the intellectual adventure of treating all the content of life as a translation of the interaction of conscious beings. Here, without doubt, we seem to have a suggestion of an "other" that is able to maintain its independence and its otherness, along with any degree of transparency or familiarity. And I mention this speculation chiefly to clarify what I consider the particular crux here, if it is not already clear.

We might imagine an intelligent being who has nothing left to learn from a sunset or even from a pain or pleasure. If we posit such an impossible case, we would then be unable to comprehend how these experiences could any longer be experiences by union with which his self has anything to gain. But, it would be urged, a person, however well you know him, is still an independent source of response, and it may be argued that here, and here only, do you find the true other of a self.

I find a difficulty in this speculation, which may rest on a misapprehension, but which I will indicate briefly because it concerns our view of externality. What we must have, on any theory, for Reality and especially for Negativity to be manifested in, is the full content of life: pain, conflict, sacrifice, satisfaction. Now, isn't there a difficulty, I ask, in deriving these contents from a universe in which nature is conceived solely as a system of persons, except by presupposing, in the "outside" or "other" of everything regarded as a person, precisely what might as well have been presupposed as the "outside" or "other" of persons commonly recognized as such? It is things, is it not, which set the problems of life for persons?. And if you transform all things into persons, the very differences that make life interesting are gone, except insofar as for practical purposes you turn the persons back into things—your food, or your own body, or the place at which you were born.

In attempting to make the "outside" adequate to the highest claims, you have, in essence, turned it into an "inside". And so, while professing to meet the problem of the outside in the highest degree, you have, it appears to me, really abandoned it altogether. If the instruments and attributes of my life are transformed into persons, I am surely reduced to emptiness and deprived of my very character, for without external activity, my character is nothing. This criticism may be mistaken, but it serves to affirm that we must perceive as actual the distinctions which give life its content. There cannot be spirit, it would seem, constituted by nothing but pure spiritual centers. Spirit is a focus, a significance, which can only be by contact with a "nature" — an external world.

I will now proceed to indicate the consequences of these ideas — consequences that are well-known, to which I have nothing to add, except this: to urge that their profound point is lost if they are not conceived in their whole depth of paradox. I will try to express them through antitheses to current opinions, which will highlight the reasons why they seem so important to me, and indeed, define their peculiar nature.

a. It is a fundamental mistake to treat the finite world, or pain, or evil, as an illusion. To the question of whether they are real or not real, the answer must be, as with all questions of this type, that everything is real so long as you do not take it for more than it is. On the view I am presenting, finiteness, pain, and evil are not accidental; they are essential features of Reality, belonging to an aspect of it which leaves its marks even on perfection itself. The view that they are illusions suggests that if we possessed complete knowledge and could feel everything, we would see and feel that there was no pain or evil at all. However, the view that contradiction is actual — and, more than that, is an exaggeration of a feature truly fundamental in reality — asserts something different. It says that if we knew everything and could feel everything, we would see and feel what finiteness, pain, and evil truly mean, and how they play a vital part in perfection itself.

The way of confronting these realities also differs fundamentally for these two theories. While it is not our business to preach, we can illustrate our view by its practical effect: It is absurd and insulting to tell a person in pain or mired in sin that such things do not exist. However, it is neither absurd nor insulting to try to help them feel that something great and precious can be made of each of these experiences. In a certain sense, the two views—that which disposes of them as illusion, and that which accepts them as immanent in perfection though not precisely as they seem—may appear to approximate. But our present task is to insist on their crucial difference, to urge that all depends on being in earnest with the idea of negativity. From such a point of view, the idea of illusion is rejected, though that of "appearance"—as something actual and yet contradictory—is accepted. I do not believe that Hegel can be held to treat evil as an illusion, even though he has used the word "illusion" in discussing the matter. As I understand it, the illusion he speaks of is not the belief that evil or finiteness is actual, but the belief that its actuality prevents the supreme end from being accomplished, whereas, in truth, it is essential to its accomplishment.

At all events, against the idea that finiteness, pain, and evil are illusions, the view here indicated would maintain that finite conscious beings actually suffer and do wrong because it is their nature to complete themselves. And the general form of this self-completion involves, as one fundamental factor, the relative loss of self. In the finite world, this is emphasized by various degrees of what we have called Logical Contradiction—that is to say, the inadequacy of the elements in which completion is sought. It would follow, and this seems to agree with the best ethical theory, that the ultimate logical structure, if I may so speak, of suffering and of evil is the same as that of satisfaction and of good. This is very noticeable, of course, in Green's theory of morality. It is undoubtedly not easy on this theory to distinguish otherwise than in degree between moral good and evil. And I believe this very difficulty is an indication that its main outline, its metaphysical fabric, is sound.

The difference, in principle, is one of the adequacy of the contents in which self-completion is sought, and the consequent degree of their tendency to give rise to discord and contradiction. But in all important satisfaction there is a thrill, which is analogous to pain, due to the tension of self-completion. And theory seems to demand that, as Plato suggested, a perfect experience should be, not indifferent or neutral as the careless reader might suppose, but such as to include and harmonize in itself the characteristics of pain and pleasure.

b. The same mode of thought would be hostile to any conception of the divine nature that should involve stability and perfection in such a sense as to exclude activity and the general form of self-sacrifice. It is not my intention to adhere to the view of those who conceive the divine being as finite, and as possibly one of a number. My intention is rather the reverse, namely, to maintain that finiteness eo ipso arises if negativity is not given its full significance in the conception of the supreme nature. Dr. E. Caird's criticism of Aristotle's Theoretic Life, when literally interpreted, clarifies this point very clearly. It is not an imperfection in the supreme being, but an essential component of his completeness, that his nature, which summarizes all Reality, should go out into its other to seek the completion which in this case alone is absolutely found. The "other" in question can only be finite experience. And it is in and because of this, and qualified by it, that the Divine nature maintains its infinity. And, therefore, it may be said that the general form of self-sacrifice—the fundamental logical structure of Reality—is to be found here also, as everywhere. Not, of course, that the infinite being can lose and regain its perfection, but that the burden of the finite is inherently a part, or rather an instrument, of the self-completion of the infinite. This view is familiar to many, but I only plead that it loses all its profound point if it is not taken with bitter earnestness.

I have used phrases that imply time—"activity," "going out of oneself," "seeking and finding"—perhaps remorselessly. The objection to predicating time of the supreme experience lies in the nature of self-completeness. And if, on the one hand, succession seems incompatible with this, on the other hand, the idea of instantaneousness or simultaneity—which is itself a temporal idea—must not be introduced here to complicate our thoughts. We must surely distinguish the conception of changing or progressing as a whole from the conception of uniting in a self-complete being characteristics which for us demand succession. If we were to be barred from ascribing content to the supreme being merely because for us all content is developed in time, the ultimate result must be that for us the supreme being will be nothing at all.

c. Finally, our point of view is hostile to the simplistic form in which questions of optimism and pessimism are usually raised as to the "surplus of pleasure over pain in the universe". Even Mr. Bradley has discussed this question with reference to the Absolute, but I cannot help thinking that it is improperly stated. What we, as factors of Reality, demand—what any factors of Reality as such must demand—is essentially, if I am right, not pleasure but satisfaction. And what is satisfaction? It is the profound attainment of ourselves. This, without doubt, implies some pleasure. But the crucial point, if I am not altogether wrong, is that in satisfaction, the pain or difficulty was a "moment"—that is, a phase which remains an element—and actively contributes to the positive attainment. Whereas, in comparing pleasure and pain as experienced facts of feeling, I presume that they retain their initial positions as strictly plus and minus quantities, respectively.

This is one point, and another follows directly from it. The quantitative comparison of pleasure and pain, even if we disregard the difficulties pointed out in anti-Hedonist polemics, betrays an inorganic point of view.

The question surely cannot be how many moments of pain you have experienced, and whether you have had enough moments of pleasure—allowing for intensities on each side—to outweigh them. Rather, the fundamental question is whether the experience has "done its work," and returned you to yourself as a complete, or at least a completer, being.

So, it would seem, the problem should be stated similarly about the universe. Not, if we could reckon up moments of equal pleasure and pain, which of the two classes would be found to outnumber the other. But rather, is there reason for thinking that pain and finiteness are elements playing a definite part in the whole such that its completeness depends upon containing them?

Broadly speaking, I suggest, experience indicates that a soul which has never known pain, like a nation which has never known war, has no depth of being, and is not a personality at all. Of course, this way of looking at the matter does not by itself dispose of the suggestion that the cost even of perfecting a soul may be too high. But the conviction that there essentially must be a certain cost corresponds to our best insight in the sphere of everyday experience. And so, in the end, if such a question as that of pleasure or pain in the Absolute holds any reality for us at all, it seems all-important from where we draw the suggestions from which we are to learn what to look for. We ought surely not to start from commonplace experiences. Instead, we should turn to those experiences in which self-expression is at its fullest—the rare moments to which Aristotle alludes in his discussion of the Theoretic life. It may be noteworthy that Aristotle consents while Plato refuses to ascribe the feeling of pleasure to the Divine nature.

And this may be connected with Aristotle's apparent omission of negativity from his conception of an ideally perfect experience. In his distinction, however, between the enjoyment of self-realization and the enjoyment of recreation, he offers a hint that we might do well to follow.

And for him as for us, apparently, the activities primarily devoted to sheer enjoyment and delight are, by the very structure of man's soul, wrested to severer forms of self-expression. So that the completest of all the creations in which as yet man has freely and spontaneously sought what at his best he most enjoys is, I presume, for us, as for Aristotle, that of poetical tragedy. This does seem to me to be a paradox worth noting. Can we seriously suppose that a nature which, when it reaches the summit of evolution so far as we have experienced it, is taking such a profound line as this, will find a perfection in any attainment which is not strongly marked with an analogous temper?

I am only using this idea to frame the question of optimism in a certain light. That is to say, to state it not as the question whether pain is, as it were, quantitatively submerged or neutralized by pleasure, but by looking for a completeness in which souls have found themselves, or realized their inherent structure.

This completeness, considered as a whole, cannot be quantitatively compared with the factors or elements, such as pain or pleasure, subordinated within it. If we had no negative factor but Contradiction as such, then I suppose completeness could only be in its abolition—that is, in an Absolute or perfection which bore in it no trace of the character present in finiteness and imperfection. But the distinction between Contradiction, as we defined it, and Negativity, seemed to be highly suggestive on this point.

It is, on the whole, an attractively simple view that the not-self means only discord and collision with the self, and that the self is experienced, and self-hood indeed exists, only by opposition to such a not-self. And that consequently, with the cessation of discordance—that is, of what we have called Logical Contradiction—the experiences of self-hood as such must cease and terminate, though Individuality proper would all the more survive and prosper. For such a view, the "responsive not-self" would have no existence. Consequently, all differentiations or sub-individualities within the Absolute would be imperfect and self-discordant in various degrees, and the Absolute itself could have no experience of self-hood. They would be mere appearances whose inner imperfection would reveal itself in their discrepancy as against an outer not-self. A conception of this kind, involving the admission that all minor individualities within the Absolute must be imperfect and self-discrepant, would certainly "cut many knots". It would release us from the difficult task of trying to understand the perfect experience as implying a society of perfect selves, and from explaining the relation of our imperfect selves to such supposed perfect differentiations of the Absolute.

But there is an obvious and all-important fact, which I already mentioned at the beginning of this chapter, that demands any such ideas should only be accepted with considerable modification. It is quite plain that our conception of the self has two sources in its relation to the not-self, and not just one.

And crucially, the sense of unity and reconciliation with the world beyond us is a far larger factor in our awareness of selfhood, and one which increases concomitantly with it, than is the mere sense of collision with the not-self. Now if we are going to argue that the sense of union with, or satisfaction in, the not-self—for example, the feeling of co-operation with a society—is not an element in furnishing us with our conception of selfhood, then we are driven to this result: that the awareness of selfhood disappears in proportion as the self expands in excellence and success. And in a certain sense, such a conclusion is tenable; and in this sense, it might give us a useful indication when we come to consider the attribution of an awareness of self to the Absolute.

But the fundamental point is here: In agreement with the whole doctrine of this chapter, we must take it that the sense of discord and the sense of concord are rooted in one and the same characteristic.

This characteristic is Negativity itself, which, though a possible attribute of things, in imperfect conjunctions takes the form of contradiction. If we are willing to dispense with the conception of a system of perfect selves as constituting the Absolute, then we may admit that in some degree, contradiction as well as harmony will attach to every finite self, because of its inherent imperfection. Therefore, we may concede that however complete the reconciliation with the not-self, however true it is that the self at its best has in its world of externality an immense affirmative expansion, yet the determination of the sense of selfhood by contradiction with the not-self is an element never altogether absent from the finite self-consciousness, and one that co-operates in giving sharpness to the recognition of self.

The finite self, then, would be essentially such as we know it—imperfect and inconsistent with itself. Though it would possess, in its nature, an element of unity and expansion, suggesting a completion which as a finite self we must conceive that it would never truly attain. As experienced in the absolute experience, where the essence of perfection is to transmute and to triumph over imperfection, it would no longer, the indication suggests, be called a "self" in the finite sense. As we have seen and shall see, its substance would lend itself to new arrangements, to the constitution of new worlds in continuity and readjustment with other selves, so that the experience would no longer be describable as constituting a system of selves.

Nevertheless, the positive affirmation of the expanding self in its not-self, which we have shown to be the truly essential element of self-consciousness—though perhaps not the limiting factor—provides an indication that cannot be disregarded. This holds true both for understanding the self in the Absolute, and for understanding the Absolute if we attempt to regard it as a self. We have argued throughout that it is in the highest of our own experiences that we must seek for the clues to the fullest reality. And the fact that we experience our self most completely precisely when we are least aware of its finite selfness is a clue that must not be forgotten. Defect and contradiction cannot constitute the really significant essence even of a finite being. It is positive awareness of an area or quality of self-maintenance that, after all, the self aspires to, even though failure and contradiction may force on it a recognition of its limits. And it is this—the real foundation of selfhood—that is in some way possessed by the self in the Absolute, and by the Absolute itself insofar as it is analogous to a self.

Thus, we have attempted to show that while contradiction and discrepancy are indeed inevitable in the constitution of the finite self, they are not the ultimate characters which the constitution of a self presupposes. And that this ultimate character, quite apart from specific speculations about the Absolute, reveals itself in increasing degrees through those experiences which exhibit the finite self as a self in the fullest sense. We have, however, admitted that much of what we habitually associate with the idea of a self in the "other" is connected with the features of apparent discord and opposition, which give the idea of freshness and independence that seems to reinforce any responsiveness we meet with in nature. And it is not in the absence of negation, but in the growth paripassu and even in the fusion of the negative and positive responses, that we find the true essence of self-consciousness as conditioned, if by a negative, yet not by a contradiction.

A strong light is thrown upon the difference between these two conceptions by a problem that is fundamental for our attitude to the finite self and finite life in general. It is allied to the problem of pessimism, but it is really more about the issue between the "lower" and the "higher" mysticism. Men have asked, from Greek times onwards at least, whether it is "better to be born or not to be born"? I do not mean this in the commonplace sense of asking whether life or the world of lives contains more pleasure or more pain, as, in my opinion, we roughly and rather unthinkingly distinguish them. On our attitude to this form of the question, I have said something already and shall have more to say later. But the point now before us is different and much more serious. It is not a survey of life by a standard taken within it, but an ultimate question as to the place and functions of finite life in the universe. This is the profound question insisted upon by mysticism in its popular and aggressive forms.

Every student of Plato must often have longed to know what Plato held to be the function and justification of terrestrial life on the whole and in the scheme of the universe. One might state the problem crudely by asking if he ever admitted that any soul was the better for undergoing or having undergone the life on earth. Did our knowledge, our morality, our love of beauty, partially and laboriously won in the conflict of sensations and desires, seem to him to be of any value, for ourselves or for the universe, which would not have equally been real—or more real—without them?

Did he consciously apply to the whole being of the finite the principle so obvious in his detailed theory, that hindrances and contradictions are opportunities and starting-points? While it would be beyond our present subject to attempt a full answer to these questions regarding Plato, they serve as an excellent introduction to the standpoint of mysticism.

Consider these evocative lines: "Earth, these solid stars, this weight of body and limb, / Are they not sign and symbol of thy division from Him?". These lines, as I understand them, show an interesting deviation towards natural mysticism in a poem which also contains a splendid expression of "immanence". And so, the mysticism of the East, at any rate in a popular stage which significantly influenced European thought largely through Schopenhauer, answers decisively: it would be better if no one were born. Self, self-consciousness, and self-will are held to be disturbances, diseases of the universe, and illusions in the fullest meaning of the word.

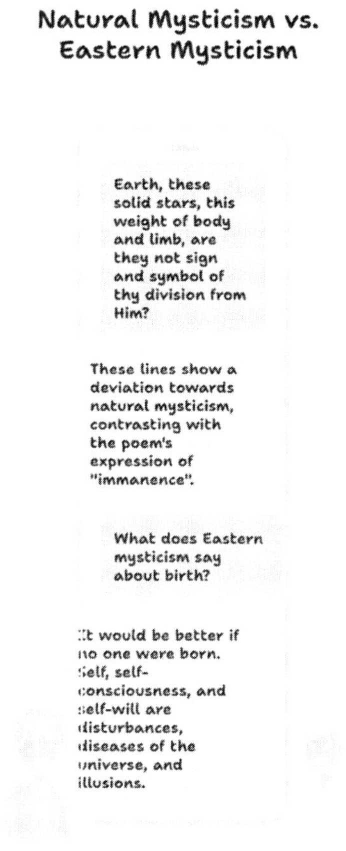

That is to say, they are not merely appearances whose contradictions point to a fuller reality, but phenomena which essentially involve the total contradiction and disappointment of the very ideas and desires that constitute them. And this disappointment and contradiction are not held to be in any way instrumental to a realization of the content of such ideas and desires in any form whatsoever. A link between such an attitude and the constructive conceptions of Western thought is indeed supplied by the reservation that though not instrumental to any fulfillment of itself, the finite world is connected with the one desirable fulfillment—its own suppression—by a law imposing certain conditions on the attainment of the goal. It cannot be suppressed by violence, for example, by suicide; the evil lies deep in the will to live, and only the suppression of this will by means which take a form akin to art, morality, and religion, can put a stop to the vicious circle of the wheel of life.

The same profound paradox is inherent in popular Christianity, and is acutely felt. And the popular solution is not unlike the solution of Schopenhauer's Buddhism. It presses itself on the earliest reflection, and we may state it in the words in which Plato refers to it: "We mortals are here on duty, and must not withdraw till we have our orders".

Heaven, we understand, though much better than what we have, would be forfeited by the attempt to grasp at it prematurely. And if our inquiry presses behind the details of the "scheme of salvation" and we ask, "But was the Fall itself a part of the scheme of salvation, and is a world with sin and atonement a better world than one without them?" it seems as if different views may be taken as to what a typical Christianity should answer. For Christianity, no doubt, sin is the greatest of evils—the evil; and the victory over it the object of the world.

But it would seem that for a Christianity which has the courage of its opinions, the idea of the victory involves the idea of the Fall. And the answer would be that the scheme of salvation, involving finiteness and sin, was essential to the nature of God and the perfection of the universe. Speaking at the level of reflective orthodoxy, it would appear hardly possible to admit that anything so deep-rooted as the connection of the doctrine of the Trinity with the Incarnation and the Atonement should be considered as an excrescence on the plan of the universe or an arrangement contrived in time to remedy an incidental aberration. Thus we are brought in sight of the philosophical conception, which has frequently been applied to the interpretation of Christian dogma, that finiteness is essential to true infinity, and that the two are continuous and interwoven, not exclusive and antagonistic alternatives.

It is from this profound point of view that we have to adjust our conceptions of the defectiveness of the self and of self-consciousness. We are, broadly speaking, to enter into the idea that finite experience, though itself defective, is neither an accidental disturbance of the "Quiet" nor a regrettable deviation from the Perfect. The absolute or infinite should present itself to us as more of the finite, or the finite at its best, and not as its extinction. "More," not in time nor in quantity, but in completeness, in progress along the path of continuity which is indicated by the nature of things.

It is at bottom a logical blunder to hold as obvious truth that merely to annul the finite is to affirm the infinite—that is, that merely not to be in the finite world is logically and per se a presumable gain. In logical phrase, the bare negation has no significance. To be nearer perfection than on Earth must mean, if it is to mean anything, not merely to be rid of terrestrial life, but to have realized it and more.

The treatment I have offered regarding the relation of self and not-self in self-consciousness is in profound harmony with these ideas. As in the antithesis of morality and religion, so in the antithesis of self-consciousness and what is more than self, it is our conviction that a positive continuity can be exhibited. And that the defects of the given not merely necessitate transcendence but positively indicate its nature.

After all, it is not the bare negation by a not-self, but reconciliation with it and expansion through its response, on which self-consciousness in its fullness depends. Satisfaction and sacrifice, which for us are opposite examples of the same fundamental structure, must both contribute of their nature to the complete experience. And such a complete experience would possess and absorb into its being all that finite selfhood exists to achieve: self-maintenance in self-transcendence.

Lecture-7

The Self and the Absolute

This lecture confronts one of philosophy's deepest questions: what the self truly is, and why it must point beyond itself to the Absolute. By tracing how finite individuality grows through self-transcendence, unity, and non-contradiction, it reveals how our highest experiences—ethical, aesthetic, and religious—offer living clues to a reality more complete than the isolated self.

Investigates how the finite self relates to and participates in the Absolute

Ladies and gentlemen, in this lecture, we embark on a profound journey to explore the fundamental nature of individuality and its relationship to the Absolute. Our primary aim is to articulate clearly what compels us to affirm the existence of an absolute being beyond ourselves. This endeavor is not merely about explaining the logical outcome of an argument; it's about grasping the deeper implications of such a reality, specifically how it reshapes our understanding of experience and guides us towards appreciating the whole. We find that current perspectives often fall short in this appreciation, even within advanced metaphysical thought.

Addressing Criticisms of a Transcendent Reality

The notion of a rational reality that transcends what is immediately given to us has faced significant challenges. These criticisms broadly fall into two categories: those questioning the very rationality of the real, and those targeting its transcendence of the given. The former, perhaps best encapsulated by Bergson's phrase, "everything is given," will be addressed later. Our immediate focus, however, is on the latter criticism, a line of thought first articulated by Aristotle in his critique of Plato's "Form of the Good" and still widely debated today.

Aristotle, in his impatient observations regarding Plato's doctrine of Form, questioned the meaning of "the thing itself," or "man himself," if its definition is identical to that of man as experienced.

He seems to ask, "What on earth can they mean by 'the thing itself' if, as is the case, the definition of man itself is the same with that of man?". Indeed, one might wonder:

If we can fully define "things as given to us" or "man as we experience him" in a self-consistent manner, without needing anything beyond that definition, what more could possibly be required?. If that were truly the case, we could simply define man and nature based on our experience, without internal incoherence or external reference, and conclude our "troublesome speculation".

However, this is precisely where the difficulty arises. When we attempt to describe man as he appears to be, we invariably discover that his "self" - that which gives character to the appearance and is essential for understanding it – lies outside the immediate portrayal.

Should we then try to define this "self of man," or indeed the "self of anything," coherently and intelligently, we find ourselves venturing far beyond what we actually possess in our immediate experience. The moment we engage in a reflective study of humanity, we are led to the realization that an individual's individuality and self-identity exist beyond their temporal presentation. As Green profoundly stated, man's nature is "in process of being communicated to him".

The True "Self" and the Platonic Ideal

If this understanding holds true, then there is a compelling reason to contrast "things themselves" or "man itself" with things and man as they are prima facie given in our experience. The "self of man" or of things is not a mere duplication of their given being. Rather, it represents that "way of being in which, in Platonic language, they can really be" - meaning, they can sustain themselves, and experience or be experienced without internal contradiction.

If this true way of being proves to be markedly different from our initial interpretations of experience, it merely reflects the universal journey of growth and education. Even if the character of things in our immediate world seems to be absorbed or vanish in their fuller realization, this transformation has strong everyday analogies, such as how our commonplace perceptions and sentiments relate to a more concrete apprehension of life's richness. Ultimately, an absolute reality must be all-inclusive, encompassing even apparent limitations.

However, to any mode of reasoning that accepts our immediate, imagined "given" as final - be it immediate experience or a divided personality - a powerful counter-argument, often overlooked, is this: "There is nothing in the world worth having, doing, or being which does not involve a self-transcendence, and an enormous self-transcendence, of the type which you deny". Consider the transformation demanded by a masterpiece of art: one scarcely recognizes oneself when under the spell of Shakespeare or Beethoven.

The challenge lies in dealing with truths that, while seemingly accepted by everyone, are genuinely believed by very few. And perhaps the most effective shield against believing these truths is the observation that they are not new. Yet, if we were to truly believe them "in bitter earnest," their novelty would become apparent.

Challenging Dualism and the "Reproach of Agnosticism"

It is often due to commonplace prejudices that interpreters have conventionally attributed a "two-world" view to Plato.

However, I contend that for Plato, the truly fundamental point was that there is, and can only be, a single world. What we commonly presume to be a world is not a world at all, precisely because it lacks the features of self-coherence and stability that characterize the "self of anything". If we insist on calling Plato a dualist, it is perhaps more accurate to adhere to his own figures of a "triplicism or quadruplism" (like the divided line), which demonstrate that "none of the lower phases are solid against the whole, so as to form par excellence a dualism".

This prejudice, evident in the popular interpretation of Plato and the general understanding of idealism, is strikingly similar to the "reproach of Agnosticism" leveled today against the metaphysical effort to establish the nature of a truly real world. This perspective seems to declare: "We have the given, and why go further?". It argues that one cannot reach anything concrete or actual, acknowledging that the "Absolute" cannot be fully possessed as an experience.

Therefore, why "dissolve what you have by hostile criticism when it leads to nothing beyond?". Similarly, devotees of "Personality" often feel that metaphysical analysis abandons or dissolves the "solid facts of individual life and will and the self," without providing a tangible replacement, viewing it as a "gratuitous abandonment of the substance for the shadow".

While these objections appear rooted in common sense, they actually stem from an attitude most opposed to true common sense: that of common sense theory. Two crucial points must be considered here. Firstly, there is a substantive unity throughout the history of philosophy in the viewpoint that compels us beyond the given. When we reject this approach, we are not merely countering a specific modern writer but confronting the entire edifice of idealistic philosophy, from Plato to contemporary thinkers, whose core position is "perfectly simple and direct". Secondly, there is a deficient disposition to seek corroboration and explanation within the very nature of our "best experience itself," and its progressive divergence from what is initially given. Even modern metaphysics seems infected by this diffidence, leading to an over-reliance on prejudices based on prima facie appearances.

The Argument a Contingentia Mundi: The Spirit of Metaphysics

The essential argument of metaphysics can be generally described as an argument *a contingentia mundi.* This refers to an inference from the imperfection of data and premises. The failure to recognize the true nature of this argument, and its consistent presence across all idealist philosophies, fundamentally depends on an inadequate conception of logical determination. If we begin with the principle that a conclusion cannot transcend its premises, either in certainty or content, then we can never accept the central position of metaphysics. Common analogies, such as water not rising higher than its source or not getting more out of a box than you put in, are entirely contrary to the nature of rational procedure as understood by metaphysical analysis.

While it's debatable whether Aristotle considered some reasoning to be analytic, his definition of the syllogism clearly describes the synthetic character by which thought builds its world: "Discourse in which certain things being posited, something else than what is posited necessarily follows on their being true". Furthermore, as induction clarifies, the premises gain "more significant, but more certain" status in the conclusion. The objection often raised is that this is only true if the conclusion affirms an independently verified fact, for which a specific premise is uniquely demanded. However, this view, I believe, profoundly underestimates the continuity and essence of the logical process.

What truly occurs in any inference is that the data and premises are brought together into a new whole. Through this new combination, their individual limitations as isolated factors are progressively removed, and a new character is made explicit

– a character that belongs to them only in their new combination. It is impossible for such a new character *not* to bring with it a step towards non-contradiction and new connections with the general whole of experience. A new meaning in a proposition, a new application of a purpose, or a new emotional disposition inevitably affects its truth, completeness, or stability.

This, then, is the nerve of logical determination: a positive work where data or premises neutralize each other's defects, giving rise to a new totality that transcends its factors. This is the fundamental process of experience in all its forms. When analyzed in propositional form, it reveals itself as logic – the "creative and originative nexus of mind as such". This principle, when abstractly stated, is called the principle of non-contradiction, but it is, in reality, a formulation of the "life of the whole" and is not subject to the formal limitations its abstract appearance might suggest.

The Positive and Constructive Principle of Non-Contradiction

Firstly, one cannot escape the application of this principle through a "logical quietism". You cannot claim safety from self-transcendence by affirming little or nothing, because all negation and exclusion fundamentally rest upon affirmation. Consistency, as demanded by the principle, cannot be achieved as long as anything remains outside your system.

The very negation that places something outside implicitly carries an affirmation that must ultimately bring it inside. Concepts like a vacuum, nothingness, or an "I" or "is" reduced to a mere point, are not self-consistent by virtue of emptiness; instead, they are "nests of contradictions".

Each is entangled in a web of relations, yet lacking explicit content, they possess no power to unify or organize them. This is an old argument, but it bears repeating, especially given the misconception that the principle of non-contradiction can be satisfied by mere emptiness and lacks "driving-power towards the concrete".

Secondly, and more specifically, the operation of the principle cannot be confined to maintaining propositions whose denial implies their assertion (e.g., "There is no truth"). Such restriction is only possible if we fail to recognize this characteristic, in its true meaning, across all the great provinces of experience, and more distinctly as those provinces become greater. We tend to believe that within the spheres of our ordinary experience, we can deny this or that without disrupting the general framework of our world. This misleads us into supposing that here we are dealing with a lower order of certainty than that of formal principles. However, this apparent freedom to deny exists only because, in every such negation, "so very much more is asserted than is touched by the negation's immediate content," allowing the negation to assert affirmative truth without being false. When we make negative observations in historical fact, beauty, or morality, our negation is always founded upon the affirmation, as a whole, of the world within which we are making a denial.

Thus, in every negation, an affirmative content is asserted, not solely in formal propositions. The difference lies in this: a true negation asserts immensely more than it denies, while a necessarily false negation (of an a priori proposition) affirms only what it denies. In the former, we highlight a contrast within the content of a vast general affirmation; in the latter, we address our negation to the entire affirmation of our world. If we were to apply the latter procedure to the former (e.g., saying "there is no morality" instead of "that is not well done"), we would be convicted of self-contradiction just as if we had said, "There is no truth". As we grasp the meaning of our negation, the world of morality and beauty would reassert themselves as both the condition and contradiction of our denials. The fuller experience, despite allowing for negation to define its system, is more truly supported by the principle of non-contradiction than simple, abstract propositions. It is because we cannot conceive denying the complete world of our experiences that we are compelled to affirm the simplest a priori truths in their negation. They are affirmed because they represent the world at its minimum. But non-contradiction gains stronger purchase "the more there is to lose by contradiction".

The Absolute and the Transformation of Life

This positive and constructive principle of non-contradiction – in other words, the spirit of the whole – is the operative principle not only of metaphysical thought but of life itself. It is, in essence, the argument *a contingentia mundi*, or the inference from the imperfection of data and premises. Overlooking differences of degree, this principle alone enables progressive and continuous experience, whether through inference, significant feeling, or expansion through action. It is what connects our perception of the Earth's surface with our conception of the Antipodes, or transforms parental instinct into wise tenderness and social beneficence. And it is the further pursuit of this principle that compels us to the conception of the Absolute. No point exists where an arrest in this process can be justified.

This, then, is the fundamental nature of the inference to the Absolute: the passage from the contradictory and unstable in all experience to the stable and satisfactory.

This transition, meticulously worked out in Plato for every aspect of life, has since formed the framework of serious philosophy. It is misunderstood if we expect it to grant us possession of an ultimate experience incompatible with our limited being.

What it truly offers is far more relevant to the transformation of our lives. It reveals to us the relative stability and reciprocal completeness of different provinces of experience, encompassing life's various values. It interprets the correlation between their worth, their reality, and their satisfactoriness to the soul.

We distort the entire inquiry and lose its truth if our arguments are covertly driven by some special form of human destiny, as if, when referring to the Absolute, we are merely thinking of Heaven. We should not expect metaphysics to predict terrestrial history, much less what lies beyond the grave. What metaphysics *can* and *always has* done in the hands of masters is, starting from *any datum*, to identify what in actual life (which is in the Absolute now) is higher and more stable, and what is more defective and self-contradictory. It indicates the general law by which the defective is absorbed into the higher. In this sense, it truly "gives us hope," and undeniably provides "knowledge and guidance". As Bradley stated, "Higher, truer, more beautiful, better, and more real, these, on the whole, count in the Universe as they count for us". And existence, on the whole, must correspond with our ideas, because "higher means for us a greater amount of that Reality, outside of which all appearance is absolutely nothing".

The Nature of Individuality and Degrees of Reality

From a logical standpoint, the criterion of self-maintenance, degree of being, or non-contradiction applies not only to fundamental abstract principles but, as Plato demonstrated, to the various worlds and levels of concrete experience. This holds true for significant sensation (as in beauty), emotion, pleasure, and pain, just as it does for strictly logical structures like science and philosophy, or for the ideas that operate in morality, social behaviour , or religion.

All these types of experience represent phases of individual living - stages where the "individual" maintains himself in different modes and degrees, achieving varying levels of completeness and consistency. Therefore, when discussing individuality, it is crucial to consider these main characteristics and avoid settling for conceptions of ourselves derived from our initial reflections on the apparently separate human being. If we base our idea of the individual on his minimum conscious being (e.g., in fear or ineffective desire), we will form a drastically different understanding of his nature compared to one based on social, aesthetic, or religious consciousness at their highest development.

Furthermore, by identifying degrees of reality with degrees of being or self-maintenance, it is logical to consider the "fuller self" as the "truer self". From this seemingly elementary platitude, profound implications arise that are habitually neglected. The individual does not reach the maximum of individuality by being exclusively self-repellent against others. If "personality" is strictly defined as being a subject of rights and duties among similar subjects, then personality itself is only possible because of an individuality that already transcends it. A system of rights and duties requires an "identity of wills" where these become a mere "machinery of daily life". Coercing and organizing an individual within a system of "persons" can only occur on the basis of a consciousness that, at its core, desires to be coerced and organized.

Thus, individuality, as the principle of reality and the consistent whole, leads us beyond strict personality. It moves beyond the self-consciousness mediated by an opposing "not-self" into a realm where we simultaneously go out of the self and into it, exemplified by the quasi-religion of social unity, knowledge, art, and religion proper. In these experiences, as the "repellent self-consciousness" diminishes and the sense of unity with the world and with humanity becomes pre-eminent, individuality is strengthened. The self, though less in opposition to a not-self, becomes "more itself" and "more at home". When freedom and spontaneity reach their climax in religion, the self no longer insists on its exclusive claim, and the entire being is devoted to service, which is perfect freedom. While these observations are familiar, their implications for the theory of personality or individuality are not readily grasped. It is clear that the height of individuality is found in experiences that intensely heighten the sense and fact of identity with humanity, nature, and God. If we seek a definition of the finite individual "per se," a fixed entity of "this much and no more," we will not find it. At his best, an individual exhibits features different from those emphasized in his normal state, and his truest self might even transcend what we currently know.

To reiterate two key points: Firstly, the minimum of individuality has no more claim to be the normal standard than the minimum meaning of a word. In matters like the communicability of feeling, the identity of human souls, or the continuity of maximum self-experience, there is no justification for basing our theories on our commonplace feelings of impotence, isolation, or self-will.

The formal separateness of "individual" centers of experience is progressively overshadowed by their material identity of content and emotions. If our theories were based on human beings singing together, fighting for a common cause, sacrificing for loved ones, or thinking with full intelligence, our attitude would transform into a logical and metaphysical difference of immense significance.

This shift would emphasize the identity of content and system where different selves are one, and where the often-unrealized continuity of the single self with itself ultimately lies. This is contrasted with the differences arising from organic sensations and limits of immediate experience, which often define "a mind" as separate from others and, for the same reason, from itself. A modern view suggests that the self, as our unity and life's good, lies not in self-consciousness against a not-self but in a content or quality of being fully realized when that antagonistic consciousness is minimal. This perspective offers a radically different understanding of self-consciousness in the Absolute from one dependent on an adverse not-self.

Secondly, comparing higher and less complete regions of experience helps us, in principle, to understand the relationship between less and more inclusive conditions of mind as a world. This addresses a fundamental difficulty in conceiving an absolute experience. Such an experience, we argue, includes and absorbs our individual experiences positively and in a fuller form, yet without reproducing them in their separate distinctness. The challenge of conceiving this fusion, absorption, and transcendence of our alternating, seemingly heterogeneous moods is a major obstacle to grasping the continuity between our defective self and a transcending perfection. No one deems it a fatal difficulty that metaphysics cannot put us in possession of perfect experience. But skepticism arises regarding the conceivability of how partial moods, which are truly part of the absolute, can subsist separately under finite conditions.

Understanding the Fusion of Moods and Interconnectedness of Experience

This difficulty can, in principle, be overcome by focusing on the distinction between forms of mental life where self-transcendence is at its minimum and where it approaches its maximum. While there's an apparent difficulty in distinguishing true self-transcendence from the alienation of self (unconsciousness of limitation), the true standard should be the amount of genuine self-identification with the content of reality.

In normal circumstances, our less complete attitudes are absorbed and united in those which are more complete. They tend to reappear in their fragmentary character only when our impotence is revealed by mental or bodily diminution. In short, as life becomes more finite, our attitudes tend to become alternative and successive rather than fused and solid. This is a necessary consequence of our degrees of impotence in a world that, though unified in principle, presents diverse aspects and opportunities. The real challenge is to understand *how* these aspects and attitudes can be fused or absorbed, not merely blended or conjoined.

Crucially, we must remember that our phases and attitudes are never wholly severed. Man is never in any phase purely feeling, purely practical, purely moral, aesthetic, intellectual, or religious. There is one kind of unity before the evolution of differences, and another, we contend, as they are absorbed and unified in perfection. Even in our intermediate reality, where differences are pronounced, there is always a unity of feeling where the self possessesa certain solidarity with itself, with others, and with nature. This provides a constant basis of repose, a faith and purpose that connects us with something beyond. For instance, morality cannot exist apart from religion - the reliance on individual will and duty is inseparable from the social and cosmic basis of life, implying reliance on a "strength and wisdom beyond man's own".

Bearing this in mind, let us consider the relationship between morality, theoretical cognition, the aesthetic attitude, and what we commonly call religion, especially in their more intense and inclusive forms. Religion, like other experiences, has many modes and levels, precluding a single answer regarding its relation to science and philosophy. In primitive forms, it shows little analogy to scientific consciousness. In developed forms, it can appear hostile. Similarly, its relation to art and morality can seem hostile or indifferent. Yet, actual life never allows its activities to become wholly detached. The logical connection inherent in consciousness continuously manifests in their interdependence. Even savage myths are an early effort to interpret reality, akin to scientific hypotheses.

It becomes a matter of convenience and degree how we estimate the relation between, say, philosophy and religion par excellence.

But we can undoubtedly find experiences where the two converge, or rather, have not been separated, and are united with much more besides. If we use "religion" to denote the frame of thought and devotion exemplified by Dante's ideal, we can illustrate the unity of a highest experience and the necessity of its dissociation according to degrees of finiteness and impotence.

In Dante's religion, for example:

- As religion par excellence, the finite individual feels his will and emotions absorbed and transformed in the perfect will, which also becomes his own.

- Inseparable yet distinct from this unity is a side of morality. The supreme will is realized through conflict; pain, evil, effort, and aspiration are potentially present in the finiteness through which the individual contributes to divine perfection. These elements provide a "depth or tension or seriousness" to the religious experience, analogous to desire persisting in satisfaction. If experienced in isolation, due to the obscuring of other aspects, this could manifest as the effort or despair characteristic of a moral attitude taken by itself.
- Furthermore, it is integral to this religion that the sensible universe is apprehended as a revelation of the Divine order, encompassing the fullest realization of the aesthetic attitude.
- What, taken separately, would be the theoretical or speculative intelligence, finds its "completest satisfaction" as "all things are seen in God," and its need for non-contradiction throughout experience is thoroughly fulfilled.

Countering Logical Pessimism and Affirming Inherent Unity

Of course, it might be argued that this highest religious experience is not one most of us can actually possess. Merely describing its constituent factors in the language of our separate behaviour s might seem to abandon the conception of its unity. The criticism suggests that if its unity were complete, the separation of experiences would disappear; and if they remain traceable as separate, their characteristic imperfection and self-contradiction are not resolved.

I do not believe this is a relevant criticism. It belongs to a type of thought I call logical pessimism – a fundamentally contentious method that juxtaposes extreme cases without the necessary analysis to reveal their continuity. This approach treats pain, pleasure, evil, and personality as "hard units, repellent and unyielding" against the claims of perfection and totality. However, our argument relies on analysis supported by the truth of living experiences. No person is confined to a single mood or behaviour ; everyone experiences moments where greater characters, intelligences, or emergencies enable them to transcend their habitual selves, apprehending how an "exaltation of his whole being" affects the currently distinguished elements of his finite consciousness. In these experiences, we grasp through life and feeling the truth that philosophical analysis insists upon – for example, that abstract morality cannot exist *per se*, and that its sharp antagonism between "ought" and "is" implies a deeper basis where "what ought to be is one with what is".

Our point now should be clearer. We assume finiteness, characterized by various kinds and degrees of impotence, to be the condition of existence for a being capable, in principle, of the religious experience we described. It is not difficult to see how the logical elements of such a "beatific vision" might persist or stand out in relative isolation, depending on the nature of the impotence and the challenges faced.

We observe daily that the finite mind, whose life unfolds in succession and choice, cannot simultaneously grasp even the highest mode of consciousness of which it is capable. But this does not negate the fundamental truth that what it *does* grasp, what "shows, as it were, through the mist," is of "one logical texture and of one emotional tissue" with that which temporary emphasis or distinction has, for a moment or a lifetime, withdrawn from its distinct apprehension.

The facts are obvious, though their importance is often unrecognized. When engaged in one activity, we cannot be engaged in another; our current actions or sufferings dictate our mood and mental attitude. In moral difficulty, we are preoccupied with wrongdoing and responsibility. In detached research, we temporarily treat the external world as self-existent. In religious exaltation, our minds enter a state of repose and absorption, involving a faith that excludes the temper of research and the attribution of full reality to the sense-perceived world. This attitude of trust and resignation, while perhaps doing less than justice to moral endeavor, represents a logical implication without which such endeavor would be uprooted. All these limitations are defects within the moods themselves, yet they are to some degree inevitable for their existence in finite subjects whose lives proceed by succession and alternation.

This matter becomes much clearer when we recall our preliminary insistence: we never truly realize in actual living the dissociation that we postulate for theoretical analysis and everyday nomenclature. We are never purely intellectual without volition, nor moral apart from being religious, nor aesthetic without practical or theoretical interest. Each of these attitudes is, in and of itself, an instance and example of all the others, even if their central characteristics differ. This familiar fact profoundly signifies the inherent unity of all experiences, which our impotence merely disguises. The challenge is to value this unity without failing to recognize plain distinctions. Thus, while our finiteness obscures and loosens the connection between things, it does not destroy it. If we pay attention, we can see how our moods, seemingly alternating at random, are in truth the limbs and features of fuller forms of mind, left outstanding in apparent separation by the mist that limits our particular world.

Redefining the Individual: Beyond Fixed Essences

A reader might then ask: "Will you plainly tell us what you take the individual finite being to be?". Conventionally, we imagine the individual as a "single and permanent spiritual unit," with a distinct nature and power of initiative (will, activity, spontaneity), perhaps outliving the body. This "soul," like "a whole living man" directing a "machine," is conceived as "itself and nothing else," distinct and exclusive against other souls, possessing its own weal and woe which determine the world's perfection. The question arises: "Is it not then a man's principal interest and value that he is permanently he and no one else, a self-complete being not essentially incapable of perfection while remaining what he is?". And if this clear conception is incorrect, what do we replace it with? "You seem to volatilise the individual into a sort of logical progression of ideas and emotions, always passing out of itself into, as it were, another theory, as a thought can blend with and be absorbed in another thought within the limits of a single mind. Is this what you mean?".

Our answer is two-fold. First, negatively, we must avoid or transcend three analogies inherent in this challenge when conceiving the individual. Secondly, affirmatively, we want to think of the individual primarily as mind, and we must learn to interpret "mind" positively, "in its own right, by what it is and does". The temptation to use comparisons from external objects or isolated mental phenomena is strong, but while helpful for suggestion or contrast, we truly need to accept mind's significance "on its own terms and as *sui generis*". It is not a "thing," nor a mere power of a thing (like the body or brain), nor even a "life," however attractive that analogy. Instead, it is a "whole" of a special kind, with its own structure and concreteness, appreciated only by experiencing "more" of it and understanding the differences between "more" and "less".

1. Three Analogies to Avoid in Conceiving the Individual The Analogy of a "Thing": While we know that an external thing is not self-subsistent and would be nothing apart from its context and reactions, the implication of this analogy on our idea of the soul is problematic. It suggests an identity that supports diversity but does not enter into or constitute it. The concept of metempsychosis, where the soul is a transferable thing compatible with any body and experience, exemplifies this extreme assumption of numerical identity. Such a notion renders ideas like the identity of souls inhabiting different bodies, or the diversity of souls within one body, meaningless.

This is akin to speaking of a chair becoming a table as fancy dictates. We find it difficult to attribute concrete value to an ideal or experience. However, Kant's critique of rational psychology and Hegel's emphasis on "subject" over "substance" made a different conception necessary. What we require is an "active form of totality within a certain mass of content," a "life of self-transformation towards the riddance of contradictions". The analogy of a thing merely suggests unaccountable, persistent identity heightened to exclusiveness, which misleads us.

2. The Analogy of a "Legal Person": The term "person" or "personality" carries many meanings and is used to assert high claims for individual nature. It is argued that an individual must be self-aware to be an object to himself and a source of aspiration. While this principle is sound for our moral activity and social obligations, involving exclusive and often repellent personalities, the "person" as a subject of rights and duties is essentially the individual in society as defined by law. As stated earlier, this legal personality already presupposes a stage of individuality that transcends it. Legal personality represents the "social machinery," the "mechanism of definite co-operation". However, the social spirit that sustains it must be beyond the system it sustains. A system of obligations cannot secure recognition unless the minds accepting them are united in a common purpose. Moreover, the social spirit itself is not the final form of individuality even in our experience. So, while an individual must at least be a person (as at a minimum, he must have the self-identity of a thing), if personality implies rigid systematic limitation against other persons and only partial union with the whole, then individuality must be capable of a form where the negative plays a more affirmative part.

3. The Analogy of "Reflective Self-Consciousness": We should not interpret individuality as limited to a self-consciousness

reflected from the contrast with a "not-self". Our main point in conceiving individuality is to maintain its freedom – its power or essential nature of self-transformation in obedience to the logic of the wholeoperating within it. We do not want to be burdened by the negative approach that suggests we cease to be individual when we fully enter into content that unites us with the whole and ourselves, simply because we are beyond the reflective consciousness of self against not-self. Individuality is positive and constructive. While diversity or affirmative negation will play a part in the system into which individuality develops, this is distinct from a contradictory negative in the form of a "not-self" resisting the expansion and affirmation of the self's system.

Mind as a World: The Affirmative Conception of the Individual

Secondly, while we may use these analogies, we must not be bound by them. Affirmatively, we can say that the individual, as we know him, is mind. His individuality centers on the sense in which he is a mind, which operates in two senses: by negation (exclusion of others) and by affirmation (unity in itself). Critically, the principle of mind's internal unity is not in harmony with its exclusiveness of others, particularly in the sense that it *does* exclude them.

This exclusiveness, when judged by the principle of self-identity, is a defect. Individuality or distinctness based purely on this is external and self-contradictory, connected to positive unity only by the corollary that unity and power go together, and where power ceases, unity finds its limit. If a person has greater power of comprehension and inclusion, such that less is outside him, and what *is* outside is less outside, his own unity and individuality are not less, but greater.

Therefore, a mind is a mind not through a principle hostile to its nature, but through a realization of that nature, to the imperfection of which realization the imperfection of its unity is correlative.

The conditions of psychical oneness, such as qualitative continuity of feeling and logical connection of ideas and purposes, simply execute on a smaller scale what is necessary to constitute a unity of mind.

There is no reason to limit this unity to any special complex of feeling and experience; indeed, it is not so limited. The best general description of the nature of mind is to call it a world. The world constituting a mind is not limited by any rigid rule.

While it's been suggested that the principle of individual distinctness is "one mind, one social function," this is an "unreal simplification" unless understood as a serviceable ideal where the content of a single mind constitutes a single conation. Consciousnesses vary in comprehensiveness.

While they are primarily centered in a range of externality focused by a single body, this immediate centeredness is not an ultimate limit. There are many conditions under which a single mind might control multiple bodies.

In sum, we are to think of the individual as a world of experience, whose center is given by the body and the range of externality it provides, but whose limits depend on his power. He is a world that realizes, in a limited manner, the logic and spirit of the whole. In principle, no increase of comprehension, no transformation of the self, is inconceivable as happening to him. Whether he continues to be a self in our limited sense is a matter of degree.

The precise "why" and "how" of these separate microcosms we call finite selves remain unanswerable questions. However, we can perceive that by their very existence, a certain "completeness through incompleteness" is achieved.

Every degree and distinct center of individuality or comprehension necessarily forms a different vision and interpretation of things, and through these various incompletenesses, a "totality of differences" emerges that, as far as we can grasp, could not be attained otherwise.

It has been suggested that the unity of the individual lies in a purpose or conation. For a finite being, whose life is in time and whose world is contradictory, purpose cannot be absent. However, this perspective often aligns with the "negative approach," as a purpose or conation can be merely the operation of a dissatisfaction seeking its removal. This is a "very negative and uncharacteristic conception".

The value of a conation depends on the nature of the contents that create the dissatisfaction and are reconciled in satisfaction. It can range from a mere escape from discomfort to a positive development harmonious with the self. If we define the individual by his conation, it should be relative to a specific type of fruition, understanding that the content underlying the individuality, as well as its demanded completion, characterize and determine that individuality.

Therefore, what we call "the individual" is not a fixed essence, but a living world of content, representing a certain range of externality.

Within this world, there is an active striving for unity and true individuality or completeness, driven by the "active spirit of non-contradiction, the form of the whole". It is neither a mere series of mental occurrences nor a power of the brain. On the contrary, it is a higher concrete than the body, which serves as its instrument for communication with spatial objects, yet is but a small part of the perceived and conceived spatial theatre.

The structure and unity of a single mind under normal conditions are clear and definite: they are a continuous interest and identity of content and quality, analyzed by psychology. Normally, there is no doubt where one self ends and another begins, nor any suggestion that selfhood is trivial or unreal.

Nevertheless, we gain a freer understanding when we conceive it on the analogy of a concrete thought, held together and apart by what it is in itself, and by nothing else in the universe. This requires banishing the idea of a fixed thing, characterized and limited by another nature apart from the experiences that grow within it. The distinctness and identity of selves, therefore, are matters of fact, depending on actual qualities and contents, offering a far higher interest and value to selfhood than if it were a mysterious, inexplicably imposed isolation without degrees. Indeed, the imperfection of psychical solidarity corresponds significantly to physical non-organization, suggesting a "struggle towards unity" in which the brain plays an indispensable part.

Lecture-8
Individuality as the Logical Criterion of Value

This lecture challenges the widespread belief that judgments of value lie beyond logic. By uncovering individuality as the true measure of worth, it shows how value, satisfaction, and reality rise together through coherence and completeness. Here we learn why what is most real is also most valuable—and how our deepest evaluations answer to the logic of the whole.

Establishes individuality as the standard through which value is recognized and affirmed

Good day, everyone. Today, we delve into a profound philosophical discussion concerning the very nature of value and whether our judgments about what is good or valuable can ever truly be supported by logic. This is a topic that has captivated thinkers for centuries, and our sources offer a unique perspective on this enduring debate, particularly challenging some contemporary views.

The Challenge to Logical Support for Value Judgments

Let us begin by addressing a prominent doctrine in intellectual circles today. Many speculative thinkers of high rank contend that the judgment of value cannot be logically supported. What does this mean in practical terms? It suggests that a value judgment cannot, through a logical process, be proven to be either right or wrong. Consequently, in real-world application, it is deemed impossible for such a judgment to be altered or influenced by criticism or argument, unless based on some fundamental misunderstanding.

Consider the words of Pringle Pattison, who states that "Every idealistic theory of the world has for its ultimate premiss a logically unsupported judgment of value—a judgment which affirms an end of intrinsic worth, and accepts thereby a standard of unconditional obligation".

McTaggart echoes this sentiment, asserting that when a judgment of value is deemed "ultimately true," it is "useless to seek for a proof or to demand one. It must be either accepted or left alone".

Even John Stuart Mill, a figure many of you are familiar with, aligns with this view, noting that "Questions of ultimate ends are not amenable to direct proof. Whatever is proved to be good must be so by being shown to be a means to something admitted to be good without proof".

This doctrine, when understood in its most straightforward and natural sense, presents a stark contradiction to the core tenets of Plato's philosophy, as well as Aristotle's comprehensive approach to the ultimate end for humanity.

It is indeed surprising, as our text points out, that such leading conceptions from these foundational thinkers are seemingly dismissed without explicit notice or a robust argument to justify their being set aside.

However, it is crucial to recognize that this contention itself can be interpreted in several subordinate ways, some of which may not entirely deny the principle we claim to share with Plato.

Exploring Subordinate Meanings and Their Limitations

Let's examine these potential subordinate interpretations to understand their scope and how they might retain some validity, before we set forth the substantive contention that opposes the doctrine's full and natural meaning.

The Infallibility of Judgment 'Pro Tempore'

One way to interpret this doctrine is to suggest that every individual, at any given moment, must treat themselves as infallible. This isn't a claim about objective truth but rather about the immediate necessity of acting on one's current judgment.

To hesitate or declare oneself in doubt offers no practical help, because even the act of suspending action or expressing doubt is itself a positive affirmation that the situation calls for such a response.

Crucially, this necessity is not confined to action, nor is its existence an argument solely for Pragmatism. Any judgment, once made, holds its ground; it can only be challenged or revised through a grounded review undertaken by means of a subsequent judgment. This applies universally to all judgments, including judgments of value. As a proponent of extreme Libertarianism has observed, we are powerless to modify even our moral valuations except by the valuation itself; it represents our current state of being as long as we remain so. While we might modify our will, our estimate of value, they argue, remains resistant to external alteration. It is within the potential for contradiction between these two—our will and our estimate of value—that freedom and wrongdoing are found.

And this much is a practical truth we must acknowledge through experience: no argument can guarantee altering a person's mind. For situations where an individual's action or judgment is paramount, we must either frame our arguments within their existing principles and accepted scale of values, or simply let the matter rest.

However, the critical point is that none of this applies solely to the judgment of value. This characteristic is a fundamental consequence of the nature of judgment as such, specifically its reliance upon our mental structure. It is equally true for theoretical considerations as for practical ones, for speculative thought as for desire. And, significantly, this immediate infallibility does not, in principle, exclude the openness of all judgment to discussion and revision.

It simply reiterates the foundational idea that at any moment, we think what we think unless and until we see a reason to think otherwise. This reinforces our long-held view that the mind operates as a logical whole.

Indeed, the common saying, "De gustibus non disputandum"—there is no disputing about tastes—is a half-truth. And to the extent that it holds any validity, it extends, as we've just seen, even to cognition. Remodeling the fundamental framework of a mind is a difficult task, and for many purposes, it is often wiser not to attempt it, but rather to adapt, to "become all things to all men".

The Distinction Between Cognition and Feeling

Another subordinate meaning might emphasize the distinction between cognition (knowing) and feeling or desire. It might be argued that to value something is to desire it or to find it pleasant, or at least to conceive of it as possessing qualities that, under certain conditions, would elicit desire or pleasure. This, it is contended, is a matter of feeling, not of reasoning. A judgment may state that something pleases, but the pleasure itself is a fact, and, as Hume would argue, reason cannot create new facts. Therefore, to judge something valuable is merely to recognize an existing fact, not to create it. The valuation, in this view, precedes the judgment.

This perspective often makes an appeal to the idea of ultimate ends or values. Even if we concede that critical examination might modify our understanding of what things or characters are encompassed by, or flow from, an ultimate end, the initial valuation of something as ultimate, it is argued, comes first. This fundamental valuation then serves as the basis for further discrimination of its nature. The core assertion here is: "The fundamental fact is that I care for some sort of thing; then you may argue upon the consequences in which that fact involves me. But you cannot by argument undo my first sense of value, nor could you impart it if I did not possess it. If there was no feeling there could be no value".

While I do not dispute the proposition that "If no feeling, then no value," it belongs, as our text suggests, to a very dangerous class of half-truths. Analogous statements like "If no knowledge, then no truth" or "If no aesthetic sense, then no beauty" are also true in this limited sense.

These are merely *sine qua non* conditions—things without which something else cannot exist. However, the simple converses of these judgments, though not commonly implied by the original, can be equally true and, in these cases, demonstrably so. For instance, it is plain that if there were no values, there could be no feeling. That is to say, unless our being experienced something as being "less or more," or having "less or greater reality or perfection" in certain experiences, there would be no underlying cause or reason for that immediate sense of heightened or lowered vitality that we associate with feeling.

Therefore, no inference can be drawn from this connection to the impossibility of arguing relevantly about the conditions of higher or lower perfection and their presence in any given instance. We are not necessarily obligated to demonstrate that argument can *de facto* modify the feeling of value in a concrete case, though such a demonstration would certainly support the relevance of argument. Our primary task is to explain the relativity of feelings of value to a standard that transcends them, such as the mind's inherent degrees of self-completeness or individuality.

The Core Mistake: Conflating Immediate and Ultimate Experiences

As a matter of fact, experience and argument, which is essentially a structured way of allowing experience to inform us, can and do modify both the feeling and the judgment of value. This happens in precisely the same manner and to the same extent that they can modify any other mood or attitude of the mind, whether it be cognitive or emotional.

The entire debate, at its heart, revolves around the intricate connection between mediate and immediate experiences. The assertion that no argument is possible concerning judgments of ultimate ends rests on a fundamental confusion and a mistake.

- The confusion lies in conflating what is immediate with what is ultimate.
- The mistake is in believing that the immediate is somehow beyond or beneath critical discussion. This idea is already false when applied to the immediate, and it becomes even more profoundly false when, through this confusion, it is transferred to the ultimate.

It is certainly true that before we can engage in arguments about questions of value, we must possess an immediate experience of what it means to care for something. We must have that initial judgment that "something can be cared for" before we can develop this understanding by considering what *must* be cared for more or less. This is analogous to the requirement that we must first apprehend the judgment that "something is true or real" before we can build a comprehensive science of logic or metaphysics.

However, these necessary minimums of experience are in none of these cases ultimate or fundamental. They are merely the starting-points from which experience develops. Their typical form, in philosophical terms, can be likened to Hegel's initial point of departure in the idea of mere being. If we were to argue that worth or value is simply the capacity to satisfy an idea, and therefore the content of the idea precedes the conception of worth, we would correctly be countered that our interest in the content of an idea *is itself* what is meant by value. This only demonstrates that a standard of value is prior to the valuation of particular things.

Even granting this answer, it remains strikingly clear that the power of an idea to interest or satisfy us is not merely a brute fact, but a matter for logical estimation.

The ultimate or fundamental interest is certainly not the *prima facie* or initial interest. And generally speaking, the immediate fact of interest, which gives us the very idea of valuing or caring about anything, stands at the opposite pole of experience from the ultimate or fundamental interest, where, upon deeper consideration, we find that all our capacity for caring would be most adequately engaged.

Furthermore, it is simply not true that there is any purely immediate experience. Immediacy is merely a form that any content can assume; it is not peculiar to any single type of experience. It is incorrect to claim that any form of liking, valuing, or caring remains unaffected by the overall shaping of one's life, or by the critical reflection that illuminates where true fullness lies. And if this holds true for immediate experience, it is immensely more so for ultimate experience.

While there might be some justification for supposing that you cannot be argued into or out of a simple experience of pleasure—though, it must be said, in many cases you absolutely can be to suggest that it is impossible to argue and explain where the ultimate power of objects or ideas to satisfy a mind truly resides (which is where their value for a mind lies) seems to contradict everyday experience, as well as the entire thrust of aesthetic, ethical, and metaphysical inquiry.

The Affirmative Argument: Individuality as the Logical Criterion of Value

Having addressed the criticisms and clarified the misunderstandings, let me now state in a positive form what this discussion intends to maintain, which I take as the essential meaning of the view I am defending.

We admit the following points:

- Firstly, a person's judgment is unequivocally *their* judgment, and it binds them until they have consciously altered it by a further judgment.
- Secondly, before one can engage in reasoned argument about the ultimate end or worth, one must already possess an experience of what it means to seek an end or to care for something as having worth.

However, it is here maintained that these are merely relevant instances of the general conditions that accompany the development of *all* experience, without exception. This applies to cognitive experience just as much as it does to emotional or practical experience. Crucially, these conditions do not interfere with the essential nature of the logical process that moves from the minimum to the maximum of experience.

Such a logical process can always be identified within the meaning or conditions of pleasure or satisfaction, or within the very character that constitutes an end. The degrees of this meaning or character can be exhibited through logical argument, and they can, to a great extent, be brought home and enforced through careful reflection, often leading to tangible practical results. We all know that it is sometimes possible to tell someone, "Now you are not really enjoying yourself," and for them to acknowledge this truth and, as a consequence, change their behaviour , leading to satisfying outcomes.

I reiterate that before we can dismiss this profound conception of an identical criterion across truth, reality, and satisfaction, we would need to confront the entire rigorous argument by which Plato arrives at his concept of the Form of the Good. This is, in essence, the same as arriving at the conception of a perfection of positive pleasure. We would also need to engage with the substantially similar arguments put forth by Aristotle.

The fundamental principle underlying these arguments is this: positive pleasure and all true satisfaction, as distinct from a mere intensity of feeling that might prove illusory, depend on the character of logical stability inherent in the objects of desire. What is more, what, in this sense, is "more real" — meaning, more at one with itself and the whole, free from internal contradiction — is also the experience in which the mind obtains a more durable and coherent satisfaction, and more completely realizes itself. This profound consideration prescribes the very nature of the ultimate good or end, which serves as the supreme standard of value and cannot itself be measured by anything else. Therefore, our proposed standard is positive non-contradiction, further developed through comprehensiveness and consistency. By this robust standard, any judgment regarding an ultimate end or value can be critically examined and estimated.

Addressing the Contingency of Satisfaction and Human Impotence

However, an immediate objection might arise: "But the facts are plainly against you!". You assert that degrees of logical stability, perfection, and reality are the standard by which satisfactoriness, worth, and the character of being an ultimate end are to be measured. Yet, it is a well-known fact that interest is selective. Vast areas of the highest and most perfect experience, whether cognitive, practical, or aesthetic, may entirely fail to hold value for the majority of minds, or even to attract their attention at all. If every experience were as indifferent for every mind as it is for some mind, then the concept of value itself would become a meaningless word. Therefore, the argument concludes, value cannot be measured by metaphysical perfection, but must be purely relative to the feeling of particular sentient beings.

This is a powerful argument, stemming from the observation of de facto impotence, upon which our particularity, though not our individuality, depends. But as we have already seen, the very nature of mind contradicts the fact of its seeming impotence. The mind, in its essence, always is more than it is aware of being.

Let's elaborate on this:

- Firstly, the complete absence of interest is fundamentally incompatible with the nature of a finite mind. Such a mind is inherently involved and entangled in the world of experience, and its degree of being cannot be separated from its fundamental implication within the world of which it is an integral member. In principle, there must be interest and value wherever there is a mind that is a member of a world. The partial and merely apparent separation between reality and value cannot be used to argue for the conceivability of a complete and absolute separation.
- Secondly, this very partial separation between reality and value signifies nothing more than that finite minds are, in their degree and direction of development, what we must term contingent. Their interests, much like their knowledge and actions, vary and halt in ways that, in detail, may seem unaccountable. However, in a general sense, we can clearly perceive these variations as mere instances of their inherent powerlessness or limitations.

It is of paramount importance, however, that the positive argument shows no signs of failure, even though the negative corroboration can only be partially demonstrated. The principle stands: wherever we have interest, and to the extent that we have it, we possess an implication in reality. And further, wherever we have a more stable and satisfactory interest, we possess a deeper implication in reality.

It is true that where a deeper implication in reality seems to be presented, we do not always find a corresponding increase in interest. It is quite evident that our participation in the real must be limited, and the specific map of these limitations is, for us, largely determined contingently.

The general explanation for this is straightforward: we are often preoccupied by certain interests, the contents of which are not such as to readily form a logical whole with certain other interests. This is analogous to being preoccupied with certain theoretical principles that, in their current formulation, resist coalescing with provinces of knowledge that *prima facie* appear open to us.

But one might rejoin: "There's more to it than that." Not only do different minds pursue different values, but a single mind might apprehend and be familiar with an object or activity of high logical perfection, yet remain relatively or even completely indifferent to it—that is, refuse to assign it value. The answer remains practically the same: the object in question is, by its very nature, excluded from forming a coherent whole in its own right with the contents that have already preoccupied that mind. Alternatively, the object is pursued and receives attention only by virtue of some interest extraneous to it, which *is* part of that existing whole of contents. Think of a student who grudgingly studies a repulsive subject for an examination, or someone who earns a living from work they detest.

There's a humorous saying, attributed to Oliver Wendell Holmes, that "in principle every man loves every woman". Yet, individuals might plead non-acquaintance, specific dislikes, or a limited capacity for affection already preoccupied. There is a truth in this joke, and it applies even more seriously to the individual's love of perfection.

It becomes clear that if we abandon the notion of "De gustibus non disputandum"—as every serious student or critic must, except in the sense that changing habitual likings is difficult—then the view we are disputing is abandoned along with it. Indeed, no one would seriously put forth their own *de facto* indifference, or that of another, as a valid argument against the intrinsic value of a scientific discovery or an artistic achievement.

Ultimately, every objective standard of worth that can be proposed must be reducible to degrees of perfection.

The Nature of Value: "Relative to Persons" vs. "Conscious States"

To shed further light on the nature of value, let us consider the proposition that "all other values are relative to values for, of, or in a person". This statement, when translated into "Nothing has value except the conscious states of conscious beings," has often, perhaps surprisingly, generated conclusions hostile to the meaning with which thinkers like Green or Kant originally affirmed it. This has certainly occurred when it has been used to support Hedonism. Another interesting application, while perhaps not explicitly contradictory to Green's type of thought, points in a very different direction from their most characteristic views.

This doctrine posits that nothing has value but the conscious states of conscious beings. Furthermore, the value of the universe possesses no unity other than that of a simple sum of these individual conscious values. This becomes even more apparent if we assume the universe as a whole is not itself a conscious being. But even if it is, the values of the conscious states of finite beings are still considered as additive amounts, to be counted in addition to the value of the universe as a single conscious being.

For those who maintain that the universe as a whole constitutes a single, overarching experience, encompassing finite beings as finite centers of experience, this discussion about the unity of value might seem of subordinate importance. Yet, it remains valuable to engage with, both for the subordinate issues it raises even within that hypothesis, and because its underlying principle bears significantly on the related question of whether the universe is, in truth, conscious.

To clarify, if we are speaking of all conscious states of all conscious beings, including everything necessary for their completion, and all possible ways of their existence or interaction, then it would indeed be true that within this totality, we must find all that is of value. This point, I believe, would be agreed upon by all who accept the doctrine found in Green and Kant. They might, upon reflection, suggest that the word "person," if taken too strictly, unduly narrows the proposition. But all would likely agree if "persons" were broadened to "conscious beings".

However, does this immediately lead us to the doctrine that the universe's value is merely the sum of the values of all conscious states of all conscious beings? I think not, at least not in the natural sense of the latter proposition, nor in the sense in which I gather it has been put forward. I understand its core point to be that the "part-values" are primary, existing prior to their sum, which is nothing more than that sum. The sum, in this view, is determined *by* the parts, and is in no way a holistic unity or standard by which those parts are themselves determined. The idea that the whole is single and primary, the source and standard of value, and that part-values are to be understood as determined by their contribution to this whole, is, I gather, precisely what is intended to be rejected.

While the two statements ("all values relative to persons" and "nothing has value but conscious states") might appear similar—after all, in both views, parts make up the whole and the whole is made up of parts—there is a fundamental difference. Those who align with Green or Mr. Bradley would likely accept the first doctrine but not the second. The second doctrine—that nothing has value but conscious states—assumes that these states could possess value if they existed in isolation, and if they were, in all respects, rightly considered as states external to one another and without any implications beyond themselves.

The first doctrine, in contrast, assigns value to them precisely in respect of what they *imply*, and because they are *not*, and should not be, regarded as states external to one another or to what they imply. This distinction, though subtle, is of fundamental importance.

If we assign value to any whole as a unified entity, it can be argued that values relative to this whole, though derived from it, must in some sense be assignable to all factors involved in the whole. However, such an assignment does not imply any inherent value in the factors taken by themselves.

This is a conception fundamentally distinct from the idea that factors possess value *as such* and *per se*, such that the value of the whole can simply be conceived as a sum of values that genuinely and primarily belong to the factors as distinct entities. This "disintegrating implication"—where value is merely an aggregate of self-sufficient parts—is, I understand, the full meaning behind the second statement.

The Meaninglessness and Valuelessness of Abstracted Consciousness

The difficulty presented by this doctrine can be illuminated by a paradox: If you treat a state of consciousness of an intelligent finite being as simply a state of consciousness, you are treating it as something which it is not. Its very essence, as we have continually emphasized, lies outside itself. Its true nature is to be a part of a "perfect world," yet in any given state, this world remains incomplete, though always implied. Therefore, a state of consciousness derives its value from the object and the individuality which must be "read into it" in order to truly appreciate it, and which, in actual experience, are never entirely separate from it.

Let us pursue this line of thought. There is a familiar argument that distinguishes consciousness from the objective relations of the conscious being—relations implied in concepts such as Truth, Beauty, Virtue, and Freedom. This argument contends that you cannot, in the final analysis, justify a preference for a state of consciousness that is true, or virtuous, or imbued with beauty, insofar as your preference is influenced by a care for these objective characteristics. Why? Because your judgment of such relations is supposedly prone to error. Therefore, when formulating a preference for one state of consciousness over another, you supposedly ought to consider nothing but the state of consciousness itself—the condition of the mind at that moment—in and by itself. This requires excluding all reference to the fact that you hold certain predicates, like true, good, or free, to be applicable to it. These predicates are deemed separable; they depend on objects outside the mental state and do not reside within the confines of the mental condition itself.

If I understand correctly, the view we are currently discussing incorporates this familiar argument, but with a slight modification. The character of the universe, which, in objective relation to the mental state, serves as the ground for the truth, freedom, or other characteristic ascribed to that state, is *not* entirely ruled out of consideration. Instead, it is admitted as a *means* to the character of the state of consciousness itself, which, in this modified view, is still considered to be the sole possessor of value.

However, this still falls short. The error of conceiving a state of consciousness in an intelligent being as being, by its very nature, confined to itself, appears to be fundamental. You cannot simply dismiss its object as a mere means to its character. Its object is a partial apprehension by consciousness of its own nature; it is a world continuous with, yet extending beyond, the conscious state itself. And crucially, you cannot truly value the fragment without an appreciation of the whole.

Consider the truth of a thought. It does not merely mean that a mental state is "so" and a separate object is also "so". While this might be the case, the thought could still be perfectly false, as in the example of a "true" conclusion derived from "false" premises. The truth of a thought means, surely, that the thought has a content and context that allow it to occupy a harmonious place within the whole spiritual structure of experience. This essential character, however, does not reside *within* the mental state itself, even though it profoundly influences the mental state. It belongs to the mental state only as it is organized within a larger whole, as emphasized by the contrast we have previously drawn.

In sum, when we value truth, beauty, virtue, and similar concepts, we are not merely valuing isolated mental states; we are valuing spiritual worlds. These worlds are simultaneously objective and subjective, and they are essentially continuous with even greater worlds. Although they are given to, and even exist within, conscious minds, they are not simply *states* of conscious minds. Furthermore, it is not clear, without specific examination and proof, that the seemingly particular consciousnesses to which they are given are separable existences, either from their own continued being or from other so-called particular beings. We might justly refuse to call such particulars "individuals" in the fullest sense, and we may certainly refuse to treat the true whole or individual as a mere sum of such particulars.

Consciousness Apart from Individuals or the Individual

Now, let us push the argument further by comparing the statement that places value in conscious states *as such* with the proposition we initially set beside it, which places value solely in "persons" or, more precisely, in individuality.

When it was asserted that all value resided in or for persons, this was because "persons" implied a capacity for being ends or worlds unto themselves. It was believed that nothing else existed in its own right or could serve as a focal point where a complex of being could cohere to fulfill a plan.

However, as has been pointed out concerning Bentham's valuation of pleasurable states, and also very ably in the analogy between the egoist's self (which they respect) and the moral cosmos (which they reject), it is quite conceivable that by attaching value solely to the state of consciousness, one may entirely lose the essential reference to the person, the unity, or the idea of an end or purpose. In the case of the egoist, they might as well deny their own totality as deny that of the cosmos. This is, *prima facie*, the very essence of any view that attaches value not to persons or to individuality, but to isolated states of mind.

As drawn out previously, you can either value these states as self-sufficient entities *per se,* or you can value them as implying a personality that constitutes their whole, or world, or end. But in the latter case, you are not valuing them *per se*. And you could not value them as you do without comprehending the personality to which they belong, or the greater world of which they are dependent fragments. This argument becomes even stronger if we substitute "individuality" for "personality," thereby avoiding the narrower implications often attached to the term "person". If all value truly resides in individuality, then we must begin from the fullest experience of individuality that we can construct, and the valuation of particular states of consciousness will then be secondary to that fuller experience, and derived from it.

This argument gains even greater force for those who believe that succession in time is merely an appearance, not the ultimate reality. In this view, the particular state of consciousness ultimately possesses no separate, distinct being. Instead, all states, as Kant suggested concerning the infinite moral progression when viewed by God, are ultimately comprehended within a deeper, similar reality.

And the crucial implication here is that that which ultimately has no distinguishable being cannot ultimately have a distinct valuation. Furthermore, the reversal of an argument previously alluded to carries us even deeper. If a person denies their unity with others, it was asked, why should they assume their unity with themselves?. But again, if they postulate their unity with themselves, how can they then deny their unity with the further stages of individuality?.

There appears to be no logical reason to draw a line at which this profound continuity must break off. The *prima facie* inference, therefore, points towards a unitary perfection residing in the complete individuality of the universe as a conscious being, which, in this ultimate sense, isthe ultimate value and the supreme standard of value.

While calling it an "end" or a "person" might carry certain dangers of misconception, to regard it as an individual whole seems no more than inevitable. This consideration extends beyond the mere subject of the unity of value and touches upon the profound unity of experience itself. It is impossible to exclude it here, precisely because it is one of the crucial consequences that demonstrate how precarious our ground is when we attempt to treat a state of consciousness as merely a state of consciousness and nothing more.

For the same reason, on the hypothesis of a universe that is conscious as a whole, the separate valuation of its life and of the finite lives that are integral to its life seems inconceivable, except in the secondary sense we have already admitted.

A finite consciousness is finite precisely because it "stops short" and does not fully realize its own inherent nature. You cannot assign it a value except through and in relation to its own full nature, which is the comprehensive whole.

You cannot, therefore, simply add the value that a finite consciousness retains, despite its shortcomings, to the value it possesses within the complete being that it inherently implies. To use an analogy: if a thing, as you currently perceive it, is worth two units, but properly understood and seen in its full scope, it is worth ten, you cannot simply add the two to the ten when calculating its full and ultimate value.

The Universe as the Unit of Value

If, in the assertion that the universe is not, as such, "good" or "bad," the emphasis is placed on the peculiar nature of these predicates as implying a quasi-moral estimate—a conceptual divorce between what *is* and what *ought to be*—then a measure of agreement is possible on this point.

If the universe is conceptualized as a perfect conscious being, then, when judged comparatively to its members, and as that which gives and *is* the standard, it is indeed relatively "good" and the fulfillment of all ideas. However, in itself, though perfect, it is not "good" in the sense that it is on one side of a contrast between what *ought to be* and that which is *not* what it ought to be but is in the process of becoming so. "Good" and "bad" are therefore not appropriate expressions by which to pose a question about it. Yet, if the question *is* raised, the universe must be pronounced "good" as opposed to "bad".

However, even though in the sense described above it is not strictly "good"—and certainly not morally good in the ordinary sense—it is nonetheless perfection itself, and the fundamental standard of all goodness and value.

Strictly speaking, you do not *value* it; you value all else *by* it. Its value is the fundamental unit, and all other values must be adjusted so as to amount to it. And this, I take it, is the very meaning of those who assert that all value resides in or for a person, just as it is the meaning of those who hold that all value is ultimately one in the perfection of the universe. Conversely, the claim that all value is solely of conscious states of conscious beings as such would then be precisely the opposite of this profound contention.

The State as a Paradigm of Unified Value

The philosophical treatment of the State in this discussion is naturally analogous to our treatment of the universe. And we can agree that the State represents an experience rightly taken as typical of the higher forms of human experience. If the "particular"—the individual understood in the common, though often incorrect, sense—is to be the ultimate, irreducible unit of value here, then that principle would have to be consistently applied throughout.

But if, in the context of the State, we can observe that individuality transcends the particular, given consciousness, then we will be prepared for a more complete transcendence as we move towards fuller, more encompassing experiences. For this reason, it is important to clarify our view on this matter. Is the value of a State, in its fullest sense, found merely in the psychical successions forming the individual consciousnesses of its constituent conscious beings, as additive amounts, each possessing value *per se*?.

Our argument remains consistent: the State, for us, represents a phase of individuality that belongs to the ongoing process towards unity, though it falls far short of its ultimate completion. We understand and accept the warning that there can be no value in anything less than a personal consciousness. This means no value in a history of mankind distinct from the persons whose experiences constitute that history or who are developed within it.

However, even granting that nothing has value which is not, in some manner, a personal consciousness, this does not resolve the crucial question of how much more than its given self at any moment such a consciousness may imply as the unit of value to which it ultimately belongs.

- First, we can argue, as we effectively did earlier, that in accepting a "personal consciousness," we have already implicitly accepted a standard that extends beyond the mere states of consciousness of a conscious being. By "person," or a being partaking in individuality (even including animals and young children in our idea), we presumably mean some kind of whole; and individual states of consciousness, by themselves, are not wholes.
- But further, the real question is whether two or more so-called "persons" can be members of the same greater whole or unity for the purposes of valuation. Are they to be valued simply as they are given, in their apparent separateness, or do they, by forming an integral part of larger wholes, acquire a value that is completely different from what they would prima facie possess?.

I hold it as an enormous concession, previously indicated, that the value of any state of consciousness is said not necessarily to be known to its subject or to any actual judge. This crucial insight removes any compulsion to interpret value as merely an immediate, obvious aspect of a given complex of experience.

It is entirely consistent with the view that the significance and implications of the complex, however latent or remote to the ordinary observer, are the true grounds of its value. Let us view this question through the lens of the Greek theory of society, at its most refined. Its famous paradox states that the value of a society lies in its happiness as a whole, not merely in the happiness of the separate individuals who compose it.

This means that if you were to assume each individual possessed the highest happiness an isolated observer would assign to them, and then simply aggregated these individual happiness to represent the community's happiness, you would fundamentally miss the true nature of the community's happiness.

"Happiness," here, can fairly be equated with value, or felt perfection. This true happiness can only be grasped by first judging the perfection of a society as a unitary body of experience—because it is within this larger unity alone that the individual conscious being can truly be all that they can be. Only then would you adjust your estimate of individual perfection in light of this greater societal perfection.

Of course, to value individuals fully and with complete understanding would be equivalent to valuing them as fully unified within the greater whole. In such a scenario, the difference between these points of view would vanish, with the crucial exception that simply valuing "states of consciousness as such" could never properly equal valuing unified individuals.

The entire view we are advocating rests on a denial of the position that "individuals" are a mere plurality, such as cannot be unified in their contributions to a common experience.

Consider, for example, the ancient theory regarding the position of slaves, a principle that applies to all imperfection and reciprocal supplementation of consciousness within any society whatsoever.

The core point is that social life and experience embody a "one-mind in a number of bodies," where individual consciousnesses, though formally separate, are materially identical in varying degrees. Therefore, in terms of value, they each assume the character of that to which they are instrumental, precisely as each individual, through their thought and loyalty (not merely as a passive means), transcends their immediate self and becomes absorbed in the total result.

Thus, a loyal servant of a statesman or scholar derives value from the latter's work; through it, the servant participates in the perfection of the whole. In the same vein, the entire society is dignified and sanctified by the knowledge, beneficence, or religion that it respects and makes possible. Conversely, it is also brutalized and degraded by the internal ills and evils it harbors. This principle, as I said, is universal.

While it certainly does not excuse the specific historical incidents of slavery, its importance, first articulated by Plato and Aristotle in relation to the child and as a partial theory of the slave's position, is absolutely fundamental for understanding the entirety of social experience. The life of any reasonably harmonious household offers a clear illustration of this concept.

It is entirely possible for a consciousness to find its end, its explanation, and its value, in what it shares with another consciousness, and in what is incompletely present in itself alone. And, ultimately, all finite consciousnesses find their value in this way. It is not only the so-called "lower" individuals who are dignified by their respect for a dim apprehension of the achievements of the "higher". The "higher, "or leading minds, conversely, draw much of their courage, dutifulness, and self-denial from their felt unity with those they lead, with the "lower". As the poet says, "God uses us to help each other so, Lending our minds out".

All this is implicitly contained for a careful reader within the class-system described in Plato's *Republic*.

The very foundation of it all is this: no phase in a particular consciousness is merely a phase of that apparent subject; rather, it is always and essentially a member of a further, more encompassing whole of experience.

This larger whole passes through and unites the states of many consciousnesses, but it is not exhausted in any single one, nor even in all of them, when taken merely as distinct states. It is true that my state of mind is uniquely mine, and yours is uniquely yours.

But not only do I experience in my mind what you experience in yours—which would still be consistent with the total independence of our two minds—but I experience it differently from you, in such a way that there is a systematic relation between the two experienced contents, and neither is intelligible or complete without the other. Once you have admitted the unity of the person with themselves, it becomes logically impossible to stop short of acknowledging their profound unity with others, with the world, and indeed, with the entire universe. And the ultimate perfection by which an individual is to be valued is their place within the perfection of these greater wholes.

Thus, the principle that all value is value of individual experience is absolutely maintained.

The difference lies primarily in what we define as "individual experience," and consequently, in the point of departure we choose for valuing it.

In all finite individuals, there is an inherent process of self-transcendence, and therefore a translocation of the point of reference in valuing.

However, not all self-transcendence is primarily social. It is therefore incorrect to claim that all good, *as such*, is social good, and it is beneficial that this common inaccuracy has been challenged.

It is a paradox of humanity that the finest qualities of human beings themselves, and the forms of experience in which humanity achieves its greatest perfection, are not, at first glance, very widely distributed.

Art, philosophy, and religion, while bearing the relationship to society we have indicated, are not immediately concerned with promoting social relations, nor are they specifically molded to serve social ends.

The doctrine we have been opposing is likely a reaction against the exaggerated claims that social good is the *only* good. However, it appears to be a mistake to push this reaction so far as to deny that the State itself is a name for a special form of self-transcendence, in which individuality strongly anticipates the character of its perfection.

Concluding Thoughts: Value as Logical Coherence and the Whole

To summarize our position:

- We concede that in the judgment of value, every person is, in a sense, infallible for themselves, but this is only true in the same way that it is true for every possible judgment.
- We agree that there must be an experience of feeling before any reasoned judgment of value can take place.
- And we concur that the unitary value of the universe, which represents the completion of individuality or perfection, should not properly be referred to as "goodness," especially not with an ethical implication. Instead, it should be conceived as perfection.
- Furthermore, we understand that all that is valuable must ultimately reside within the comprehensive whole of conscious experience, or within the aggregate, or coming together in some specific manner, of conscious states of conscious beings.

The core questions we have addressed are: Can the judgment of value be logically supported? And does the whole which possesses value simply lie in the sum of the values of conscious states, understanding those states as distinct and successive, and their values as mere addable quantities?.

The answer to both, it appears, is resounding: Before you can truly judge anything, you must perceive it in its full nature. And the nature of any conscious state of a conscious being is not to be found within itself, unless, by a deliberate reference to the overarching whole, we have specifically trained ourselves to discern it there.

Therefore, we firmly adhere to Plato's profound conclusion: the objects of our likings possess as much of satisfactoriness—which we identify with value—as they possess of reality and truth. And this, I submit, is not merely a subjective preference, but a logical standard, and a standard that inherently involves the whole of experience.

It is through this lens of comprehensiveness, consistency, and non-contradiction that we can truly begin to understand and evaluate the rich tapestry of value in our world.

Lecture-9

Freedom and Initiative

This lecture redefines freedom by challenging the idea that it means escape from determination. It reveals freedom as the active, creative logic of the self—a world shaping itself through its contents. By linking initiative to coherence, responsibility, and artistic creation, it shows how genuine freedom deepens individuality and gives lasting value to action.

Discusses freedom as the active expression of individuality and its role in shaping value

Ladies and Gentlemen, fellow seekers of truth and understanding, Today, we delve into a profound exploration of Freedom, Initiative, and the Self's Logic, drawing upon a comprehensive philosophical perspective that seeks to unite seemingly disparate aspects of our experience. Our journey aims to clarify the intricate relationship between individual existence and the broader universe, ultimately revealing how genuine freedom is not found in isolation, but in a deeper, more integrated understanding of the self.

The Self as a "World in Oneself" and its Foundation

Our fundamental premise, the very cornerstone of this discourse, is that individuality means being a world in oneself. This isn't merely a poetic notion; it implies a special kind of self-determination inherent in every finite individual. You might recall our earlier discussions, particularly in Lectures III, IV, and V, where we emphasized what some might perceive as the dependence of the finite individual upon the external or mechanical world. An astute critic might even label this approach as akin to materialism or naturalism.

However, let me hasten to clarify: our conviction has always been that the truth, or the real, is the whole. Our deepest anxiety has been to avoid neglecting any crucial factor, to prevent any fundamental antithesis from arising that would subordinate mind or spirit to excluded elements. Elements, once excluded, tend to remain both hostile and superior, undermining the very essence of what we seek to uphold.

Thus, the seemingly counter-intuitive truth is that our primary object and ideal has always been that of freedom. If our mind or spirit attempts to draw solely upon itself, in a narrow, introspective sense—opposing an inner self to the external world—we believe it fundamentally misunderstands its own procedure, transforming the very logic of the self into fallacy and superstition. We have deliberately risked misunderstanding to shed all biases against particular forms of appearance, challenging them only when, in isolation, they claim an unreal predominance.

Indeed, it is crucial to understand that our apparent materialism or externalism is materialism or externalism with a profound difference. We champion it as the very fulness and genuine purport of concrete idealism. Any interpretation that implies a reactionary temper is unequivocally rejected. For us, the true connection throughout existence is logical and synthetic, not merely causal in the popular sense of a simple, undifferentiated repetition of connections. The old adage, "Everything is what it is, and not another thing," holds true in the sense that the interdependence of different appearances does not simply reduce one into another. Consider, for example, the external world. It cannot be a self-subsistent entity. But there's a world of difference between exhibiting it as the condition and complement of spiritual being and attempting to reduce it to mere inwardness or subjective imagery. While it's a fundamental truth that "everything is another thing or more than one other thing" as appearances are transfigured by progressive experience, this truth loses all meaning if it suggests that differences are simply absorbed without bringing their former selves to the transfigured whole.

The Concrete Universal and the Vindication of Freedom

This brings us to the very type of Individuality we have championed from the outset: what we described as the concrete universal—or, more generally, as a world or cosmos. Far from conceding to Determinism, Materialism, or Naturalism in a way that is hostile to Idealism or spiritual freedom, our contention is precisely that no other conception offers any loophole whatever by which Freedom can be saved, or a creative, constructive, and initiative character vindicated for the self.

Let us briefly reiterate the essence of this idea. The essence of Individuality, as we understand it, is to be a world in oneself. A being possessing this character must be no other world than itself; the individual, as individual, is unique. This uniqueness is merely a corollary of the ultimate ideal of organization. Even among finite beings, the positive character of originality is minimally impaired by de facto overlapping or recurrence; it resides in what a person is, not in what they are not.

This concept of being a "world in oneself" applies to even the most finite individual. In them, however incompletely, we witness what it means to have experience, or, in the most general sense, to be conscious. Indeed, we cannot apply the term "being" in its full sense to anything but the whole of a consciousness or an experience. Anything else, like a mountain or a tree (assuming no consciousness), exists only derivatively, as a fragment or abstraction within consciousness. We cannot meaningfully grasp it except as a portion of the experienced or the experiencing, or both in an undivided moment.

Self-Determination and the Logic of the Cosmos

While this might seem like common ground today, it carries a crucial corollary: the character of self-completeness, of being a cosmos, inherently brings with it its own mode of self-determination and initiative. It is illogical to conceive of a being as a unity in diversity of content, yet assume that the nature of this content is indifferent and won't influence the responses and transformations of the whole.

A timeless observation, yet profoundly true, is that our fears for freedom often stem from a desire to "swim without going into the water". In more serious terms, it's a lack of faith in the Absolute. We cling to a desire to keep our individuality unspotted by the world, unstained by the content of life. The inevitable consequence of this stance is that we are driven to view the self as a slave of circumstance.

On the contrary, the conception of consciousness we are presenting is, in principle, that of a system of content, "come alive" according to certain arrangements. Through these arrangements, the Absolute allows minor worlds, formally distinct and of varying degrees of fullness, to constitute its union with externality—a union that is itself the Absolute. The overwhelming impression of such a law of arrangements subserving life, evident in the organic world and animal intelligence, cannot be dismissed. The rich gradation of animal minds poses an insurmountable challenge to theories that posit finite consciousnesses as simply distinct, self-subsistent differentiations of the Absolute.

It is far more natural, and consistent with plain facts, to suppose that feeling or consciousness emerges where, and to the extent that, they are called forth by content to be experienced. Their appearance is conditioned by those peculiar phenomena of the external system that, in countless degrees, pave the way for the growth of microcosms. This perspective realizes something akin to what monadism demands: that every possible gradation of reality must be occupied, and thus the Absolute is enriched by experience of all conceivable grades and varieties of content. Ultimately, this illustrates our point: a finite individual is in essence a cosmos, which is a portion of the cosmos, bringing relatively to perfection and full experience that which in and through correlated externality, the Absolute has to manifest and appropriate.

The Emergence of the Self: A Developmental Process

The idea that the ego or self is relatively late and artificial, along with the protracted discipline of a living body or succession of bodies it presupposes, reinforces this conclusion. While objections to the "eternal self" (in the sense of a pre-existing, static entity) might seem to challenge this, they actually serve to illustrate our point. To put it simply, if we accept the provisional reality of succession in time, there is absolutely no gain in positing higher appearances before their conditions are present. We must believe they emerge when their conditions are present, and not before.

The self is experienced when a persistent mental system has been developed, capable of opposition to a not-self. While it may seem strange, the self might be active *before* it is fully experienced, in the underlying unity of feeling from which the unity of consciousness grows. However, this is largely a distinction of dates of appearance. As Green constantly reiterated, understanding *how* we reach the experience of the eternal self is different from the truth *that* we possess it. There is a puzzling question as to why the animal mind, so continuous with the human mind, seems to arrest its development earlier. While a more complete evolution would be easier to explain, we must accept this fact without letting it dictate our understanding of human experience. We reiterate: Mind is best regarded as a cosmos, and as working out its behaviour by the logic of a cosmos.

Addressing the Determinism Objection: Green and the "Circumstances"

A significant difficulty arises when we present these facts, particularly concerning Green's account of the self-conscious moral agent. The core criticism is this: if self-consciousness, as a common and identical principle, is the same for all moral agents, and the only difference between individuals lies in their content (which includes what is experienced by the self), then any assignable difference in content—even character or disposition—ultimately traces back to data and environment, including bodily inheritance. In essence, it becomes a difference of circumstances.

Given this, the argument proceeds, if the principle of self-consciousness is common, then differences between individuals are externally accounted for. The self, in its distinctiveness, is said to spring from circumstance, not from its own initiative. In short, what determines the individual comes from without, from surroundings, not from self-consciousness. Thus, determinism seemingly triumphs; the spiritual principle accounts for nothing distinctive; the body and circumstances make the man what he is. The criticism is that, for Green, the difference between one self and another lies *simply* in circumstances.

Our initial rejoinder might seem obvious: "No, not *simply* in circumstances, but in what a man makes of his circumstances." We observe different minds emerging from practically the same circumstances, yet making entirely different worlds of them. However, against a determined antagonist, this answer might not entirely hold. The antagonist would concede the appearance but insist that it's superficial. While minds and immediate externals differ, the difference in minds, interests, and capacities is, by hypothesis, dependent on circumstances and cannot be attributed to the endowment of self-consciousness, which is a common character.

The Deeper Response: The Self as Inclusive and Transcendent

Such a thoroughgoing deterministic interpretation cannot be met with compromise. It demands a more thorough point of view than its own. We believe this perspective is already embedded in what we've advanced.

Following Green, we do not wish or need to exclude "circumstances" from the determinant and distinctive features of the self. On the one hand, the self, in its quality and content, bears the banner of its place and time; it is what it includes. Its finitude, imperfection, self-contradiction, and exclusivity stem from the impotence that causes it to include so little.

On the other hand, and this is crucial, its true and ultimate nature lies outside it, in the whole upon which its impotence bears witness. And it is precisely through the impact of that whole, in all its forms, in what we mean by struggle and circumstance, that its own nature is progressively communicated to it. Therefore, it is a superficial, external observation to merely note that all particular selves share the identical feature of self-consciousness.

This self-consciousness is, in other words, a conation towards the unity of a harmonious cosmos, or towards the completed system of an eternal self. The abstract generality of this truth does not establish an abstract character for the partly individualized conations that constitute concrete selves. The striving towards unity and coherence is the striving of the self as a living system of content. The fact that this content has its origin "without" is simply a corollary of the central truth that every self is a special "within," dealing with a specific group of elements from that world-life in which all experience is one.

In sum, we maintain that no ideal of freedom lies in the direction of isolating the self from the world. On the contrary, freedom lies in the direction towards unity and coherence. All that becomes one with the self is capable of contributing (even through apparent contradiction and the effort it stimulates) to this satisfaction of the inherent logical tendency.

So, to the criticism, "Your individual conation takes its line not from a self-conscious entity within it, but from outward circumstance, which is given to the self, and not created by it," we offer this reply: "That, on the whole, and despite disagreeing with the last five words ('not created by it'), is, as we understand the matter, what the self is there for and consists in—to convert externality into inwardness.

It is to elicit the conation, the need, or the teaching, that underlies the circumstances out of which, and by means of which, it becomes a self. It is the working, the 'logic, ' of this relative totality of experience that constitutes the freedom of the concrete self." This freedom, we argue, affirms the self as a part of the eternal deed in which the Absolute sustains its living whole of experience.

The Challenge of Predetermination and the Nature of Causation

The critic, however, might persist, raising the objection of predetermination. Even if the difference in origin between individuals, rooted in the world beyond them, doesn't impeach their essential individuality, the fact remains that "it all comes from somewhere". Previously existing circumstances, united in a center that brings no *new positive element*, seem to work out their inevitable resultant with present conditions. As Kant argued, it seems to make no difference whether the sequence is physical or psychical; the essential point is predetermination—the power of a past, which is no longer a present, to prescribe what the present is to be. This perspective appears to intensify determinism into fatalism, describing individual action and world history as the "rattling off of a chain of results inevitably decreed". "Tout estdonne" - "Everything is given".

We needn't dwell excessively on the answer to this difficulty, as it emerges clearly from Kant's noumenon/phenomenon distinction and Green's doctrine of the eternal self. Those who deny that a world of consciousness carries its past in its present, or that the logical determination of an outcome (like a conclusion from premises) is fundamentally different from determination by a past that is simply "past and gone" (like physical causation), will remain unmoved by familiar arguments. For those who have grasped the working of a living mind or individual cosmos—the relation of a want to a motive, a motive to a volition, a volition to the self's structure—such reiteration would be tedious.

Logic, Life, and Artistic Creation: The Indivisible Energy of Reason

However, we can frame this argument in a more aggressive, universally applicable way, particularly addressing recent speculations that tend to exclude logic and intelligence from life, creation, and initiative. This tendency even extends to "intuition" in philosophy, which ought to relate to intelligence as Hegel's Reason relates to Understanding.

We previously asserted—and this might have caused surprise—that the recent tendency to separate imitation and invention, repetition and creation, fails most utterly in its treatment of the creative imagination of art.

The truth is, once you break in two the indivisible energy of reason, assigning one part to likeness and the other to difference, you render both utterly and finally impotent and inconceivable. We see this in the prevalent view that condemns logical intelligence to solely spatial considerations, solids, geometry, and repels it from dealing with life. Yet, a truer philosophy has suggested that man's reason, strictly speaking, can understand nothing *but* the organism.

In the account of artistic creation as a pure incarnation of the new and unaccountable, we recognize the same irrational severance of identity and diversity. This severance, throughout the tradition in question, stems from working with "likeness and unlikeness" instead of "identity and difference". The crucial distinction is that likeness, being a repeated effect, cannot be subserved by difference between terms, whereas identity, as a co-operative universal, is best subserved by difference. Likeness leads to class relations; identity leads to organic wholes.

What this theory of "pure difference" truly implies is that in artistic creation, in genius and imagination, you have pure difference without identity, pure novelty issuing from no determinate connection, pure irrationality and unaccountableness. The work of art, it is claimed, cannot be predicted from its matter and author; it is beyond reason and intelligence, just as life, in these speculations, is beyond logic.

This is a less common but thoroughly relevant form of the freedom controversy than that focused solely on moral volition. A decision here carries implications for all other areas.

It is a natural notion that the creative imagination of the artist is a faculty of origination de novo. Phrases like "creative" or "productive" hold a certain magic. In early stages of art and aesthetic training, the imaginative process is often contrasted with logical derivation from reality, much like the "ought" is contrasted with the "is" in imperfect moral theory. This tendency is reinforced by the obvious difference between a work of art and a calculation. An artist might say they "didn't know how it came to them," while a calculation seems "common form," analyzable step-by-step. Of course, science also has genius, though perhaps less specialized.

However, even with the fullest weight, this comparison amounts to very little against our main thesis. It only means that in calculation, we deal with relatively simple and definite matter, easily fixed, combined, and communicated. We are merely reproducing skeleton elements of microcosms, not the full effect of their concentrated contents.

It's unsurprising that, within narrower limits than we imagine, one mind can largely replicate another's work in these areas.

But when the whole person is concerned, the case is entirely different. It is then natural that one mind cannot wholly substitute for another, and the outcome of one "world of content" cannot be reproduced by another whose contents are different. This is all that the appeal to impossibility of prediction truly corroborates. Prediction means doing a thing before it is done. This is only possible when conditions are certainly determinable and can be assembled at will. In anything dependent on the *entire response of a mind's content*, such a possibility is absurd, unless a smaller mind falls within a greater mind, allowing for some substitution. In that case, prediction of main lines of action is possible.

Therefore, the supposed impossibility of predicting or constructing a work of art by anyone other than its author adds nothing new in principle to the argument. This argument only points to a difference in the *matter* dealt with, not a fundamental difference in the creative principle itself. The creative nature of artistic achievement rests on the same principle as all advance and completion effected by the spirit of logic, which lies in the continuity of the universal.

All logical process is the re-shaping of a world of content by its own universal Spirit. There is no repetition, not even the recurrent application of a word, that is devoid of this creative element. And in creative production *par excellence*, we simply have the same thing at its fullest.

As we gain aesthetic insight and experience, the penetrative imagination reveals itself as the higher form of the creative. We come to feel that not the invention of novelty, but the logic which lays bare the heart and structure of things, and in doing so purifies and intensifies feeling, is the true secret of art. Of course, we cannot predict a painter's or poet's incarnation of thought; if we could, we would *be* them. But this isn't because we are *too* rational, but because we are not rational enough. We lack the "fundamental brainwork" and the capacity for the infinitely delicate logic of expression.

If we say the process isn't rational because it's largely unconscious, we commit a serious confusion. The process itself is an intense and exquisitely adjusted and organized consciousness, often plainly logical. It is not, however, *another* consciousness watching and analyzing the first. And in this sense, all logical process without exception is unconscious. You cannot make the working function of a syllogism into its major premise, nor predict its conclusion from an inactive, watching consciousness.

The spirit of logic, when at work, deals with what is before the mind and reshapes it; but it is not itself a part of what is before the mind. In this, it shows kinship with creative imagination, which, at its best, turns towards the penetrative. It is "creative" because profound penetration reveals positive treasures beyond the average mind, not because it deviates into arbitrary fantasy.

In short, all logical activity is a world of content reshaping itself by its own spirit and laws in the presence of new suggestions.

A syllogism is in principle nothing less, and a Parthenon or "Paradise Lost" is in principle nothing more. This, then, is the nature and type of originality and initiative we seek to vindicate for our conative development, whether practical or intellectual. Our actions and ideas flow from our world, like a conclusion from premises, or a poem from its author's spirit. Do we demand a more complete originality? Would a creativeness beyond that of King Lear or the Sistine Madonna still hold human interest? When we say "continuity," we mean "logic". If we deny logic, we sever production from its roots in human nature.

While art is not governed by the purpose of representing the actual world but has its own autonomous growth, the main principle holds. Even in what we consider the freest creation, the unchallenged domain of productive originality, there is nothing which is not one in nature with the remoulding of a cosmos by its own yearning for totality. This is the synthetic vitality of the logical spirit.

This creative freedom of art is what we offer as the type of the characteristic logic or movement of the self. It is difficult to conceive or desire an initiative more complete, or one consistent with a self that is anything at all. Life itself, often cited as true continuity, is merely a lower phase of an analogous logic, related to human activity as a hill to a Turner sketch. We are offered a share in the eternal deed which constitutes reality. A self, then, appears as the active form of totality, realizing itself in a mass of experience, as a striving towards unity and coherence. Its self-determination is that of a logical world, analogous to a conclusion emerging from premises, where a new and transfigured whole transcends its data. This nature is most identifiable in the triumphs of art and poetry. The eccentricities of purely freakish fancy are logical breaches of continuity, while great art intensifies and expands the possibilities of man and nature, leading to a deeper, more thorough logical continuity. To brand this kind of initiative as a "rattling off of a preformed chain" is to reject the very continuity that makes life interesting. If we desire a creativity more "free" than this, we will find no analogy in knowledge, practice, or art. This is our conception of a self, of "what it is to be a self," and of "what it is to be" free or self-determined.

The Emptiness and Timelessness of Self-Consciousness

Let us consider two common difficulties in grasping this view.

1. The Emptiness of Self-Consciousness: The idea that self-consciousness or the bare subject-object relation is the principle of the self might seem empty and abstract. In this sense, the concept *is* empty, lacking specific content within its definition. This is inevitably true, stemming from self-consciousness as the principle of the whole. It is inconceivable for the principle of the whole to be occupied *ab initio* by a determinate, partial content.

If we ask whether mind or self-consciousness is indifferent, divorced from all content like pure water, the answer is that its content *is* the Absolute. It is always more proper to content that approaches the Absolute's character. However, the question "Does the bare fact that I am a self-consciousness bind me *a priori* to a determinate form of life, habit, or character?" is absurd. The power of self-consciousness is to make a self out of circumstances. This would be impossible if we were circumstantially determinate *antecedently* to circumstance. We must understand that everything comes from somewhere, and self-consciousness, the active form of totality, gives everything its character, becoming the center where all elements, in their degree, influence the whole. The emptiness of self-consciousness as such is an inevitable condition of its fulness in actual individuals. Any experiences fulfilling general conditions can constitute self-consciousness, and this truth in no way impeaches its value. If self-consciousness is the highest and most significant of finite experiences, what other condition could we expect? The keynote is that a true self is something to be made and won, held together with pains and labor, not something given to be enjoyed.

2. The Timelessness of the Self: The timelessness or eternity ascribed to the fundamental self by idealism has also caused difficulty. But it is quite simple: Time itself is a hybrid experience. Succession alone is insufficient to constitute it, just as it is insufficient to constitute a self. The crucial point lies in interpreting the continuity of content necessary for experiencing duration through succession.

Those who see succession as ultimately mere appearance will speak of the self, as it becomes a present whole, approximating eternity. Others see succession and continuity as inseparable factors of a fundamentally temporal reality.

However, once the hybrid or dual nature of time (and space) is admitted, the facts about the finite self are less disputed. "Duree," understood as the operative concentration of the self's past history at the growing point of the present, is akin to the relative timelessness of a finite self. If timelessness is an essential constituent of time, then saying a finite being is temporal (has "duree") implicitly includes what the eternal self theory demands. The finite has succession—it's not "all there"—which no one denies. The difference lies in the emphasis on how externality and successiveness accompany degrees of self-completeness, and the recognition that the self's true being lies beyond its fullest actual realization. The distinctive being of the self is inversely proportional to its dependence on externality and successiveness.

Logic vs. Fatality: Perfect Determination

The crucial distinction separating determinateness from determinism is that between logic and fatality. By logic, we understand, with Plato and Hegel, the supreme law of nature of perfect experience. It is the impulse towards unity and coherence (the positive spirit of non-contradiction) by which every fragment yearns towards its whole, and every self towards its completion in the Absolute. The Absolute itself is both an incarnation and satisfaction of this logic. While higher attainments are more concrete and inclusive, and lower experiences more restricted, it is the fundamental truth that logic is the mainspring, and practice is a subordinate feature of its movement.

Fatality, conversely, would be a movement or succession without love or logic, with moments external to each other, like the unconscious processes of physical nature. A true theory acknowledges room for externality, not as a self-subsistent real, but as an element of dissociation essential to the whole's order and emphasis. It only becomes the menacing form of fatalism or determinism when we treat it as subsistent in its own right and use it to interpret conscious experience. Compared to logical determinateness, fatality is an imperfect, relative, and indeterminate form of connection. It presents the paradox of a universal operating without its own being, like the reaction of a body in its sleep.

For our current purpose, this means externality or physical determination is imperfectly determinate. It is sensitive only to certain factors of a situation. It is not the awareness of a whole reshaping itself according to the full significance of its contents. We must understand physical causation not as the type of perfect determinateness, but as a region of abstract, external contexts between unawakened beings, contrasted with a living, concrete world of appreciation where the whole quality of every element can bear upon and respond to every other.

Therefore, determinateness and determinism are in principle opposed. Determinateness is fullest in the Absolute and God, and in all experience, determination and value go together.

Ultimate value resides in the whole, and value increases with participation in it, meaning the transfiguration of experience by the fullest vitality of all elements bearing upon all. This is the ideal of the logic of a self, and the concept of determinism – a causation that is partial and unawakened – is thoroughly antagonistic to it.

It has been said that God could only impart Himself by imparting a self. We complement this truth by asserting that a self can only be a self insofar as it *is* the self.

The desire to escape the principle of self-determination and non-contradiction is, though it may seem otherwise, a desire to shirk responsibility. What the ordinary advocate of freedom demands as "the power to have acted otherwise" is, paradoxically, to act and not to act, or to act without accountability.

It is to repudiate, not accept, responsibility – the qualification of the self by its behaviour . When offered the truth that their act shall be their own and themselves, they flee. They wish to remain uncommitted and undeveloped, even in the moment of action. But if uncommitted after thousands of actions, they remain uncommitted after the thousand and first. The point is that, in their view, the act does *not* characterize the self.

The Problem of the Evil Self

Now, let us turn to the problem of the evil self, which tests our understanding of individuality and completeness. We identify three typical forms of imperfection:

- The animal self.
- The naive or elementary good self.

- The bad self, proper—the rebellious or positively negative self.

If badness is a defect of individuality, an imperfectly informed logic, a failure to construct a whole, why aren't the first two types, which clearly exhibit incompleteness, pre-eminent cases of the evil self? How can we distinguish badness from mere imperfection?

1 The Animal Self: The bodily needs and desires shared with brute creation are an obvious example of the imperfect self, often exploited by ethical philosophy and popular morality. However, it is plain, as the Greeks knew, that the animal content of life is the common root of man's purposes, both good and bad. It is not to be negated, except in the sense of transformation. The form of imperfection that would consist in remaining a brute beast cannot actually exist in a human consciousness. The animal basis is imperfect like data without a theory, not like a theoretical structure capable of narrowness or self-contradiction. It wouldn't even amount to an imperfect human self.

2 The Naive or Elementary Good Self: This presents a more serious difficulty. Consider the life of a simple, uncultured, but kindly and honorable person. In our analogy, such a life, compared to the average, is decidedly imperfect, claiming a low rank of individuality. Their mental equipment omits vast provinces of experience and couldn't handle the complexities of advanced civilization. If defective individuality is like a failure of theoretical grasp, lying in openness to contradiction, then surely this is an example. It might be argued that this forces us to the absurdity of saying ignorance is vice, because a wicked, cultured mind might have a far wider range of knowledge and capacity for unification. This apparent fact—that an ignorant mind can be good, and a cultured one bad—is commonly

alleged against us. Yet, this objection leads to a striking verification of our view.

Socrates' "ignorance is vice" referred to ignorance of the good, which for him meant the unification of life. The unification of life has fundamental necessities and outlying corollaries. The essential matter is that the naive or simple self of everyday morality consists of the principles fundamental to the unification of life. The contention that "wisdom is goodness" ultimately transforms into the justified contention that "goodness is wisdom". Like possessing a sound fundamental principle in science without specialized knowledge, naive morality is imperfect, but it possesses the essential and fundamental conditions of unification. Scientific or artistic aptitudes are outlying corollaries and completions.

Thus, naive morality and religion, though imperfect, are not ranked as comparable to the bad self, nor are they wholly surpassed in value by isolated higher developments of civilized mind. (We concede that they are morally and religiously defective due to their limitation). This is because they possess the essential and fundamental conditions of unification, which scientific or artistic aptitudes, for example, are posterior and dependent upon. A person is good insofar as their being is unified at all in any sphere of wisdom or activity. While perfection in one part of the mind affects others, simple morality can more nearly stand alone, and its absence shakes the whole foundations of life and mind. It is, in respect to life as a whole, like a failure of belief in the first principles of rational system to scientific intelligence.

This is the true distinction between morality (commonly so called) and intellectual/aesthetic excellence. It is a distinction of degree between the more and less fundamental ideas that govern life. It is not the current distinction between intellectually held ideas and ideas effective in action. Ideas that form the main structure of the mind cannot but be operative. Ideas whose content claims such a place but are inoperative because inadequately held are not truly knowledge. The presence of inoperative ideas in moral matters is vastly exaggerated. Inoperative ideas are those not carried out into the connections that would constitute their meaning and power. A selfish man does not truly know the value of unselfishness. Goodness is wisdom, and this truth has significant ramifications.

We've seen that the animal self is too primitive to be an imperfect human self, and the naive self, though imperfect, is a sound foundation.

3 The Evil Self: This is different in kind. Here, we encounter the phenomenon of two quasi-rational systems in active antagonism, claiming different principles for identical data. We can find considerable positive unification in a system that we nevertheless recognize as evil. Just as a theory can have high organization but be rejected for a more solid one, the evil self is not evil in itself. A suggestive fact is how highly desirable objects and interests can enter into the very fabric of an evil life.

The evil self is evil because, and insofar as, it is antagonistic to the good. However highly organized it may be in itself, it is inevitably, through this antagonism, the adversary of unification of experience, and the vehicle of contradiction in the very heart of the self. Questions arise: Is evil a species of good? Could the self be equally divided, making it hard to pronounce which is good or evil?

For our purpose, we've seen enough: not every imperfect self is *pro tanto* an evil self. And an evil self, in itself, may show a higher degree of consistency and coherence (due to its positive aim, not its negative aim) than many imperfect or non-moral good selves. It is the difference between inadequacy and developed contradiction. This confirms our conception of maximum individuality or unification of experience as the standard of real and good, and thus our conception of logic as the law of the self's striving.

If so, the evil self is a case of the logical striving of the self after unity, which has brought it into contradiction with a fuller and sounder striving. This raises the question of self-determination: Can the inherent drive towards unification take the shape of a bad self, as a logical necessity? And is this fatalistic?

Certainly, the bad will is a logical necessity in the self that develops it, no less than the good will. Its point is lost unless it is a development of the self in the same sense as the good will. The only difference is that it has seized a false clue, essentially incapable of achieving the unification the will sets out to do, thus leading to antagonism with unified life and ultimately with itself.

There is no metaphysical difficulty here. Moral evil is inherent in morality. It is not something alien to the world; it has a relative right to be. It is involved in finiteness, though its special shapes arise from the logic of individual finite beings.

That this should be embodied in the work of selves is part of the contradiction belonging to finite life, where harmonious self-affirmation is impossible. Moral evil, we might say, is good hostile to good. As hostile, it demands amendment, but in its positive nature, it contributes to the whole's vitality.

Is this doctrine dangerous, suggesting fatalism or predestination to evil? This applies equally to good and evil: Does a necessary action imply a necessary agent? Does "cannot but be such and such" mean the agent "cannot help" making it?

The primary principle governing this discussion is that the attitude of moral judgment and responsibility is only one among other attitudes and spheres of experience. It is an aspect of reality, isolated by our importance, that would appear differently in the whole.

It must not be set up as absolute. The feeling that "it all depends on me, and I, and I only, can determine and am responsible," is right and true in the face of a moral decision. The factors of the will and the law of action are presupposed in being a self. The question is how that self will reshape itself. At that moment, the self's absolute independence is a fact and an element in determining behaviour .

However, metaphysical theory, viewing the self in its basis of moral solidarity with the natural and social world, and in its special relations with others that forbid isolation, recognizes that this independence, though a fact, is only a partial fact. Both views are true and represent reality in their degree.

It is fatal to confuse them or set them in antagonism as if they belonged to the same situation. In a moral emergency, everything depends on the individual will, and it is right to recognize this. But it is also true that the individual will has far deeper roots than what we commonly take to be the individual mind, and its task is set by the universe.

The Determinist relies on this deep-rootedness, but not entirely justifiably. While they rightly urge that ideas about volition shouldn't affect presupposed positive influences, their metaphysical position is hostile to self-determination. They construe the self and motives by analogy with non-self entities, and their term "necessary" conveys a process irreconcilable with true moral deliberation.

With our present theory, this is not the case. It does not narrow the scope of moral deliberation. It recognizes the self as operative in its own nature, as creative and originative according to its own law—the only law of creativeness that prevails in the universe.

It recognizes a necessary act—an act which *must* be what it is—but not a necessary agent, because nothing but the agent determines the act.

There is no meaning in applying "must" or "cannot help it" to the agent, except in the sense that everything is what it is. In other words, nothing past, nothing external, is operative in the agent's choice. It is all gathered up and made into the agent himself, and its remodelling in him is one with his creative production of a new deed.

This supplements the strictly moral attitude ("It is I, and I only, who have to act") with a wider metaphysical recognition (akin to religion's).

This recognition acknowledges that I, through my goodness or badness, through my moral judgment and decision (a burden I cannot escape), am yet more or less completely doing the work of the universe. As and because I am myself, I am acting as a member in a greater self, continuous with it, and dyed with its colors.

The Ideal of Contingency: A Misinterpretation of Freedom

The ideal that seems irrepressible in discussions of Freedom, Initiative, and Individuality is the ideal of Contingency. To establish contingency "in the heart of things" is the motto of moralistic idealists and some scientific thinkers. The aim of this lecture, however, is to defend a wholly different set of suggestions.

The bias towards contingency arises from a misinterpretation of the demand for creative initiative, combined with a failure to appreciate the true nature of logical process. Our effort has been to bring the conception of moral and individual initiative closer to the idea of logical determination, and thus into comparison with the forms of creative activity most undeniably recognized as yielding the highest human value.

It is notable that the tendency to confuse creative determination with arbitrariness and contingency appears in popular ideas of art and originality, no less than in morality.

From our perspective, not only logical theory, but the entire doctrine of thought and emotion's aesthetic expression, social right and duty, religious aspiration, and the achievements of science and philosophy, is fatal to the ideal of contingency. It is being master of and mastered by content, with its transfiguration as it reshapes itself towards the whole, that confers logical stability and exalts individuality.

Lecture-10
Nature, the Self, and the Absolute

This concluding lecture draws together nature, self, and the Absolute into a single, living vision of reality. It shows how external nature and inner consciousness are not rivals but complementary moments of one experience, and how finite selves transmute limitation into meaning. Here the unity of being emerges as something we already live, not merely something we think.

Concludes by synthesizing nature, individuality, and the Absolute into a coherent vision of being

Good morning, everyone. Today, we delve into a profound philosophical discussion concerning the intricate relationship between Nature, the Self, and the Absolute, drawing deeply from the insights presented in our lecture material. This is not merely an academic exercise, but an exploration of concepts that touch upon our everyday experience and fundamental understanding of reality.

Let us begin by grappling with the very notion of Nature. The lecture posits Nature as the environment of selves, something we often consider to be self-existent. However, it immediately challenges this clear-cut division, noting that the line between Nature and Mind is not fixed. Consider, for instance, the idea of Nature possessing Beauty. Is that an inherent quality of Nature, or something perceived and attributed by a mind?

The difficulty in speaking intelligibly about a relation between Nature and the Self arises because each term seems inconceivable without the other. Any attempt to draw a rigid line between them will inevitably contain an element of arbitrariness.

If we were to define Nature narrowly, as the "homogeneous world of units adapted for calculation" known to mathematical physics, then the distinction would be simple, but the relation would hold no interest. In this abstract sense, Nature would be a specialized abstraction, serving to reduce the world's appearances to comparable formulae, effective for understanding external conditions, but falling far short of what Nature means to the common person or the poet.

However, the lecture urges us to consider a broader, richer understanding of Nature. If we interpret Nature as the "universe in space and time interpreted as a living system"—a meaning that lies at the very root of all art and poetry—then the distinction becomes much harder to maintain.

In this view, it becomes difficult to exclude the "spiritual side of the higher organisms," and any further spiritual beings implied by their existence, from Nature itself. If any distinction remains, it would simply be that of part and whole, implying a relationship that points towards a more unified view.

This brings us to a crucial distinction of kind that is highly relevant to our purpose: what does the environment, the world of things and facts as we experience it, contribute to the being of the self?Nature, in this sense—the spatial, external, objective world, complete with its beauty and usefulness—is nearly everything, yet "not quite everything".

It is challenging to pinpoint where it ceases to be; the line between subject and environment cannot always be drawn at the same point. This is because the self, in a fundamental way, "draws its material from Nature". Even as the self confronts its objective surroundings, it utilizes this very material to cultivate the "feeling of selfhood". For everyday sentiment and perception, Nature differs only in degree from what it is for the artist and poet. It is the "world in space and time, with all its secondary qualities, and moreover, with all the interpretations and emotions by which in our experience it is taken as qualified". Crucially, the lecture asserts that in this sense, Nature "could be nothing apart from a self which at least must be sentient".

Despite this, Nature is not "created by the self taken apart from the detail of the environment," because such a self would be nothing. While the self may be said to "make its own environment," this is only by selection, always dependent on "the given," and never arbitrary. It is an affair of interests, motives, preferences, and reasons, implying that "something does not come from nothing, but from something in particular".

The self, which actively shapes its environment, is itself "all soaked in environment," leading to the profound statement: "You cannot say where self ends and environment begins".

Nature, conceived as an environment, encompasses "the whole detail of thing and fact which enters into the world of the self". The extent to which we treat it as qualified by the self's interpretations and emotions is a matter of degree, and it consistently includes influences from our own bodies, friends, animals, and external events involving other human beings.

Therefore, the distinction between Nature and the Self ultimately becomes akin to the distinction between circumstance and character.

It is a distinction of points of view. Anything in ourselves or our environment can be considered Nature if it is not viewed in the light of a self's behaviour . Conversely, anything belongs to a self when details of our world are seen as interconnected parts within the "total reaction of a mind".

This framework is consistent with common usage when contrasting Nature with fine art, morality, politics, or economic activity. For instance, being born in the Highlands or Lowlands, in town or country, or of a strong or feeble race, are all "natural facts" and "obvious pieces of environment". However, our attitude towards these facts, or towards other things because of them, "belongs to myself, and is the sort of stuff or substance in which myself consists". So, Nature is the "world in space and time, abstracted from our momentary attitude and considered as self-existent," yet "possessed of qualities which presuppose it to be in relation with a cognitive sentient purposive and emotional being".

This leads us to the intimate connection between Nature and Mind or Self. The core question we must discuss is precisely what Nature "has to do with mind or self". It is undeniable that Nature is, in some sense, "plastic and responsive to finite subjective mind" and thus can be considered "expressive" of mind, its embodiment, or a "crystallisation or hieroglyph of it". However, the lecture immediately points out that this familiar idea conceals two fundamentally antagonistic lines of thought: one starting from the idea that mind and nature are akin, and the other from the idea that they are complementary and prima facie in opposition.

Let us first examine the idea of kinship, often leading to Pan-psychism. If our impression of unity between Nature and Mind leads us to emphasize kinship or resemblance, we might arrive at the contemporary notion of the Universe as a "society of spirits".

In this view, the constituent parts of Nature are seen as members of this society, their external form being the "body" and their behaviour the "language and conduct" of actual spiritual beings other than ourselves. This perspective suggests that Nature literally possesses a purpose and significance akin to our own, communicable to us based on our sympathy and insight.

However, the lecture offers a strong critique of Pan-psychism. It argues that if Pan-psychism is carried through consistently, all externality is dissolved away, meaning that outward appearance would be infinitely resolvable into spirits. If, on the other hand, we admit that externality *must* exist as a counterpart to spirit, then there is no principled reason to deny that parts of Nature, where subjective mind seems a superfluous hypothesis, are simply "externality or the counterpart of subjective mind elsewhere". For Pan-psychism to be necessary, the "resolution into spirit must be universal".

The lecture frankly confesses that Pan-psychism appears to reveal a "poverty of philosophical imagination". It treats the profound opposition and inseparability of mind and externality as if it were merely a collection of centers of experience. It undermines the very complementariness of mind and nature, on which their inseparability depends, by reducing one into the other and thereby destroying the "speciality of function for which the one is needed by the other". Why, the lecture asks, should we insist on reducing "to a homogeneous type the contributions of all elements to the whole"? What then becomes of the material aspects of life – our food, clothes, country, or even our own bodies? Our relation to these things is "essential to finite being," and if they were also subjective psychical centers, their subjective quality, if fully realized, would "destroy their function and character for us".

Furthermore, the work for which finite mind is necessary and valuable is primarily "guidance, including will, and appreciation, including emotion". In the lower organic world, and much of the automatic workings of human and animal bodies, "there is no need of finite mind for will or guidance". The mind we might presume in a newt or an orchid, if any, could not guide processes like organic "restitution" or fertilization, which even the highest human intellect could barely contrive and which show no signs of conscious guidance. It would be contrary to our convictions to assume subjective mind is present in a degree irrelevant to any functions it could perform. While some rudimentary shrinking from hostile conditions might exist in higher animals, even that is doubtful in lower forms. A "marvellous work of guidance" occurs, but not by finite subjective mind.

It is more challenging to limit the value of mind for appreciation. One might ask, "Why should not a plant enjoy its own being, or a mountain or the sea feel its own power and persistence?" However, the lecture notes that appreciation loses interest as its object loses distinctiveness, and our capacity for distinctive apprehension diminishes as we descend the organic scale. While we might attribute some appreciation to higher animals, we likely overstate it; they probably do not "know" their own appearance, and their apparent pride comes from immediate feeling of life, not self-awareness. Even their highest appreciative quality, such as love and loyalty, disappears where distinctive family relations cease. Thus, in the lower organisms, "the function of appreciation can hardly be supposed to exist as a raison d'etre of subjective mind".

Instead, this appreciation is "emphatically present in the onlooker," the higher finite spiritual beings who "appreciate and understand the lower organic world very far better than that world can be supposed to appreciate and understand itself". This argument applies even more strongly to the inorganic world; a mountain or lake, even if it had a dim subjectivity, could neither guide nor appreciate itself as a poet could. Its function is as an object to another's subjectivity, an "externality correlative to finite mind," not as a subject itself. Therefore, Pan-psychism is deemed a "gratuitous hypothesis," failing to acknowledge the "complementary functions of subjective mind on the one hand and externality on the other as together essential to any complete form of conscious experience".

Having critiqued the kinship view, let us now turn to the complementary perspective. If we start from the idea of externality—a world with systematic spatial and temporal determinations, endowed with all its secondary and tertiary qualities—as something complementary to subjective mind, something without which mind "would not be itself, would not be a self, would not be anything". In this case, Nature would still be plastic and responsive to finite subjective mind, but its external world would not, in principle, be resolvable into subjective centers. Instead, it would hold a "distinctive place and function as externality," acting as the "source and storehouse of all positive properties, contents, and distinctions". We could still call it a symbol of mind or an expression of will or intelligence, but these descriptions are incomplete. It is, in fact, "the very content of our consciousness embodied in a form in which we learn to recognise it".

However, the lecture emphasizes that this doesn't mean mind superfluously recognizes its *own* content in Nature. Rather, "the content of mind is the content of Nature because Nature is the instrument or element of the Absolute by which the mind's own "nature" is communicated to it". Conversely, the content of Nature is the content of mind because "it is only in the sphere of mind that Nature reveals, to begin with, anything at all, and a fortiori, that she reveals the possibilities of life and spirituality that are shut up within her". Indeed, it is "all but impossible to distinguish Nature from mind," and "to separate them is impossible". If you ask what in Nature is not mind, the answer is "the fragmentary or disconnected qua fragmentary or disconnected". If you ask what in mind is not Nature, the answer is "the spirit of totality, the attitude which makes everything alive in its bearing on the whole". This means we must not "libel Nature by saying that she has no meaning, no will but simply borrows from ours". On the contrary, "we have them to give her only because we take them, nay, we are and exist by taking them, from her".Mind has nothing of its own but the "active form of totality"; "everything positive it draws from Nature".

The lecture highlights a striking, often overlooked parallel between mind and life. Discussions that emphasize the self-sufficiency of life and mind as guides or initiators ignore this crucial parallelism. There is no inherent "credit or merit" due to life or mind over the natural environment for furnishing "definite and special lines of variation, peculiar contrivances, adaptations, principles". Instead, everything points to the conclusion that life and mind are "the appearance at different stages of an omni-potential principle, which elicits its whole definite content and development from its surroundings".

For life, this is natural selection; for finite mind, it is a wider sense of the same process. The strength of this principle lies in its "emptiness"—it brings no content that could resist the organization of all contents.

Even within life, reactions are determinate, just like in the mechanical world, demonstrating a contrast between uniformity of response and adaptation and qualitative variety of new developments.

These new developments are not due to "miraculous guidance" from life or mind *per se* but arise from relevant stimuli. The "real miracle lies in the significance hidden in Nature as a whole," coupled with the "omni-potentiality of life and mind" to elicit organisms, selves, and civilizations from what is latent in Nature.

Thus, external Nature, in this view, is not a "masked and enfeebled section of the subject-world," but is that "from which all finite subjects draw their determinate being and content". Nature becomes the vehicle of life and subjective mind under certain unknown conditions. We cannot ascribe independent being to it, especially considering its character as we perceive it. It is "idle and superfluous" to give Nature a mind of its own; "Our minds are its own mind".

This perspective, however, does not deprive Nature of its own being or make it merely subservient to human ends. Instead, it teaches that "Nature teaches us what are the ends of the universe" and we are capable of learning them. Humanity's power lies in "making its own the ends which the universe through Nature teaches it to appreciate".

Moving towards the Absolute, the lecture proposes that the system of the universe can be described as a "representative system," where Nature, or externality, "lives in the life of conscious beings". This characteristic is essential, not incidental. Nature, though a system in space and time, could not exist if it were purely in space and time, because space and time themselves are "hybrid forms of being"—externality and succession presupposing a degree of unity. Therefore, "Nature thus, exists only through finite mind". And reciprocally, "finite minds again exist only through nature". Every finite mind "focus[es] and draw[s] their detail from some particular sphere of external nature," expressing and interpreting its significance. The ultimate 'why' remains unknown, but this arrangement allows the "value of all that the universe contains" to be elicited through finite minds, leading to a "fuller unity". Every instinct, every feeling of joy, energy, or love in the animal world, is an outcome of external conditions focused in life and mind, destined to culminate in the "complete experience which is the life of the whole".

The lecture then addresses the perplexity surrounding the conception of the Absolute, attributing it to our "unreally hypostasised notion of the consciousness of finite minds". We cling to the "superstition" that regards minds as "substances, crystal-nuclei, fallen or celestial angels". A more accurate notion of mind might be gleaned from animal minds, which are less burdened by these traditional human soul concepts.

The discussion transforms if we realize that every focus of consciousness is an "effort," subject to "constant and enormous fluctuations," to grasp and internalize the "value and significance of a world". Far from being a strange assumption, the "transmutation, reinforcement, and rearrangement" of conscious experiences by inclusion in a "fuller and more extended